FINANCE FOR ALL?

D1366940

A World Bank Policy Research Report

FINANCE FOR ALL?

POLICIES AND PITFALLS IN
EXPANDING ACCESS

THE WORLD BANK
Washington, D.C.

© 2008 The International Bank for Reconstruction and Development / The World Bank

1818 H Street NW
Washington DC 20433
Telephone: 202-473-1000
Internet: www.worldbank.org
E-mail: feedback@worldbank.org
All rights reserved

1 2 3 4 5 10 09 08 07

ISBN: 978-0-8213-7291-3
eISBN: 978-0-8213-7292-0
DOI: 10.1596/978-0-8213-7291-3

Cover photo: Comstock.
Cover design: Critical Stages.

Library of Congress Cataloging-in-Publication Data

Demirgüç-Kunt, Aslı, 1961–
    Finance for all? : policies and pitfalls in expanding access / [by Aslı Demirgüç-Kunt, Thorsten Beck, and Patrick Honohan].
        p. cm.
    Includes bibliographical references and index.
    ISBN 978-0-8213-7291-3 -- ISBN 978-0-8213-7292-0 (electronic)
1. Financial services industry--Developing countries. 2. Banks and banking--Developing countries.
I. Beck, Thorsten. II. Honohan, Patrick. III. World Bank. IV. Title.
    HG195.D46 2007
    332.109172'4--dc22
                                                                            2007033387

Contents

Figures

Foreword

ACCESS TO FINANCIAL SERVICES VARIES SHARPLY AROUND THE WORLD. In many developing countries, less than half the population has an account with a financial institution, and in most of Africa less than one in five households do. Recent development theory sees the lack of access to finance as a critical mechanism for generating persistent income inequality, as well as slower growth. Without inclusive financial systems, poor individuals and small enterprises need to rely on their own limited savings and earnings to invest in their education, become entrepreneurs, or take advantage of promising growth opportunities. Financial sector policies that encourage competition, provide the right incentives to individuals, and help overcome access barriers are thus central not only to stability but also to growth, poverty reduction, and more equitable distribution of resources and capacities.

The World Bank Group has long recognized that well-functioning financial systems are essential for economic development. The work of its financial sector has, over the years, emphasized the importance of financial stability and efficiency. Promoting broader access to financial services, however, has received much less attention despite the emphasis it has received in theory. The access dimension of financial development has often been overlooked, mostly because of serious data gaps in this area. Empirical evidence that links access to financial services to development outcomes has been quite limited, providing at best tentative guidance for public policy initiatives. The increasing emphasis by policy circles in recent years on building more inclusive financial systems thus highlights the need for better data and analysis.

Measuring access to finance, its determinants, and its impact has been the focus of a major research effort at the Bank in recent years.

This research has included case-study analyses of specific policies and interventions, as well as systematic analyses of extensive cross-country and micro data sets. *Finance for All?* presents first efforts at developing indicators illustrating that financial access is quite limited around the world and identifies barriers that may be preventing small firms and poor households from using financial services. Based on this research, the report derives principles for effective government policy on broadening access.

The report's conclusions confirm some traditional views and challenge others. For example, recent research provides additional evidence to support the widely-held belief that financial development promotes growth and illustrates the role of access in this process. Improved access to finance creates an environment conducive to new firm entry, innovation, and growth. However, research also shows that small firms benefit the most from financial development and greater access—both in terms of entry and seeing their growth constraints relaxed. Hence, inclusive financial systems also have consequences for the composition and competition in the enterprise sector.

The evidence also suggests that besides the direct benefits of access to financial services, small firms and poor households can also benefit indirectly from the effects of financial development. For example, the poor may benefit from having jobs and higher wages, as better developed financial systems improve overall efficiency and promote growth and employment. Similarly, small firms may see their business opportunities expand with financial development, even if the financial sector still mostly serves the large firms. Hence, pro-poor financial sector policy requires a broader focus of attention than access for the poor: improving access by the excluded nonpoor micro and small entrepreneurs can have a strongly favorable indirect effect on the poor.

Expanding access to financial services remains an important policy challenge in many countries, with much for governments to do. However, not all government action is equally effective, and some policies can be counterproductive. Policy makers need to have realistic goals. For instance, while access to formal payment and savings services can approach universality as economies develop, not everyone will or should qualify for credit. There are instances where national welfare has been reduced by overly relaxed credit policies.

Government policies in the financial sector should focus on reforming institutions, developing infrastructures to take advantage of technological advances, encouraging competition, and providing the right incentives through prudential regulations. The report discusses experience and evidence of different government interventions—such as those through taxes, subsidies, and direct ownership of institutions—illustrating how they sometimes tend to be politicized, poorly structured, and beneficial mainly those who do not need the subsidy. In the absence of thorough economic evaluations of most schemes, their net effect in cost-benefit terms also remains unclear.

Despite best efforts, it seems likely that provision of some financial services to the very poor may require subsidies. Generally speaking, the use of subsidies in microcredit can dull the incentive for innovative new technologies in expanding access, with counterproductive long-term repercussions for the poor. Besides, evidence suggests that for poor households credit is not the only—or in many cases, the principal—financial service they need. For example, in order to participate in the modern market economy even the poor need—but often cannot access—reliable, inexpensive, and suitable savings and payments products. Subsidies may sometimes be better spent on establishing savings and payment products appropriate to the poor.

This report reviews and synthesizes a large body of research, and provides the basis for sound policy advice in the area of financial access. We hope that it will contribute to the policy debate on how to achieve financial inclusion. While much work has been done, much more remains to be learned. The findings in this report also underline the importance of investing in data collection: continued work on measuring and evaluating the impact of access requires detailed micro data both at the household and enterprise level.

The World Bank Group is committed to continuing work in the area of building inclusive financial systems, helping member countries design financial system policies that are firmly based on empirical evidence.

François Bourguignon
Senior Vice President and Chief Economist
World Bank

Michael Klein
Vice President, Financial and
Private Sector Development, World Bank
Chief Economist, IFC

The Report Team

THIS POLICY RESEARCH REPORT WAS WRITTEN BY ASLI DEMIRGÜÇ-KUNT, Thorsten Beck (both with the Development Research Group), and Patrick Honohan (Development Research Group and Trinity College Dublin), under the general supervision of L. Alan Winters (Development Research Group). It draws heavily on the results of the on-going research program in the Finance and Private Sector Team of the Development Research Group at the World Bank. Original research as background for this report includes work by the authors and by Meghana Ayyagari (George Washington University), Robert Cull, Xavier Gine, Leora Klapper, Luc Laeven (now at the IMF), Ross Levine (Brown University), Inessa Love, Vojislav Maksimovic (University of Maryland), Maria Soledad Martinez Peria, David McKenzie, Sergio Schmukler, Colin Xu, and Bilal Zia.

The peer reviewers for the report were Franklin Allen (Wharton School), Stijn Claessens (IMF), Augusto de la Torre, Michael Fuchs, Richard Rosenberg (CGAP), and Guillermo Perry. The authors also benefited from conversations with and comments from Finance and Private Sector Board members, members of the UN Advisors Group for Building Inclusive Financial Systems, participants of the 2007 IMF-World Bank Dutch Constituency meeting in Moldova, and the 2007 WBER-DECRG conference on Access to Finance in Washington, DC. While the analysis in this report needs to satisfy scientific standards and hence is mainly based on academic research, the study has also benefited from extensive discussions with policy makers and advisers in the course of operational support for World Bank diagnostic and policy development work in the financial sector.

The authors are also grateful to Priya Basu, Gerard Caprio (Williams College), Shawn Cole (Harvard Business School), Gerrardo Corrochano, Carlos Cuevas, Uri Dadush, Enrica Detragiache (IMF), Quy-Toan Do, Samir El Daher, Aurora Ferrari, Francisco Ferreira, Inderbir Dhingra, Matthew Gamser, Alan Gelb, Michael Goldberg, Arvind Gupta, Santiago Herrera, Alain Ize, Eduardo Levy-Yeyati, Omer Karasapan, Shigeo Katsu, Aart Kraay, Anjali Kumar, Rodney Lester, Latifah Osman Merican, Pradeep Mitra, Ashish Narain, Tatiana Nenova, David Porteous, Roberto Rocha, Luis Serven, Patrick Stuart, and Willem van Eeghen for comments.

The authors would like to acknowledge the editorial assistance of Mark Feige. Edward Al-Hussainy and Subika Farazi provided excellent research assistance and Agnes Yaptenco superb administrative support. Polly Means contributed to cover design and graphics. Report design, production, and dissemination were coordinated by the World Bank Publications team. We are grateful to Stephen McGroarty and Santiago Pombo Bejarano in the Office of the Publisher, and to Arvind Gupta, Merrell Tuck-Primdahl, and Kavita Watsa for assistance in dissemination.

Financial support from the Knowledge for Change Program is gratefully acknowledged.

The findings, interpretations, and conclusions of this policy research report are those of the authors and do not necessarily reflect the views of the World Bank, its executive directors, or the countries they represent.

Abbreviations

ATM	automated teller machine
DFI	development finance institution
FDI	foreign direct investment
GDP	gross domestic product
MFI	microfinance institution
ROSCAs	rotating savings and credit associations
SBA	Small Business Administration (United States)
SME	small and medium enterprise

Overview and Summary

FINANCIAL MARKETS AND INSTITUTIONS EXIST TO MITIGATE THE effects of information asymmetries and transaction costs that prevent the direct pooling and investment of society's savings. Financial institutions help mobilize savings and provide payments services that facilitate the exchange of goods and services. In addition, they produce and process information about investors and investment projects to enable efficient allocation of funds; to monitor investments and exert corporate governance after those funds are allocated; and to help diversify, transform, and manage risk. When they work well, financial institutions and markets provide opportunities for all market participants to take advantage of the best investments by channeling funds to their most productive uses, hence boosting growth, improving income distribution, and reducing poverty. When they do not work well, opportunities for growth are missed, inequalities persist, and in the extreme cases, costly crises follow.

Much attention has focused on the depth and efficiency of financial systems—and for good reason: well-functioning financial systems are by definition efficient, allocating funds to their most productive uses. Well-functioning financial systems serve other vital purposes as well, including offering savings, payments, and risk-management products to as large a set of participants as possible, and seeking out and financing good growth opportunities wherever they may be. Without inclusive financial systems, poor individuals and small enterprises need to rely on their personal wealth or internal resources to invest in their education, become entrepreneurs, or take advantage of promising growth opportunities. Modern development theories increasingly emphasize the key role of

Finance is an essential part of the development process—

—and a well-functioning system needs broad access, as well as depth

access to finance: lack of finance is often the critical element underlying persistent income inequality, as well as slower growth.

Thus, access to finance helps to equalize opportunities and reduce inequalities—

Earlier theories of development postulated that a rise in short-term inequality was an inevitable consequence of the early stages of development. However, it is increasingly recognized that inequality can adversely affect growth prospects—which implies that wealth redistribution can spur development. Despite the emphasis that financial market imperfections now receive in theory, development economists have tended to advocate the adoption of redistributive public policies to improve wealth distribution and to foster growth. However, since financial market imperfections that limit access to finance play an important role in perpetuating inequalities, financial sector reforms that promote broader access to financial services need to be at the core of the development agenda. Indeed, if financial market frictions are not addressed, redistribution may have to be endlessly repeated, which could result in damaging disincentives to work and save. In contrast, building inclusive financial systems focuses on equalizing opportunities. Hence, addressing financial market imperfections that expand individual opportunities creates positive, not negative, incentive effects. While theory highlights the risk that selectively increased access could worsen inequality, both cross-country data and evidence from specific policy experiments suggest that more-developed financial systems are associated with lower inequality. Hence, though still far from conclusive, the bulk of the evidence suggests that developing the financial sector and improving access to finance are likely not only to accelerate economic growth, but also to reduce income inequality and poverty.

—but the access dimension of financial development has often been overlooked

Access to financial services—financial inclusion—implies an absence of obstacles to the use of these services, whether the obstacles are price or nonprice barriers to finance. It is important to distinguish between access to—the possibility to use—and actual use of financial services. Exclusion can be voluntary, where a person or business has access to services but no need to use them, or involuntary, where price barriers or discrimination, for example, bar access. Failure to make this distinction can complicate efforts to define and measure access. Financial market imperfections, such as information asymmetries and transaction costs, are likely to be especially binding on the talented poor and on micro- and small enterprises that lack collateral, credit histories, and connections. Without inclusive financial systems, these individuals and enterprises with promising opportunities are limited to their own savings and earnings. This access dimension of financial development has often been overlooked, mostly because of serious data gaps on who has access to which financial services and a lack of systematic information on the barriers to broader access.

This report is a broad-ranging review of research work, completed or in progress, focusing on access to finance. The report presents indicators to measure financial access, analyzes its determinants, and evaluates the impact of access on growth, equity, and poverty reduction, drawing on research that uses data both at the firm and household level. The report also discusses the role of government in advancing financial inclusion, and these policy recommendations are stressed throughout the report. Although much remains to be learned, a significant amount of empirical analysis has been conducted on these issues over the past years. As with any review, taking stock of all this research also allows us to identify the many gaps in our knowledge and helps chart the way for a new generation of research in this area.

The report pays particular attention to the following themes:

- *Measuring access.* How well does the financial system in different countries directly serve poor households and small enterprises? Just how limited is financial access? Who has access to which financial services (such as deposit, credit, payments, insurance)? What are the chief obstacles and policy barriers to broader access?
- *Evaluating the impact of access.* How important is access to finance as a constraint to the growth of firms? What are the channels through which improved access affects firm growth? What is the impact of access to finance on households and microenterprises? What aspects of financial sector development matter for broadening access to different types of financial services? What techniques are most effective in ensuring sustainable provision of credit and other financial services on a small scale?
- *Adopting policies to broaden access.* What is the government's role in building inclusive financial systems? Given that financial systems in many developing countries serve only a small part of the population, expanding access remains an important challenge across the world, leaving much for governments to do. Not all government actions are equally effective, however, and some policies can be counterproductive. The report sets out principles for effective government policy on broadening access, drawing on the available evidence and illustrating with examples.

This report presents access indicators, evaluates impact, and provides policy advice

Outline of this report

THIS OVERVIEW INTRODUCES THE MAIN MESSAGES of the report, pulling together theory, data, and analysis. It then presents the key policy implications of this material and highlights some of the challenges in the implementation of these recommendations. It concludes with directions for future research.

Chapter 1 starts with analyses of the theoretical models that illustrate the crucial role access to finance plays in the development process, particularly its influence on both growth and income distribution. Then the chapter examines various data sets to assess the ability of both firms and households to access financial services, to identify barriers to access, and to provide an empirical foundation to better understand the welfare impacts of broader financial access.

Chapter 2 focuses on the ability of firms, particularly small firms, to access financial services. It investigates not only the implications for growth and productivity for individual firms, and the economy at large, but also the impact that restrictive financial access can have on the structure of the economy. The chapter also explores which aspects of financial sector development matter for access to external finance— looking at banks, markets, and nonbank finance, and focusing especially on the role of foreign banks.

Attention turns to households and microentrepreneurs in chapter 3, which examines whether an emphasis on financial sector development as a driver of economic growth is consistent with a pro-poor approach to development. After reviewing the theory, empirical evidence at both the micro and macro levels is presented. The chapter then analyzes the barriers to access and how they can be overcome, with particular consideration given to the promise and limitations of microfinance.

An analysis of the government's role in facilitating access to financial services is presented in chapter 4. The chapter starts with a discussion of the important role that institution-building must play in improving access in particular and financial development in general. It then turns to measures to boost market capacity, improve competition and efficiency, and regulate against exploitative and imprudent practices. This is followed by a discussion of the impact that governments can have by owning or subsidizing financial service providers; as an example, the case of government-backed credit guarantee schemes is looked at in some depth. Before concluding, the chapter considers key issues in the political economy of access.

The first step to improving access is measuring it—

—but the paucity of data presents methodological challenges

While data on the financial sector are often considered to be readily available, systematic indicators of access to different financial services are not. Indeed, access is not easy to measure, and empirical evidence linking access to development outcomes has been quite limited because of lack of data. Existing evidence on the causal relations between financial development, growth, and poverty is consistent with theory. However, most of the evidence comes either from highly aggregated indicators that use financial depth measures instead of access or from micro studies that use financial or real wealth to proxy for credit constraints.

One of the key problems in assessing financial inclusion is that— unlike indicators of financial depth—an analysis of aggregated data sets has limited value. Simply knowing how many deposit accounts there are, for example, does not reveal much. Some individuals or firms may have multiple accounts, while others have none; moreover, regulatory authorities generally do not collect data on individual account holders. Therefore the best data would be generated by census or survey, which would allow researchers to measure financial access across subgroups. Few such surveys exist for households, however, and the data sets that are available are often not compatible from one country to the next.

In the absence of comprehensive micro data, researchers have sought to create synthetic headline indicators, combining more readily available macro data with the results of existing surveys. These headline indicators indicate that households around the world have limited access to and use of financial services: in most developing countries less than half the population has an account with a financial institution, and in many countries less than one in five households does (figure 1).

Survey data on the access of firms to finance are more plentiful—although there are concerns about the representativeness of the surveys, particularly with regard to the inclusion of the informal sector (which is larger than the formal sector in many countries). Survey data indicate that less than 20 percent of small firms use external finance, about half the rate of large firms. And in three regions, at least 40 percent of firms report that access to and cost of finance is an obstacle to their growth (figure 2).

Figure 1 Proportion of households with an account in a financial institution

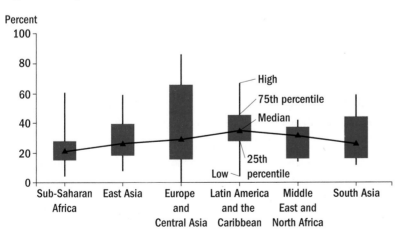

Source: Honohan (2006).

Note: Figure shows the highest and lowest national percentages, as well as the median and quartiles, for the countries in each region.

Figure 2 Percentage of firms reporting finance as a problem

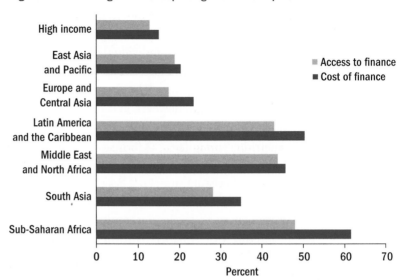

Source: Investment Climate Survey (ICS) responses by enterprises in 76 countries, grouped by region.

Note: Figure shows the percentage of firms reporting access to finance or cost of finance as a severe or major obstacle to firm growth.

Identifying barriers to access: physical access, eligibility, and affordability

Why do large proportions of the populations in many developing countries not use financial services? Identifying the barriers that prevent small firms and poor households in developing countries from using financial services not only helps researchers understand the reasons for financial exclusion but also provides hints as to which policies could be helpful in removing these barriers and broadening access. One major constraint is geography, or physical access. While some financial institutions allow clients to access services over the phone or via the Internet, some require clients to visit a branch or use an automated teller machine (ATM). While an ideal measure would indicate the average distance from household to branch (or ATM), the density of branches per square kilometer, or per capita, provides an initial, albeit crude, indicator. For example, Spain has 96 branches per 100,000 people and 790 branches per 10,000 square kilometers, while Ethiopia has less than 1 branch per 100,000 people and Botswana has 1 branch per 10,000 square kilometers.

Another barrier is the lack of proper documentation. Financial institutions usually require one or more documents for identification purposes, but in many low-income countries, most people—especially those not employed in the formal sector (who are usually poor)—lack such papers.

Finally, many institutions have minimum account-balance requirements or fees that are out of the reach of many potential users. For example, it is not unusual for banks to require a person opening a checking account to make a minimum deposit equivalent to 50 percent of that country's per capita gross domestic product (GDP).

While barriers to access vary significantly across countries, lower barriers tend to be associated with more open and competitive banking systems. Such systems are characterized by private ownership of banks, including foreign ownership; strong legal, information, and physical infrastructures (such as telecommunication and road networks); regulatory and supervisory approaches that rely heavily on market discipline; and substantial transparency and media freedom.

However, access indicators are just that—indicators. While they are linked to policy, they are not policy variables. Thus, creating indicators is only the beginning of the effort. Analytical work collecting and using in-depth household and enterprise information on access to and use of financial services is necessary to understand the impact of financial access and to design better policy interventions. Better data and analysis will help researchers assess which financial services—savings, credit, payments, insurance—are most important in achieving development outcomes for both households and firms, and will inform efforts to narrow down which cross-country indicators to track over time.

Barriers to access vary significantly across countries

Evaluating the impact of access to finance for firms

One of the important channels through which finance promotes growth is the provision of credit to the most promising firms (figure 3). Many firms, particularly small ones, often complain about lack of access to finance. Recent research using detailed firm-level data and survey information provides direct evidence suggesting that such complaints are valid in that limited access stunts firms' growth. This finding is supported by studies based on census data and individual case studies using detailed loan information.

Access to finance, and the institutional underpinnings associated with better financial access, favorably affects firm performance along a number of different channels. Improvements in the functioning of the formal financial sector can reduce financing constraints for small firms and others who have difficulty in self-financing or in finding private or informal sources of funding. Research indicates that access to finance promotes

Access to finance can promote new-firm entry, growth, innovation, optimum size, and risk reduction—

Figure 3 Finance helps firms grow faster

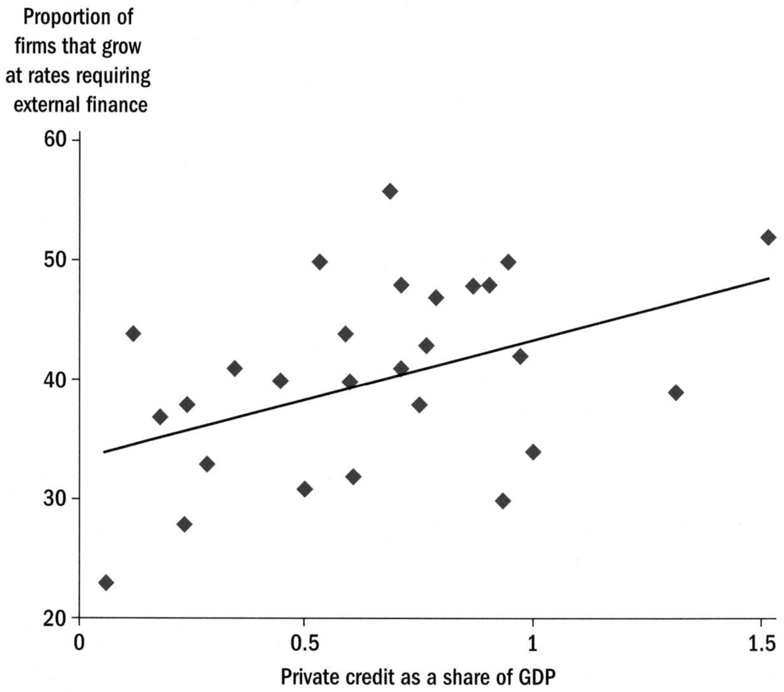

Proportion of
firms that grow
at rates requiring
external finance

Private credit as a share of GDP

Source: Demirgüç-Kunt and Maksimovic (1998).
Note: The graph plots the proportion of firms that are able to grow faster than they would if they had no access to external finance against financial development as measured by private credit/GDP.

more start-ups: it is smaller firms that are often the most dynamic and innovative. Countries that strangle this potential with financial barriers not only lose the growth potential of these enterprises but also risk missing opportunities to diversify into new areas of hitherto unrevealed comparative advantage. Financial inclusion also enables incumbent firms to reach a larger equilibrium size by enabling them to exploit growth and investment opportunities. Furthermore, greater financial inclusion allows firms the choice of more efficient asset portfolios as well as more efficient organizational forms, such as incorporation.

—to the benefit of the economy in general

If stronger financial systems can promote entry of new firms, enterprise growth, innovation, larger equilibrium size, and risk reduction, then it is almost inescapable that stronger financial systems will improve aggregate economic performance. Improved finance does not raise aggregate firm performance uniformly, however, but rather transforms the structure of the economy by affecting different types of firms in different ways. At any given level of financial development, smaller firms have more difficulty accessing external finance than do larger companies. But with financial development and greater availability of external finance, firms that were formerly excluded are given opportunities. Research shows that small firms benefit the most from financial development—both in terms of being able to enter the marketplace and of seeing their growth constraints relaxed. Hence, inclusive financial sectors also have consequences for the composition of and competition in the enterprise sector.

Firms finance their investments and operations in many different ways, depending on a wide range of factors both internal and external to the individual firm. The availability of external financing depends not only on a firm's own situation, but on the wider policy and institutional environment supporting the enforceability and liquidity of the contracts that are involved in financing firms. And it also depends on the existence and effectiveness of a variety of intermediaries and ancillary financial firms that help bring providers and users of funds together in the market. Bank finance is typically the major source of external finance for firms of all sizes. Modern trends in transactional lending suggest that improvements in information availability (for example, through development of credit registries) and technological advances in analysis of this improved data (for example, through use of automated credit appraisal) are likely to improve access of small and medium enterprises (SMEs) to finance. Provided that the relevant laws are in place, asset-based lending such as factoring, fixed-asset lending, and leasing are other technologies that can release sizable financing flows even for small and nontransparent firms.

Use of modern transactional lending by banks helps reach more firms

However, relationship lending (which relies on personal interaction between borrower and lender and is based on an understanding of the borrower's business and not just on collateral or mechanical credit scoring systems) will remain important in environments with weak financial infrastructures and strong informal economic activity. Because relationship lending is costly for the lender, it requires either high spreads or large volumes to be viable. If the customer's creditworthiness is hard to evaluate, then there may be no alternative to relationship lending. Indeed, limited access to credit in some difficult environments may be attributable to the reluctance of existing intermediaries to do relationship lending on a small scale.

—but relationship lending will remain important for informal economic activity

Foreign banks are likely to increase access for SMEs—

The role of foreign banks in improving access has always been controversial, partly for political reasons. The growing market share of foreign-owned banks in developing and transition economies has resulted from a number of forces, including the privatization of long-established state-owned banks and the sale of distressed banks in the aftermath of banking crises (often after being financially restructured at the expense of the host country government). Foreign owners bring capital, technology, know-how, and independence from the local business and political elites, but debate continues over whether they have improved access. Most foreign banks are relatively large and do not concentrate on SME lending, sticking mostly to the banking needs of large firms and high-net-worth individuals. However, the increased competition for large customers can drive local banks to focus more on providing profitable services to segments they had once neglected. The balance of a large body of evidence suggests that a country that allows foreign banks to operate within its borders is likely, over time, to improve financial access for SMEs, even if the foreign banks confine their lending to large firms and government. In contrast, the performance of state-owned banks in this dimension has tended to be poor.

—and the role of nonbank finance is likely to increase

Nonbank finance remains much less important than bank finance in most developing countries, but it can play an important role in improving the price and availability of longer-term finance to smaller borrowers. Bond finance, for example, can provide a useful alternative to bank finance. The emergence of a large market in external equity requires strong investor rights; where these are present, opening to foreign capital inflows can greatly improve access and lower the cost of capital, with spillover effects for smaller firms. This is true for portfolio equity investments, foreign direct investment (FDI), and private equity, all of which are likely to become increasingly important in the future.

Evaluating impact of access to finance for households

Over the long term, economic growth helps reduce poverty and can be expected to lift the welfare of most households. Evidence suggests not only that finance is pro-growth but that it reduces income inequality (figure 4) and is pro-poor. How important in this process is the direct provision of financial services to poor households and individuals? Existing evidence suggests that indirect, second-round effects through

Figure 4 Finance and income inequality

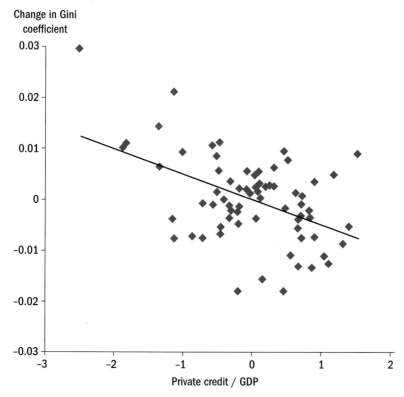

Source: Beck, Demirgüç-Kunt, and Levine (2007).
    Note: The figure is a partial scatterplot of growth of Gini coefficient vs. private credit/GDP, controlling for initial levels of Gini.

more efficient product and labor markets might have a greater impact on the poor than direct access to finance. First, aggregate regressions yield more robust results of a dampening effect of finance on inequality and poverty, while micro studies, which do not consider spillover effects, provide a more tenuous picture. Similarly, calibrated general equilibrium models that take into account labor market effects suggest that the main impact of finance on income inequality comes through inclusion of a larger share of the population in the formal economy and higher wages. Hence, the evidence so far seems to suggest that direct provision of financial services to the poor may not be the most important channel through which finance reduces poverty and income inequality. Therefore, fostering more efficient capital allocation through competitive and open financial markets should remain an important policy goal, and it is as relevant for reduction of poverty and inequality as it is for overall economic growth.

Financial exclusion extends beyond the poor in many countries—

In many countries, however, access to financial services is limited to only 20–50 percent of the population, excluding many nonpoor individuals and SMEs. That being the case, improving the quality of the services provided and the efficiency with which they are provided without broadening access is not enough: it would leave large segments of the population and their talents and innovative capacity untapped. The provision of better financial access to these excluded nonpoor micro- and small entrepreneurs can have an especially favorable indirect effect on the poor. Hence, to promote pro-poor growth, it is important to improve access not only to the poor but to all who are currently excluded. That is not to say that improvements in direct access for the poor should be neglected. The benefits here may be more modest in the long run, but they can be immediate.

—but there are barriers to increasing access

There are many reasons for the limited access to financial services, especially in the case of the poor. The poor may not have anybody in their social network who understands the various services that are available to them. Lack of education may make it difficult for them to fill out loan applications, and the small number of transactions they are likely to undertake may make loan officers think it is not worthwhile to help them. As financial institutions are likely to be located in rich neighborhoods, physical distance may also matter—banks simply may not be near the poor. Even if financial service providers are nearby, some poor clients may encounter prejudice—being refused admission to banking offices, for example. The poor face two significant problems in obtaining access to credit services. First, they typically have no collateral and cannot borrow against their future income because they tend not to have steady jobs or income streams that creditors can track. Second, dealing with small transactions is costly for the financial institutions.

Joint lending and dynamic incentives may increase inclusion—

The new wave of specialized microfinance institutions serving the poor has tried to overcome these problems in innovative ways. Loan officers come from similar backgrounds and go to the poor, instead of waiting for the poor to come to them. Group-lending schemes improve repayment incentives and monitoring through peer pressure, and they also build support networks and educate borrowers. Increasing loan sizes as customers demonstrate their ability to borrow and repay reduces default rates. The effectiveness of these innovations in different settings is still being debated, but over the past few decades, microfinance institutions have managed to reach millions of clients and have achieved impressive repayment rates. Even though subsidies are often involved, researchers are reconsidering whether it might be possible to make profits while providing financial services to some of the world's poorest. Indeed, mainstream banks have begun to adopt some of the techniques used by the microfinance institutions and to enter some of the same markets. For many, however, the most exciting promise of microfinance is that it could reduce poverty without requiring continuous subsidies.

Has microfinance been able to meet its promise? While many heartening case studies are cited—from contexts as diverse as the slums of Dhaka to villages of Thailand to rural Peru—it is still unclear how big an impact microfinance has had on poverty overall. Methodological difficulties in evaluating impact, such as selection bias, make it difficult to reach any solid conclusion. So far, the evidence from microeconomic studies, taken together, does not unambiguously show a reduction in poverty. Additional research—ideally using more field experiments—is needed to convince the skeptics.

—but the welfare impact of microfinance is not clear—

One of the most controversial questions about microfinance is the extent of subsidy required to provide access. Although group lending and other techniques are employed to overcome the obstacles involved in delivering services to the poor, these mechanisms are nevertheless costly, and the high repayment rates have not always translated into profits. Overall, much of the microfinance sector—especially the segment that serves the very poor—still remains heavily dependent on grants and subsidies. Recent research confirms that there is a trade-off between profitability and serving the very poor.

—and much of the microfinance sector relies on grants and subsidies

Microfinance has traditionally focused on the provision of credit for very poor entrepreneurs, and enthusiasts often emphasize how microfinance will unleash the productive potential of these borrowers, leading to productivity increases and growth. Yet much of microcredit is not used for investment. Instead, a sizable fraction of it goes to meet important consumption needs. These are not a secondary concern. For poor households, credit is not the only, or in many cases the priority, financial service they need: good savings and payments (domestic as well as international) services and insurance may rank higher. For example, one reason why the poor may not put any savings in financial assets may be the lack of appropriate savings products.

The poor need other services in addition to credit—

The question, then, has two parts: Should finance for the very poor be subsidized, and if so, is microfinance the best way to provide those subsidies? The answer requires comparing costs and benefits of subsidies

—and the very poor will require subsidies to access financial services

in the financial sector with those in other areas, such as education and infrastructure. The clear need for the latter set a high threshold if scarce public funds are to be diverted to subsidizing access. Within the financial sector, the case for subsidizing savings and payments services, which can be seen as basic services necessary for participation in a modern market economy, seems stronger than that for credit. In the case of credit, interest rate subsidies in particular do not seem to be the way to go, given their negative incentive effects on repayment, the likelihood that much of the subsidy will in practice be diverted away from the target group, and the chilling effect on unsubsidized service providers just starting to provide small-scale credit. Instead, policies that encourage entry in general are more promising, as are policies that promote the adoption of novel techniques (such as those that take advantage of the already wide and increasing availability of mobile phones). Once in place, such techniques lower the unit cost of service delivery to the poor.

Policies to broaden access

Perhaps more important, improving financial access in a way that benefits the poor to the greatest extent requires a strategy for inclusion that goes well beyond credit for poor households. Since expanding access remains an important challenge even in developed economies, it is not enough to say that the market will provide. Market failures related to information gaps, the need for coordination on collective action, and concentrations of power mean that governments everywhere have an important role to play in building inclusive financial systems. Not all government action is equally effective, however, and some policies can be counterproductive. Direct government interventions to support access require careful evaluation, something that is often missing. Our discussion is selective, setting out principles for effective government policy, drawing on and generalizing lessons from specific examples that illustrate how other issues can be approached.

It is important to have realistic goals

Even the most efficient financial system supported by a strong contractual and information infrastructure faces limitations. Not all would-be borrowers are creditworthy, and there are numerous examples where national welfare has been reduced by overly relaxed credit policies. Access to formal payment and savings services can approach universality as economies develop. However, not everyone will—or should—qualify for credit.

Deep institutional reform ensuring, above all, security of property rights against expropriation by the state is an underlying, albeit often long-term, prerequisite for well-functioning financial systems. Prioritizing some institutional reforms over others, however, would help focus reform efforts and have a positive impact on access in the short to medium term. Recent evidence suggests that information infrastructures matter most in low-income countries, while enforcement of creditor rights is more important in high-income countries. Another finding is that in relatively underdeveloped institutional environments, procedures that enable individual lenders to recover on debt contracts (for example, those related to collateral) are more important in boosting bank lending compared with those procedures mainly concerned with resolving conflicts between multiple claimants (for example, bankruptcy codes). Given that it is potentially easier to build credit registries and reform procedures related to collateral compared with making lasting improvements in the enforcement of creditor rights and bankruptcy codes, these are important findings for prioritizing reform efforts.

Encouraging the development of specific infrastructures (particularly in information and debt recovery) and of financial market activities that can use technology to bring down transaction costs will produce results sooner than long-term institution building. Specific activities include establishing credit registries or issuing individual identification numbers to help establish and track credit histories; reducing costs of registering or repossessing collateral; and introducing specific legislation to underpin modern financial technology—including leasing and factoring, electronic finance, and mobile finance.

Encouraging openness and competition is also an essential part of broadening access, because they spur incumbent institutions to seek profitable ways of providing services to previously excluded segments of the population and increase the speed with which access-improving new technologies are adopted. Foreign banks have an important role to play in expanding access, as discussed above.

In this process, providing the private sector with the right incentives is key; hence good prudential regulations are a necessity. Competition that helps foster access can also result in reckless or improper expansion if not accompanied by the proper regulatory and supervisory framework. As increasingly complex international regulations—such as those envisaged in the advanced versions of the Basel II system—are imposed on banks to help minimize the risk of costly bank failures, it is important

Reforming institutions—

—developing financial infrastructures to take advantage of technological advances—

—encouraging competition—

—and providing the right incentives

to ensure that these arrangements do not inadvertently penalize small borrowers. That can happen if banks are not able to make full allowance for the potential risk-pooling advantages of including SME loans in their overall loan portfolio. Research suggests that while banks making small loans have to set aside larger *provisions* against the higher expected loan losses from small loans—and therefore they need to charge higher rates of interest to cover these provisions—they should need relatively less *capital* to cover the risk that they will lose more than they have anticipated.

A variety of other regulatory measures is needed to support wider access. Sometimes the most effective measure is not the most obvious one. For example, interest ceilings fail to provide adequate consumer protection against abusive lending. Increased transparency and formalization and enforced lender responsibility are more coherent approaches, along with support for the overborrowed (such as assistance in finding a viable workout plan or formalized personal bankruptcy schemes). However, delivering all of this is can be administratively demanding.

The role for direct government intervention is limited

The scope for direct government interventions in improving access is more limited than often believed. A large body of evidence suggests that efforts by government-owned subsidiaries to provide credit have generally not been successful. Direct intervention through taxes and subsidies can be effective in certain circumstances, but experience suggests that they are more likely to have large unintended consequences in finance than in other sectors. For example, with direct and directed lending programs discredited in recent years, partial credit guarantees have been the direct intervention mechanism of choice pushed by SME credit activists. However, these are often poorly structured, embody hidden subsidies, and benefit mainly those who do not need the subsidy. In the absence of thorough economic evaluations of most of these guarantee schemes, their net effect in cost-benefit terms also remains unclear.

In nonlending services, the experience has been mixed. A few government financial institutions have moved away from providing credit and evolved into providers of more complex financial services, entering into public-private partnerships to help overcome coordination failures, first-mover disincentives, and obstacles to risk sharing and distribution that impede outreach to SMEs by banks. Ultimately, these successful initiatives could have been undertaken by private capital, but the state had a useful role in jump-starting these services.

Political economy concerns are key in implementing policies to expand access

A comprehensive approach to financial sector reform aiming at better access must take political realities into account. If the interest of powerful incumbents is threatened by the emergence of new entrants financed

Main messages of this report

FINANCIAL MARKET IMPERFECTIONS THAT LIMIT access to finance are key in most development theories. Lack of access to finance is often the critical mechanism behind both persistent income inequality and slow economic growth. Hence financial sector reforms that promote broader access to financial services should be at the core of the development agenda.

Access is not easy to measure, and empirical evidence linking access to development outcomes has been quite scarce due to lack of data. Initial efforts indicate that financial access is quite limited around the world and that barriers to access are common. Further research to assess the impact of access on outcomes such as growth and poverty reduction will require better micro data, particularly data derived from household and enterprise surveys.

Empirical evidence suggests that improved access to finance is not only pro-growth but also pro-poor, reducing income inequality and poverty. Hence financial development that includes small firms and the poor disproportionately benefits those groups.

Providing better financial access to the nonpoor micro- and small entrepreneurs can have a strongly favorable indirect effect on the poor. Spillover effects of financial development are likely to be significant. Hence, to promote pro-poor growth, it is important to broaden the focus of attention from finance for the poor to improving access for all who are excluded.

Provision of financial services to the very poor will require subsidies. If subsidies for credit damage the ability and incentives of the microfinance industry and the financial sector more generally to make use of innovative new technologies in providing access for the nonpoor, their effect on the poor could be counterproductive.

However, for poor households, credit is not the only—or in many cases, the principal—financial service they need. Subsidies may be better spent on savings and payment systems because those services are necessary for participation in a modern market economy.

Government policies should focus on building sound financial institutions, encouraging competition (including foreign entry), and establishing sound prudential regulation to provide the private sector with appropriate incentive structures and broaden access. Governments can facilitate the development of an enabling financial infrastructure and encourage adoption of new technologies, but attempts at direct intervention (through subsidies, for example, or ownership of financial institutions) are more likely than not to be counterproductive.

by a system that has improved access and outreach, lobbying by those incumbents can block the needed reforms. Given that challenges of financial inclusion and benefits from broader access go well beyond ensuring financial services for the poor, defining the access agenda more broadly to expand access for all, would include the middle classes and help mobilize greater political support for advancing the agenda around the world.

Directions for future research

While this report reviews and highlights a large body of research, it also identifies many gaps in our knowledge. Much more research is needed to measure and track access to financial services, to evaluate its impact on development outcomes, and to design and evaluate policy interventions.

More theory work—

New development models link the dynamics of income distribution and aggregate growth in unified models. There are good conceptual reasons for believing that financial market frictions play an important role in the persistence of income inequalities, but there is too little theory that examines how reducing these frictions may affect the opportunities faced by individuals and the evolution of relative income levels. Future theoretical work could usefully study the impact of financial sector policies on growth and income distribution within the context of these models and provide new insights.

—and more comprehensive and consistent data

Lack of systematic information on access is one of the reasons why empirical research on access has been limited. The efforts described above in developing cross-country indicators of access are only first steps in this direction. This work should be continued and expanded, both in terms of country coverage and coverage of institutions and different services available. Building data sets that benchmark countries annually would help focus policymaker attention and allow better tracking and evaluation of reform efforts to broaden access.

Furthermore, while cross-country indicators of access are useful for benchmarking, any assessment of the impact of access on outcomes such as growth and poverty reduction requires data at the household and enterprise level. Few household surveys focus on financial services. Efforts to collect this data systematically around the world are important in improving the understanding of access. Indeed, household surveys are often the only way to get detailed information on who uses which financial services from which types of institutions, including informal ones.

A better understanding of the impact of finance

Emerging evidence suggests that financial development reduces income inequality and poverty, yet researchers are still far from understanding the channels through which this effect operates. The finance-growth channel is better understood: firms' access to finance has been shown to have significant payoffs in many areas, from promoting entrepreneurship and innovation to better asset allocation and firm growth. But how does finance influence income distribution? How important is direct provision of finance for the poor? Which is more important: improving the functioning of the financial system so that it expands access to existing customers, or broadening access to the underserved (including the non-poor who are often excluded in many developing countries)?

Results of general equilibrium models and evidence at the aggregate level hint that a narrow focus on giving just the poor better direct access is not the best policy. Instead, the poor will benefit most by policies that broaden access in general; moreover, spillover effects of financial development are likely to be important for the poor by improving employment opportunities and wages. However, simply improving competition and the available services for those already served by the financial system is not likely to be enough either. In many countries improving efficiency will require that access be broadened beyond concentrated incumbents, since a large proportion of the nonpoor as well as the poor are currently excluded. Hence the efficiency and access dimensions of finance are likely to be closely linked, but more research is needed to sort out the relative importance of these effects on growth and poverty.

In evaluating impact, randomized field experiments are promising. These experiments operate by varying the treatments of randomly selected subsamples of the surveyed households or microentrepreneurs. For instance, they could be offered different financial products, or different terms and conditions, or different amounts of training in financial literacy. Such random variation allows the researchers to make reliable inferences about how removing barriers and improving access will affect growth and household welfare. While this report discusses some of this research, more experiments need to be conducted in different country contexts, focusing on different dimensions of access. Ultimately, it is this welfare impact that should determine which access indicators should be tracked and how policy should be designed.

Policies to broaden access can take many forms, from improvements in the functioning of mainstream financial products to innovations in microfinance. Lack of careful evaluation of different interventions makes it difficult to assess their impact and draw broader lessons. Careful research in this area would also help improve design of policy interventions to build more inclusive financial systems.

Randomized field experiments may provide insights on welfare impact

CHAPTER ONE

Access to Finance and Development: Theory and Measurement

FINANCE IS AT THE CORE OF THE DEVELOPMENT PROCESS. BACKED by solid empirical evidence, development practitioners are becoming increasingly convinced that efficient, well-functioning financial systems are crucial in channeling funds to the most productive uses and in allocating risks to those who can best bear them, thus boosting economic growth, improving opportunities and income distribution, and reducing poverty.[1] Conversely, to the extent that access to finance and the available range of services are limited, the benefit of financial development is likely to elude many individuals and enterprises, leaving much of the population in absolute poverty. This access dimension of financial development is the focus of this report.

Improving access and building inclusive financial systems is a goal that is relevant to economies at all levels of development. The challenge of better access means making financial services available to all, thereby spreading equality of opportunity and tapping the full potential in an economy. The challenge is greater than ensuring that as many people as possible have access to basic financial services. It is just as much about enhancing the quality and reach of credit, savings, payments, insurance, and other risk management products in order to facilitate sustained growth and productivity, especially for small and medium-scale enterprises. Although the formal financial sector in a few countries has achieved essentially universal coverage of the population, at least for basic services, some financial exclusion persists even in many high-income countries (and, because they find it difficult to participate fully in those sophisticated economies, financial exclusion can be an even more serious handicap for those affected).

Well-functioning financial systems can boost growth and reduce poverty

Financial market frictions can generate poverty traps

Theoreticians have long reasoned that financial market frictions can be the critical mechanism for generating persistent income inequality or poverty traps. Without inclusive financial systems, poor individuals and small enterprises need to rely on their personal wealth or internal resources to invest in their education, become entrepreneurs, or take advantage of promising growth opportunities. Financial market imperfections, such as information asymmetries and transactions costs, are likely to be especially binding on the talented poor and the micro- and small enterprises that lack collateral, credit histories, and connections, thus limiting their opportunities and leading to persistent inequality and slower growth. However, this access dimension of financial development has often been overlooked, mostly because of serious gaps in the data about who has access to which financial services and about the barriers to broader access.

Measuring access can be difficult

Despite the emphasis financial access has received in theory, empirical evidence that links broader access to development outcomes has been very limited, providing at best tentative guidance for public policy initiatives in this area. Financial inclusion, or broad access to financial services, implies an absence of price and nonprice barriers in the use of financial services; it is difficult to define and measure because access has many dimensions. Services need to be available when and where desired, and products need to be tailored to specific needs. Services need to be affordable, taking into account the indirect costs incurred by the user, such as having to travel a long distance to a bank branch. Efforts to improve inclusion should also make business sense, translate into profits for the providers of these services, and therefore have a lasting effect.

This chapter reviews the theoretical models—

The purpose of this chapter is twofold. First, it briefly reviews the theoretical models that incorporate capital market imperfections to illustrate how improved access to finance is likely to reduce inequality as well as promote growth and, through both channels, lead to a reduction in poverty. Many types of policy measures aimed at reducing poverty and inequality through redistributive measures such as land reform can have adverse side-effects on incentives. If the underlying causes of inequality are not removed, the effect of such redistributive measures may be only temporary and require repetition. A complementary development strategy would directly address the underlying causes, including capital market imperfections (in addition to redistributive policies). Financial sector reforms to achieve this goal can represent a first-best policy to promote growth and poverty reduction and would also make redistribution more effective and sustainable.

Second, the chapter presents indicators of access to and use of financial services that households and small firms are likely to need. Developing better indicators of access to finance is essential to strengthen the link between theory and empirical evidence and to investigate the channels through which a more developed financial system promotes development, both in terms of growth and poverty reduction. Indeed, the extent of direct access to financial services by households and small enterprises varies sharply around the world, with very limited access in many countries.

—and presents access indicators for households and small firms

Theory: The Crucial Role of Access to Finance

Modern development theory studies the evolution of growth, relative income inequalities, and their persistence in unified models. In many of these models, financial market imperfections play a central role, influencing key decisions regarding human and physical capital accumulation and occupational choices. For example, in theories stressing capital accumulation, financial market imperfections determine the extent to which the poor can borrow to invest in schooling or physical capital. In theories stressing entrepreneurship, financial market imperfections determine the extent to which talented but poor individuals can raise external funds to initiate projects. Thus, the evolution of financial development, growth, and intergenerational income dynamics are closely intertwined. Finance influences not only the efficiency of resource allocation throughout the economy but also the comparative economic opportunities of individuals from relatively rich or poor households.

This crucial focus on the financial sector in economic modeling has been strengthened with the historical development of views on the links between economic growth and income inequality. It was long believed that the early stages of economic development would inevitably be accompanied by inequality and concentrations of wealth. Pointing to the fact that rich people's marginal propensity to save is higher than that of the poor, theoreticians argued that the need to finance large, indivisible investment projects in the process of development implied that rapid growth would need wealth concentration, leading to a fundamental trade-off between growth and social justice. More generally, Kuznets (1955, 1963) reasoned that this trade-off meant that inequality would increase in the early stages of development until the benefits of growth spread throughout the economy. Some of the earlier empirical evidence

Empirical evidence suggests that the link between growth and inequality is ambiguous

from the United States and other developed countries supported the Kuznets hypothesis. But evidence from developing countries was not so supportive.[2]

The importance of providing incentives to reward the productive efficiency of enterprise and investment might seem to imply that growth and inequality must be positively linked, but empirical studies suggest that this is not always so. In particular, while very low inequality is indeed empirically associated with rapid subsequent growth, the highest rates of growth are associated with moderate inequality. Furthermore, high levels of inequality seem to reduce subsequent growth.[3]

Modern development theory highlights the role of finance

Helping to explain these findings, more subtle theories have explored precise mechanisms whereby inequality might adversely affect growth. Financial market imperfections are often at the core of this line of thought because inequalities persist because of these imperfections.[4] For example, in the model of Galor and Zeira (1993), it is because of financial market frictions that poor people cannot invest in their education despite their high marginal productivity of investment. In Banerjee and Newman's model (1993), individuals' occupational choices are limited by their initial endowments. The structure of occupational choices—whether people can become entrepreneurs or have to remain wage earners—in turn determines how much they can save and what risks they can bear, with long-run implications for growth and income distribution.[5] Hence, these models show that lack of access to finance can be the critical mechanism for generating persistent income inequality or poverty traps, as well as lower growth.

Wealth redistribution and financial development

One implication of these modern development theories is that redistribution of wealth can foster growth. Indeed, this has been the main policy conclusion drawn by many readers of these theories. This thinking rationalizes a focus on redistributive public policies such as land or education reform. However, if it is the capital market imperfections that lead to these relationships and necessitate redistribution, why neglect policies that might remove capital market imperfections? Nevertheless, some theories take credit constraints or other frictions as exogenous. In others, static information and transaction costs endogenously yield adverse selection and moral hazard frictions that impede the operation of financial markets. In either case, researchers take capital market imperfections as given and suggest different redistributive policies to promote growth, focusing on schooling, saving, or fertility changes. This is true even though the literature also notes that if financial market imperfections continue to exist, absence of a virtuous circle a la Kuznets may also necessitate *permanent* redistribution policies.[6]

A more effective and sustainable development approach would directly address financial market imperfections, without causing adverse incentive effects. Most redistributive policies create disincentives to work and save, although the economic magnitudes of these disincentive effects are a subject of intense debate (Aghion and Bolton 1997). As Demirgüç-Kunt and Levine (2007) argue, these tensions vanish when focusing on financial sector reforms. Reducing financial market imperfections to expand individual opportunities creates positive, not negative, incentive effects. Hence these arguments are very consistent with modern development theories *yet* emphasize putting financial sector reforms that promote financial inclusion at the core of the development agenda. Addressing financial sector imperfections can also appeal to a wider range of philosophical perspectives than can redistributive policies inasmuch as the latter are directly linked with equalizing *outcomes*, whereas better functioning financial systems serve to equalize *opportunities*.

Extensive empirical evidence suggests a significant and robust relationship between financial depth and growth. More recent micro evidence using firm-level data sets suggests that better-developed financial systems ease financial constraints facing firms. This finding illuminates one mechanism through which financial development influences economic growth. Furthermore, researchers recently have shown that financial depth reduces income inequality and poverty and is thus particularly beneficial for the poor.[7] This evidence is reviewed in detail in the coming chapters. Although these results are encouraging, the link between theoretical models and empirical evidence has not been very close because of a lack of data on access to financial services. While theory focuses on the importance of broader access and greater opportunities (that is, financial inclusion), relatively little empirical evidence links access to finance to development outcomes, and there is little guidance for policies on how best to promote access.

Financial depth, or development more generally, can have direct and indirect effects on small firms and poor households. Greater depth is likely to be associated with greater access for both firms and households, which will make them better able to take advantage of investment opportunities, smooth their consumption, and insure themselves. However, even if financial development does not improve direct access for small firms or poor households, its indirect effects may also be significant.

Financial sector reforms can improve incentive structures

Empirical evidence on financial access is limited

25

For example, the poor may benefit from having jobs and higher wages, as better-developed financial systems improve the efficiency of product and labor markets and promote growth. Similarly, small firms may see their business opportunities expand with financial development, even if the financial sector still mostly serves the large firms.

Before access can be improved, it has to be measured

Only now are many questions about access beginning to be answered. Just how limited is financial access around the world? What are the chief obstacles and policy barriers to broader access? How important is access to finance as a constraint to growth or poverty alleviation? Which matters more: access by households, or access by firms? Is it more important to improve the quality and range of services available to those firms and households who might already have access (intensive margin), or to provide basic services to those who are completely excluded (extensive margin)? How important is direct access to finance for the poor and small firms compared with economywide spillover effects of greater financial development through more efficient product and labor markets? The development of indicators of access to financial services is the first step in answering all these questions. Before we can improve access, or decide whether and how to do it, we need to measure it.

Measurement: Indicators of Access to Finance

The financial sector is often thought of as being particularly well documented by statistical data. In advanced securities markets, data on transactions and prices are often available on a minute-by-minute basis. Across countries, indicators of the depth of banking systems, capital markets, and insurance sectors are widely available. Indicators such as the total value of bank claims on an economy's private sector expressed relative to gross domestic product, the turnover of shares (relative to total stock market capitalization), and the spread between lending and deposit interest rates have become standard measures of financial sector development. These indicators are also the basis for a large literature assessing the impact of financial depth and efficiency on outcomes in the real sector, such as per capita GDP growth, and exploring the determinants of financial sector development.

Much less is known about how inclusive financial systems are and who has access to which financial services. How many borrowers are behind the total value of outstanding loans of a country's banking system? How many depositors are represented by the statistic on total deposits? Or taking the perspective from the demand side, what share of the population uses deposit accounts? What share of the population has taken out a loan? Unlike data on financial depth, these statistics are not readily available. Until recently, there has been little systematic information on who is served by the financial sector in developing countries, which financial institutions or services are the most effective at supporting access for poor households and small enterprises, or what practical and policy barriers there may be to the expansion of access. Better data are needed to advance research on financial inclusion, and significant efforts have recently been made in this direction.

Unlike measures of financial depth—where data from individual institutions (or trades in the case of the capital market) can be aggregated relatively simply to obtain consolidated figures[8]— data on financial use cannot easily be constructed in this way. For instance, the total number of all bank accounts far exceeds the number of customers served, as households and enterprises may have business with several banks (or multiple accounts with a single bank). Further, regulatory entities traditionally do not collect data on individual accounts or account holders (unless they are large ones), because this information has not been considered useful for macroeconomic stability analysis. Researchers have therefore used a variety of different data sources and methodologies to infer the actual share of households or enterprises that use financial services. Many of these data collection efforts are recent, and researchers have just started to relate them to real sector outcomes. As more data become available and more systematic data collection efforts get under way, one can expect more and better analysis.

Financial inclusion, or broad access to financial services, is defined here as an absence of price or nonprice barriers in the use of financial services. Of course this does not mean that all households and firms should be able to borrow unlimited amounts at prime lending rates or transmit funds across the world instantaneously for a fraction of 1 percent of the amount. Even if service providers are keenly competitive and employ the best financial technology, prices and interest rates charged and the size of loans and insurance coverage on offer in a market economy will necessarily depend on the creditworthiness of the customer. As discussed in later chapters of this report, subsidies and regulation can influence this outcome to some extent. But the application of modern techniques in information and communications technology is more important in improving the prices,

Aggregate data can be misleading

What does access mean?

terms, and conditions on which financial services are available—regardless of whether services are provided at home or abroad.

Improving access, then, means improving the degree to which financial services are available to all at a fair price. It is easier to measure the use of financial services since use can be observed, but use is not always the same as access. Access essentially refers to the supply of services, whereas use is determined by demand as well as supply.

Distinguishing between voluntary and involuntary exclusion

To illustrate the differences between access and use, remember that even wealthy customers in advanced financial systems will choose not to use some financial services. Some moderately prosperous customers, especially older individuals or households, may not have any wish to borrow money, even if offered a loan at a favorable interest rate. Still, almost all households need to use some financial services, such as payments services, to participate in a modern market economy, and in a few of the most advanced economies, use of at least some basic services from the formal financial sector is essentially universal.

Moreover, some specific financial products are not attractive to some customers on ethical or religious grounds; nonusage in this case cannot be attributed to lack of access—although access might be an issue here if acceptable alternatives are not being offered. The case of *Sharia*-compliant financial products can be relevant here, a topic that is discussed in chapter 4.

For specific classes of financial services, the distinction between access and use can be significant (box 1.1). The challenge is to distinguish between voluntary and involuntary exclusion and, among those that are excluded involuntarily, between those that are rejected due to high risk or poor project quality and those that are rejected because of discrimination or high prices, which makes financial services or products unaffordable. While rejection due to high risk and poor project quality is not necessarily worrisome, rejection due to discrimination and high prices is, particularly if equilibrium prices are too high, excluding large portions of the population. In addition, even if the underlying cost structures are the same in different countries, a given price would lead to greater exclusion in poorer countries.

Poor people could be involuntarily excluded due to lack of appropriate products or services; they may need simple transaction accounts rather than checking accounts that entail the risk of incurring severe overdraft charges when the timing of payments and receipts goes wrong. Microentrepreneurs might be reluctant to take out loans that require

Box 1.1   Access to finance vs. use: voluntary and involuntary exclusion

WHAT DISTINGUISHES USE OF FINANCIAL SERVICES from access to financial services? To what extent is lack of use a problem? The figure below illustrates the difference between access to and use of financial services.[a] Users of financial services can be distinguished from nonusers, and there are important distinctions among nonusers. On the one hand are those who do not use financial services for cultural or religious reasons or because they do not see any need. These nonusers include households who prefer to deal in cash and enterprises without any promising investment projects. These nonusers have access, but they choose not to use financial services. From a policy maker's viewpoint, nonusers do not really constitute a problem because their lack of demand drives their nonuse of financial services. On the other hand are the involuntarily excluded who, despite demanding financial services, do not have access to them. There

are several different groups among the involuntarily excluded. First, there is a group of households and enterprises that are considered unbankable by commercial financial institutions and markets because they do not have enough income or present too high a lending risk. Second, there might be discrimination against certain population groups based on social, religious, or ethnic grounds (*red-lining*). Third, the contractual and informational framework might prevent financial institutions from reaching out to certain population groups because the outreach is too costly to be commercially viable. Finally, the price of financial services may be too high or the product features might not be appropriate for certain population groups. While the first group of involuntarily excluded cannot be a target of financial sector policy, the other three groups demand different responses from policy makers—a topic that is discussed in chapter 4.

Distinguishing between access to finance and use

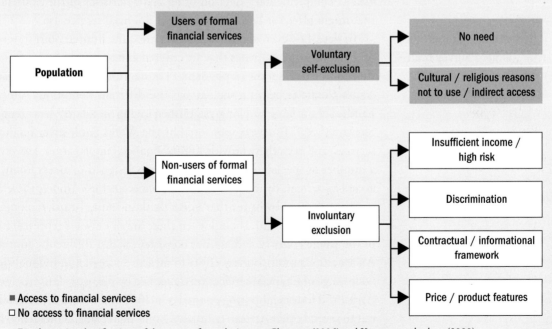

■ Access to financial services
□ No access to financial services

a. For alternative classifications of the reasons for exclusion, see Claessens (2006) and Kempson and others (2000).

them to pledge their personal assets as collateral, a common practice in most developing countries. In contrast, voluntary exclusion could result from lack of awareness of products if financial institutions do not target their marketing toward certain groups. Also, individuals can access services indirectly, for example, by using an account that belongs to somebody else in the household. And finally voluntary exclusion could also result from lack of financial literacy. Defining the "access problem" is challenging (box 1.2). It also requires a wealth of different data sources that researchers are just starting to collect. In the remainder of this chapter, we discuss some of these initial efforts and point to ongoing and future work.

Measuring access to, and use of, financial services

Recent data compilation efforts have made progress toward better measurement of both access to and use of financial services. Consider first the measurement of the use of financial services. Ideally, one would like to have census data on the number and characteristics of households that have a bank account or an account with a bank-like financial institution. In the absence of census data, one would at least like to have survey-based measures that are representative of the whole population and of important subgroups, again collecting information about the types of financial services they are consuming, in what quantities, and at what price, as well as complementary data on other characteristics of the household that might affect or be affected by their financial service use.

Research is hampered by limited survey data—

To date, however, survey-based data are quite limited both in terms of the number of countries that are covered and the amount of information collected about the respondents. The data are often not comparable across countries because the surveys use different definitions. Only a handful of the large and long-established Living Standard Measurement Surveys (LSMS) surveys sponsored by the World Bank cover financial services, and even these provide limited financial information. However, a number of specialized household surveys designed to assess financial access have been conducted in developing countries. Among these are surveys prepared by or for the World Bank in India, Brazil, Colombia, and Mexico (box 1.3), though even these are not always representative of the whole country and are not consistent across different countries. An ambitious multicountry effort to measure access of individuals to a wide range of financial services was launched by Finmark Trust in South Africa and four neighboring countries in 2002 and has since been rolled out to several other African countries. Some data come as incidental by-products of surveys designed for other purposes; this is the case for the

Box 1.2 Access to finance: supply vs. demand constraints

WHY DOES ONE OFTEN HEAR ABOUT AN ACCESS problem in credit markets but not about an access problem, say, for toothpaste? One of the basic rules of economics is that prices adjust so that at market equilibrium, supply equals demand. Hence, if demand for toothpaste exceeds the supply for it, the price of toothpaste will rise until demand and supply are equated at the new equilibrium price. If this price is too high for some, they will not use toothpaste. But all who are willing to pay the price will be able to use it. So if prices do their job, there should be no access problem.

In a famous paper, Stiglitz and Weiss (1981) provide a compelling explanation for why credit markets are different.[a] They show that information problems can lead to credit rationing even in equilibrium. That is because banks making loans are concerned not only about the interest rate they charge on the loan but also about the riskiness of the loan. And the interest rate a bank charges may itself affect the riskiness of the pool of loans, either by attracting high-risk borrowers (adverse selection effect) or by adversely affecting the actions and incentives of borrowers (moral hazard effect). Both effects exist because even after evaluating loan applications, the banks do not have complete information on their borrowers. When the interest rate (price) affects the nature of transaction, market equilibrium may not occur where demand equals supply.

The adverse selection aspect of interest rates is a consequence of different borrowers having different probabilities of repaying their loan. The expected return to the bank obviously depends on the probability of repayment, so the bank would like to be able to identify borrowers who are more likely to repay. It is difficult to identify good borrowers, which is why a bank uses a variety of screening devices, including the interest rate. Those who are willing to pay high interest rates may, on average, be worse risks; they are willing to take higher risks to gain higher returns if

successful, but such high returns are generally associated with a higher probability of failure, making it less likely that the loans will be repaid. As the interest rate rises, the average "riskiness" of those who borrow increases, possibly reducing the bank's profits.

Similarly, as the interest rate and other terms of the contract, such as collateral requirements, change, the behavior of the borrower is likely to change. Stiglitz and Weiss show that higher interest rates lead to moral hazard, that is, they induce firms to undertake riskier projects with lower probability of success but higher payoffs when successful.

In a world with imperfect and costly information that leads to adverse selection and moral hazard problems, the expected rate of return to the bank will increase less rapidly than the interest rate and, beyond a point, may actually decrease, as shown in figure A. The interest rate at which the expected return to the bank is maximized, r^*, is the "bank-optimal" rate. The bank will not want to raise the interest rate above this rate, even though demand may still exceed the funds available for lending. This also suggests that the supply of loans will be backward-bending, at interest rates above r^*.

Figure A

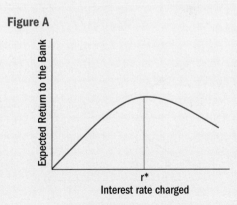

Note: D = demand, S = supply; r = interest rate.

(continued)

Box 1.2 *(continued)*

Clearly, it is conceivable that at r^*, the demand for funds (D^*) exceeds the supply of funds (S^*) as shown in figure B. In the absence of rationing, with excess demand for loans, unsatisfied borrowers would offer to pay a higher interest rate to the bank, bidding up the interest rate until demand equals supply at r^M. Although supply does not equal demand at rate r^*, it is the equilibrium interest rate. Since it is not profitable to raise the interest rate when the bank faces excess demand for credit, the bank will deny loans to borrowers who are observationally indistinguishable from those who receive loans. The rejected applicants would not receive a loan even if they offered to pay a higher rate. Hence they are denied access. Determining empirically whether an individual or firm has access to finance but chose not to use it or was rationed out is complex, and the effects of adverse selection and moral hazard are difficult to separate (see chapter 3).

What about other financial services, such as deposit or payment services, which do not suffer from information problems? Why do these areas of finance suffer from access problems? For those types of financial services, nonprice barriers become important. For example, some individuals will have no access to financial services because there are no financial institutions in their area, as is the case in many remote rural areas. Or the small transactions the poor demand may involve high fixed transaction costs, which makes them too costly to be offered: it costs as much for the bank to accept a $1 deposit as it does to accept a $1,000 deposit. Poorly designed regulatory requirements may also exclude those who do not meet the documentation requirements of opening an account, such as not having a formal address or formal sector employment. Some would-be customers may be discriminated against for some reason. For all those individuals the supply curve is vertical at the origin, and the supply and demand for services do not intersect, again leading to an access problem (as shown by S^0 in figure C). Of course, credit markets can also suffer from these nonprice barriers in addition to the type of rationing discussed above.

Price can also be a barrier. Even when nonprice barriers are overcome and the supply (S') and demand do intersect, the equilibrium price for these services (including the fees, minimum requirements, and so forth) may be very high, making them unaffordable for a large proportion of the population. This is an access problem of a different nature

Figure B

Note: D = demand, S = supply; r = interest rate.

Figure C

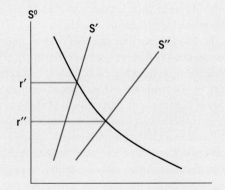

Note: D = demand, S = supply; r = interest rate.

Box 1.2 *(continued)*

since there is no rationing, but it still represents a policy problem because the high price often reflects lack of competition or underdeveloped physical or institutional infrastructures, leading to financial exclusion. These are matters that may call for public policy interventions to increase competition among providers and build relevant institutional and physical infrastructures, hence shifting the supply curve to the right (*S''*), reducing prices, and making financial services affordable for a larger part of the population. These government policies are discussed in chapter 4.

a. For other explanations, see, for example, Keeton (1979) and Williamson (1987).

European Commission's Eurobarometer, which covers all member states of the European Union (European Commission 2005).[9] Different surveys have different primary objectives: the questions in the South African survey reflect the original motivation for doing the survey, which was to assess the political and commercial climate for expanding access to finance, rather than to underpin research designed to build a comprehensive picture of economic and financial decision making. Findings based on surveys of individuals cannot easily be compared directly with those from surveys of households.[10] Different survey methodologies and their impact on the quality of information gathered are the subjects of an ongoing research effort at the World Bank.

Thus, despite some interesting insights from individual household surveys that focus on financial services, lack of cross-country comparability between survey instruments still prevents documentation of cross-country differences and thus analyses of supply and demand constraints. Altogether, household or individual survey data providing substantial financial services information currently exist for fewer than 40 developing countries and are inconsistent across countries in representativeness, measurement, and definition of financial services and products.[11]

Lack of consistent cross-country, micro data on use of financial services has led researchers to consider the information contained in more easily collected indicators such as the number of loan or deposit accounts in a country. Of course the total number of accounts is not the total number of users: people might have several accounts with one institution or accounts with several institutions. Further, a number of accounts might be dormant, a particularly common occurrence in many postal savings banks with

—and a lack of cross-country consistency

Box 1.3 Measuring access through household surveys

EXISTING HOUSEHOLD SURVEYS FOCUSING ON financial services in India, Brazil, Colombia, and Mexico give some insights into the information that can be obtained from such survey instruments beyond simple measures of use of financial services. Indeed, household surveys are necessary to obtain detailed information on who uses which financial services from which types of institutions, including informal ones. These surveys include questions on why people do not use financial services, which help researchers distinguish between use and access issues and between demand and supply factors.

For example, in the United States, 87 percent of the adult population has a bank account, compared with 48 percent in rural Upper Pradesh and Andhra Pradesh, India; 43 percent in 11 urban areas in Brazil; 41 percent in Bogota, Colombia; and 25 percent in Mexico City (48 percent when compulsory savings for borrowers are included). A comparison of U.S. and Mexican households reveals interesting differences about why some do not have bank accounts:

Main reasons for not having a bank account

Reason	United States (%)	Mexico (%)
Do not need account/no savings	53	7
Want to keep records private	22	2
Not comfortable with banks/don't trust	18	16
Fees and minimum balance too high	45	70
Inconvenience-location and hours	10	2
Lack of documentation	10	3

Although these figures are not strictly comparable because multiple reasons were allowed in the U.S. survey but not in the Mexican one, voluntary exclusion reasons—such as no need or an unwillingness to use banks—appear to be much higher in the United States compared with Mexico City. Survey responses also suggest that involuntary exclusion because of affordability is a more important deterrent in Mexico, with 70 percent of those without accounts citing high fees and minimum balances. These figures also indicate that supply factors in Mexico play a more important role in limiting access.

Sources: Caskey, Ruiz Duran, and Solo (2006); Kumar (2005); World Bank (2004).

free pass-book savings accounts and inefficient documentation systems. Nevertheless, Beck, Demirgüç-Kunt, and Martinez Peria (2007b) and Honohan (2006) show that nonlinear combinations of such aggregate indicators of loan and deposit accounts are sufficiently highly correlated with the actual proportion of households using financial services in countries for which this information is available from household surveys.

Indeed, in the absence of micro data that are more accurate but costly to collect, combining these indicators allows estimates to be made of the share of the population with accounts at formal or semiformal financial intermediaries for most countries (box 1.4). Figure 1.1 maps the main cross-country variations in this synthetic "headline" indicator. More than 80 percent of households in most of Western Europe and North America have an account with a financial institution, while the share is below 20 percent in many countries in Sub-Saharan Africa. The Russian Federation and many other countries of the former Soviet Union show usage ratios between 60 and 80 percent, a legacy of the state-run savings bank from communist time. Latin America exhibits a high variation in usage, ranging from less than 20 percent in Nicaragua to more than 60 percent in Chile. Usage across Asian countries varies much less and is mostly in the 40 to 60 percent range.

These headline indicators show that access to finance or, more precisely, use of financial services is positively, but not very closely, correlated with economic development and financial depth. Take first the correlation with economic development. The proportion of households with an account in a financial institution is higher in more developed

Creating synthetic headline indicators from surveys and aggregate data

Figure 1.1 Fraction of households with an account in a financial institution

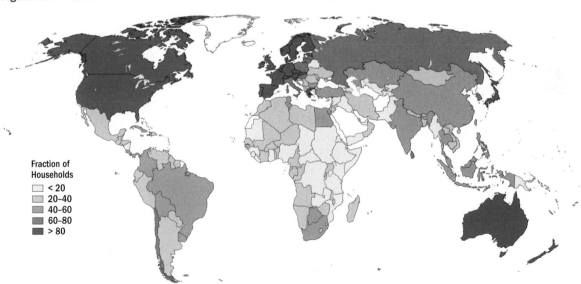

Fraction of
Households
☐ < 20
☐ 20–40
☐ 40–60
☐ 60–80
☐ > 80

Sources: Beck, Demirgüç-Kunt, and Martinez Peria (2007b); Christen, Jayadeva, and Rosenberg (2004); Peachey and Roe (2006); and Honohan (2006). See also box 1.4.

Box 1.4 Households' use of financial services: estimating the headline indicator

AN EXACT STATISTIC ON THE NUMBER OF households that use formal financial services can be inferred only from household surveys. However, only around 34 countries have household surveys containing this information, and researchers have therefore turned to proxy indicators to estimate the share of the population using financial services (For estimates by country, see appendix table A.1).

Beck, Demirgüç-Kunt, and Martinez Peria (2007b) compile loan and deposit account data through surveys of bank regulators for a cross-section of countries and document the large variation in these indicators across countries (see appendix table A.2). In Austria there are three deposit accounts for every inhabitant; in Madagascar, there are only 14 for every 1,000 inhabitants. In Greece there is almost one loan account for every inhabitant; in Albania, there are just four for every 1,000 inhabitants. The ratio of deposit and loan accounts per capita increases with income, although the average deposit or loan account balance relative to income per capita decreases with income, indicating that poor people

and smaller enterprises are better able to make use of these services in more developed countries (figures A and B). Still there is great variation among developing countries. For example in Bolivia, the average loan amount is 28 times GDP per capita, while it is only a third of GDP per capita in Poland. In Madagascar, the average deposit account balance is nine times GDP per capita, while it is only 4 percent of GDP per capita in Iran.

These aggregate indicators are not only interesting measures in their own right, but when no household surveys are available, they also can be used to predict the proportion of households using bank accounts. Regressing the share of households with deposit accounts obtained from household surveys on their aggregate indicators of deposit accounts and branch penetration, Beck, Demirgüç-Kunt, and Martinez Peria (2007b) show that the predicted share of households with deposit accounts resulting from this regression provides a reasonably accurate estimate of the actual share of households with deposit accounts obtained from household surveys

Figure A. Number of loans and deposits per capita, by income quintile of countries

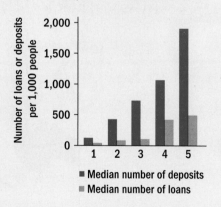

■ Median number of deposits
■ Median number of loans

Figure B. Loan and deposit size/GDP per capita, by income quintile of countries

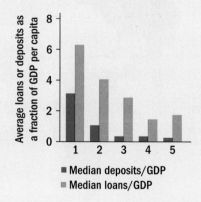

■ Median deposits/GDP
■ Median loans/GDP

Box 1.4 *(continued)*

(figure C). Hence it is also possible to obtain from aggregate indicators out-of-sample estimates of the proportion of households using a bank account, although the fit is likely to be poorer.

In parallel efforts, Christen, Jayadeva, and Rosenberg (2004) collected information on individual institutions that are considered socially oriented or alternative financial institutions, that is, institutions that target low-income clients and are not profit maximizers, such as microfinance institutions, postal savings banks, credit unions, and state-owned agricultural and development banks, while Peachey and Roe (2006) collected information on the member institutions of the World Savings Bank Association. These different efforts give a first indication of financial services provided by different providers. Honohan (2006) combines data from all three sources

to estimate a headline indicator of access. Using data on number of accounts in financial institutions as a proportion of population and an average account size as a proportion of GDP per capita (or estimated values where they do not exist) as regressors, he estimates a nonlinear regression relationship between these variables and the actual share of households with a financial account obtained from survey data. Where there is no survey data, a "predicted" share of households is obtained using the regressors and regression coefficients. Hence, the headline indicator pieces together the values of households using financial accounts from surveys when available, and this predicted value when survey data are not available. This indicator can then be used to map the share of the adult population with use of financial accounts for most of the world, as illustrated by the map in figure 1.1.

Figure C. Actual vs. fitted values of share of households with deposit accounts

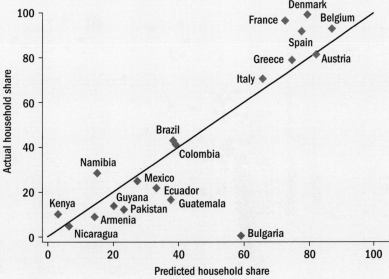

countries, approaching 100 percent for some of the richest (figure 1.2). Use of financial services increases steeply as per capita GDP approaches $10,000, and converges to near universal use at income levels above $20,000. However, countries show significant differences at similar levels of economic development. On the one hand, countries in Western Europe have typically higher rates of usage than does the United Kingdom or the United States, despite similar levels of GDP per capita. On the other hand, a higher proportion of households holds accounts in financial institutions in low-income countries in South Asia than in low-income countries in Sub-Saharan Africa.

The correlation between financial access and economic development is weak, albeit positive

Similarly, indicators of financial use show a positive but imperfect correlation with indicators of financial depth, such as credit to the private sector divided by GDP (figure 1.3). This correlation shows that access really is a distinct dimension: financial systems can become deep without delivering access to all. Take Colombia and Lithuania as examples. Both countries have similar levels of private credit to GDP at around 20 percent, but 70 percent of households in Lithuania have accounts, compared with 40 percent in Colombia. Similarly, over 85 percent of

Figure 1.2 Economic development and use of financial services

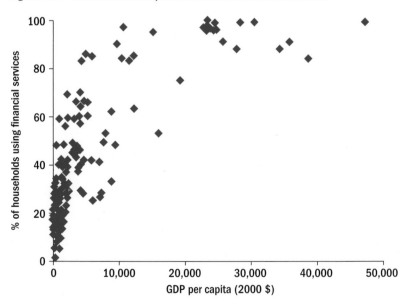

Sources: Beck, Demirgüç-Kunt, and Martinez Peria (2007b); Christen, Jayadeva, and Rosenberg (2004); Peachey and Roe (2006); Honohan (2006); World Bank (2002, *World Development Indicators*).

Figure 1.3 Financial depth vs. use

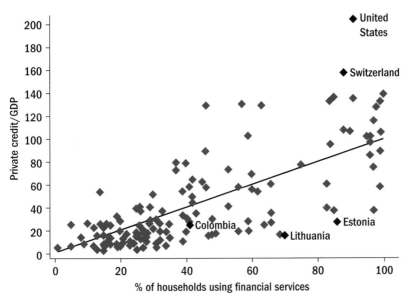

Sources: Beck, Demirgüç-Kunt, and Martinez Peria (2007b); Christen, Jayadeva, and Rosenberg (2004); Peachey and Roe (2006); Honohan (2006); and updated version of Beck, Demirgüç-Kunt, and Levine (2000).

households have accounts in Estonia and Switzerland, but while Estonia's financial depth is around 20 percent, Switzerland's is over 160 percent. The positive but imperfect correlations of financial services usage with economic development and financial depth raise questions regarding the drivers of cross-country differences in financial use and access. The correlations also suggest that there might be room for policy reforms to increase the level of financial inclusion—an issue that is addressed throughout this report.

It is important to understand not only the actual use of financial services, but also access across its different dimensions. Collecting indicators of and barriers to access and comparing them to usage and other country characteristics will enable researchers and policy makers to better understand the reasons for low access and to design policies to close the gaps (box 1.5). It is also important to assess the quality of access as well as quantity. For example, services may be available but may not be customized to different needs, or points of delivery may be too few, or delivery may take a very long time. The following discusses several dimensions of access and the indicators that have been collected to proxy for them.

Identifying barriers to access

Box 1.5 Creating indicators of access barriers to deposit, payments, and loan services

FINANCIAL SERVICES ARE PROVIDED IN THE informal and the formal sector by banks, postal savings banks, credit unions, finance companies, microfinance institutions, and a whole range of other formal and quasi-formal nonbank institutions. Given the dearth of data on access, however, the initial data collection effort has focused on commercial banks, which are the dominant institutions in the formal financial sector. (Furthermore, policy implications regarding improving access are also more relevant for the formal financial sector given that the ability of informal finance to scale up and meet the financing needs of a growing economy is not clear; see box 3.5 in chapter 3). Conducting a survey of up to five large banks in each of more than 80 countries, Beck, Demirgüç-Kunt, and Martinez Peria (2007a) developed indicators of access for three types of banking services—deposits, loans, and payments—across three dimensions—physical access, affordability, and eligibility (for breakdowns by country, see appendix tables A.4–A.7).

Barriers such as availability of locations, minimum account and loan balances, account fees, fees associated with payments, documentation requirements, and processing times are found to vary significantly both across banks and across countries. Indicators of access barriers are also found to be negatively correlated with actual use of financial services, confirming that these barriers can exclude individuals from using bank services. The correlations of these indicators with country characteristics also have important policy implications for broadening access.

This is a first effort in documenting access barriers around the world. Next steps include broadening the study's coverage of both countries and banks and documenting the barriers imposed by nonbank financial intermediaries. Finally, urban-rural differences, as well as the role of customer characteristics, such as differences in gender and age, are important areas where further work will focus. The World Bank Group plans to expand and update these indicators within the context of its *Getting Finance* indicators.

Physical access barriers can be overcome by technology

Consider first geographic access. Branches have been the traditional bank outlet. Hence geographic distance to the nearest branch, or the density of branches relative to the population, can provide a first crude indication of geographic access or lack of physical barriers to access (Beck, Demirgüç-Kunt, and Martinez Peria 2007b). As in the case of usage, geographic access varies greatly across countries. Low-income Ethiopia has fewer than one branch per 100,000 people, while Spain has nearly one for every 1,000 people. Similarly, Spain has 79 branches for every 1,000 square kilometers, while sparsely populated Botswana has one branch for every 10,000 square kilometers. ATM penetration, rather than branch penetration, shows an even wider dispersion in geographic access (figure 1.4). These indicators are only crude proxies for geographic access, however, since branches and ATMs are never distributed equally across a country but are clustered in cities and some large towns. A better measure would be the average distance from the

Figure 1.4 Branch and ATM penetration by income quintile of countries

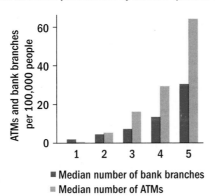

■ Median number of bank branches
▨ Median number of ATMs

Source: Beck, Demirgüç-Kunt, and Martinez Peria (2007b).

household to the branch or ATM, but these data are available for very few countries. Nevertheless, the branch and ATM density figures are highly correlated with aggregate loan and deposit accounts per population and the synthetic headline indicator introduced above, suggesting that they do contain access-relevant information (for branch and ATM penetration by country, see appendix table A.3).

A focus on branches and ATMs ignores other delivery channels that have gained importance over the past decades. Among these are nonbranch outlets, such as correspondent banking agreements, where bank services are sold by nonfinancial corporations on behalf of the banks, and mobile branches, where trucks drive through remote areas providing financial services at a scheduled frequency. Phone finance allows clients to do financial transactions such as payments or even loan applications over the phone. Electronic finance (e-finance) allows clients to access services through the Internet. While correspondent bank agreements and mobile branches have helped extend geographic outreach of financial institutions in many countries, phone and e-finance have been introduced primarily to reduce transaction costs for already existing customers and to make service delivery more effective for financial institutions. Any of these delivery channels, however, can reduce the costs of access and thus potentially increase the use of financial services.

While no cross-country data are available on the importance of these different alternative delivery channels, a recent bank-level survey, discussed in box 1.5, sheds some light on their use. Asking banks whether they accept loan applications in nonbranch bank outlets, over the phone, or over the Internet, Beck, Demirgüç-Kunt, and Martinez Peria (2007a) find a large variation across countries. According to this survey, bank customers in Australia, Chile, Denmark, Greece, South Africa, and Spain can submit their loan applications in nonbranch outlets, over the phone, or over the Internet. At the other extreme, loan applicants in Armenia, Ethiopia, Nepal, Sierra Leone, Thailand, Uganda, and Zambia have to travel to bank headquarters or a branch to submit their loan application. While this measure is of course not the only or even the most important determinant of access, it is notable that Chile, for example, has 418 loan accounts per 1,000 people, while Thailand has only 248.

Lack of documentation can create eligibility barriers

Limited geographic or physical access to a bank is only one type of barrier that potential customers face. By limiting eligibility, documentation requirements can be another important barrier to access. For example, banks in Albania, the Czech Republic, Mozambique, Spain, and Sweden demand on average only one document to open a bank account, whereas banks in Bangladesh, Cameroon, Chile, Nepal, Sierra Leone, Trinidad and Tobago, Uganda, and Zambia require at least four documents, including an identity card or passport, recommendation letter, wage slip, and proof of domicile (figure 1.5). Given the high degree of informality in many developing countries, only a small proportion of the population can produce these documents. Sixty percent of the population in Cameroon works in the informal sector and is thus unable to produce a wage slip. People in rural areas in Sub-Saharan Africa—61 percent of the overall population—are often unable to provide a formal proof of domicile. Limiting banking services to customers within the formal

Figure 1.5 Number of documents required to open a checking account

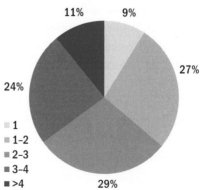

Legend:
- 1
- 1–2
- 2–3
- 3–4
- >4

(11%, 9%, 27%, 29%, 24%)

Source: Beck, Demirgüç-Kunt, and Martinez Peria (2007a).

economy or formal society thus automatically excludes a large share, if not the majority, of people in many low-income countries. Improvements on this dimension would not require great sophistication or cost.

Perhaps even more important than barriers of physical access and documentation are barriers of affordability. Standard bank account charges seem absurdly high when related to average national per capita GDP. To open a checking (transactions) account in Cameroon, a person needs more than $700, an amount higher than the per capita GDP of the country. On average, in 10 percent of the countries sampled, an amount equal to at least 50 percent of per capita GDP is necessary to open a checking account.

Likewise, the cost to the customer of maintaining these accounts varies widely as a percentage of average per capita GDP. In Uganda the figure is 30 percent, whereas customers in Bangladesh pay no annual fees. Perhaps not surprisingly, there are 229 deposit accounts for every 1,000 people in Bangladesh, but only 47 for every 1,000 people in Uganda. Obviously, much of the cross-country variation here reflects the fact that bank charges do not vary as much across countries as income does, imposing a much greater burden on individuals in poor countries and making access more difficult. High minimum balances to open and maintain bank accounts and high annual fees can constitute high barriers for large parts of the population in the developing world. Checking accounts also often come as expensive packages with costly overdraft facilities that can easily be incurred accidentally by those with low and volatile incomes, resulting in great risks.

Assuming, somewhat arbitrarily, that poor people cannot afford to spend more than 2 percent of their annual income on financial services, just the fees on checking accounts can exclude more than 50 percent of the population in some African countries such as Kenya, Malawi, and Uganda from having a bank account (figure 1.6).[12]

Payments services—for paying bills and sending domestic or international money transfers—are an important service for many low-income households, but again these services are too costly in many countries. For example, the cost of transferring $250 internationally—a typical amount of remittance—is 5–10 percent of this amount for half of the sampled countries and varies from 30 cents in Belgium to $50 in the Dominican Republic (figure 1.7). The fees associated with ATM transactions (for a relatively small transaction of $100) are also above 40 cents in Pakistan and Nigeria, and average 10 cents across countries, while the use of ATMs is free in 50 percent of the sample countries.

Affordability barriers: fees and minimum balances

Figure 1.6   Share of the population unable to afford checking account fees

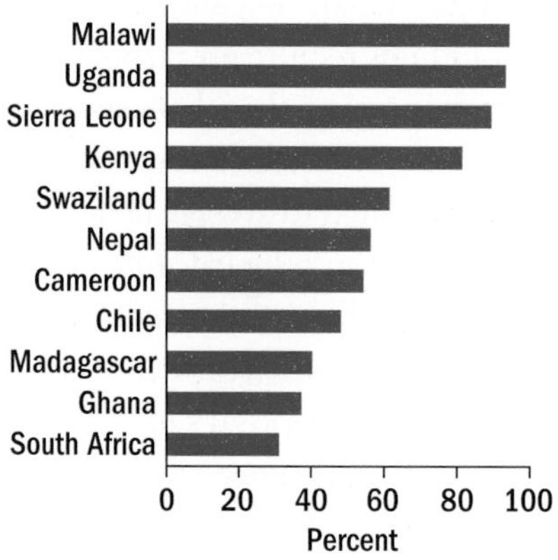

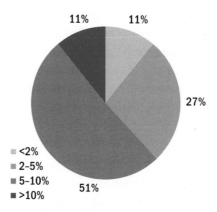

Source: Beck, Demirgüç-Kunt, and Martinez Peria (2007a).

Figure 1.7   Cost of transferring funds abroad as a percentage of $250

Source: Beck, Demirgüç-Kunt, and Martinez Peria (2007a)

A lack of appropriate products and services

Lack of appropriate products and services for low-income households and microenterprises is another important barrier to access financial services. Availability and affordability of consumer and mortgage loans vary quite a bit around the world. Banks in Nepal reported that the minimum amount a consumer can borrow is 12 times per capita GDP, whereas in richer countries it is possible to borrow amounts smaller than 10 percent of per capita GDP. Mortgage loans, where they exist, can also be subject to high fees and high minimums. Furthermore, it can take more than 10 days to process a credit card application in the Philippines, more than 20 days to process a consumer loan application in Pakistan, and more than two months to process a mortgage loan application in Chile.

Surveys of firms over the past 10 years have greatly expanded the information available about financing patterns of and access constraints on small firms and even microenterprises across countries. These sources include the Regional Program on Enterprise Development (RPED) studies for Sub-Saharan Africa in the 1990s; Business Environment and Enterprise Performance Surveys (BEEPS) for the transition economies; the World Business Environment Survey (WBES), conducted across 80 countries in 1999–2000; and the Investment Climate Surveys (ICS), conducted since 2002 and available for almost 100 countries. These surveys include micro-, small-, and medium enterprises that are not captured in data sets based on published financial statements. In addition to specific firm information, these surveys contain an array of questions on the business environment in which the firm operates, information that allows in-depth analysis of the relationships between firm investment, productivity, growth, and financial and institutional obstacles. Doubts have been raised about how well these surveys actually represent the population of firms for a specific country, a concern that could be fully allayed only by using census data, which are unavailable for most developing countries. Even census data that are available mostly cover only formal sector firms, representing, in many developing countries, a small fraction of the total number of firms, formal and informal.[13]

These surveys ask firm managers to what extent access to and cost of external finance constitute obstacles to their operation and growth, with higher numbers indicating higher obstacles. In general, small firms in both the WBES and ICS report financing constraints to be among the most important business constraints they face (figure 1.8). The geographic variation is large. Firms in East Asian and European countries rate financing as a minor constraint on average, while in the Middle East and Sub-Saharan Africa, financing constraints are much more severe. Variation is also wide within regions, particularly in Latin America, the Middle East, and South Asia. For example, the average Chilean firm reports that neither access to finance nor its cost are important constraints to growth, whereas the average Brazilian firm reports both as important growth constraints.

These surveys show that more than 40 percent of large firms, but just over 20 percent of small firms, use external finance for new investment (figure 1.9). While large firms finance about 30 percent of their new investment by external finance, small firms only finance 15 percent externally.

Looking at firms' use of and access to finance—

—managers' perceptions of financial exclusion vary widely

Figure 1.8   Financing and other constraints faced by small firms

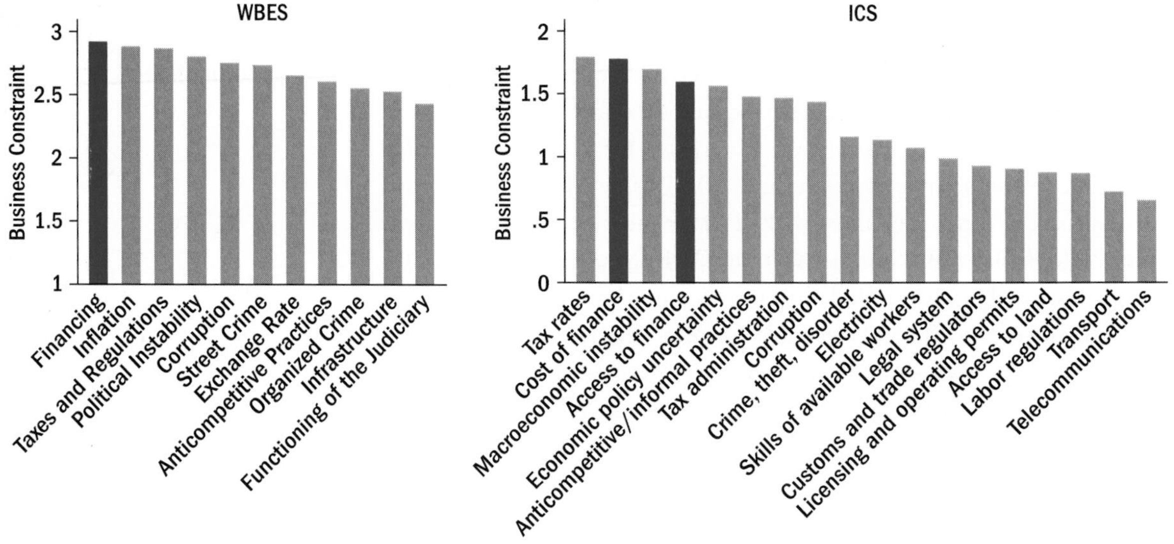

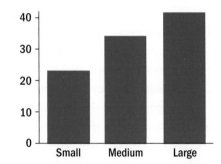

Source: WBES and ICS.

Note: WBES covers small firms in 80 countries; ICS covers those in 71 countries. The figures show the mean response of firms rating obstacles on a scale from 1–4 in WBES (1 = no obstacle; 4 = major obstacle) and 0–4 in ICS. In WBES, a firm is defined to be small if it has 5–50 employees; in ICS, small firms are those with 1–20 employees.

Figure 1.9   Percentage of firms using external finance, by firm size

Source: ICS.

Note: ICS covers 71 developing countries. Small firms are those with 20 or fewer employees; medium firms are those with 20–99 employees; and large firms are those with 100 or more employees.

Looking across regions, use of external finance by firms varies considerably. For example, some firms in East Asia finance almost 60 percent of their new investments with external finance. Within regions, there are big differences here too—while the average firm in the Philippines finances less than 8 percent of its new investment externally, this figure is 77 percent for the average Thai firm. Out of all financing sources, bank finance is the most common, for firms of all sizes (figure 1.10).

Firm-level surveys suggest that the share of small firms with bank credit varies from less than 1 percent in Pakistan to almost 50 percent in Thailand. Analyzing WBES data on financing patterns, Beck, Demirgüç-Kunt, and Maksimovic (2008) find that small firms and firms in countries with poor institutions use less external finance, especially bank finance. Small firms do not use disproportionately more leasing or trade finance compared with larger firms, so these financing sources do not compensate for lower access to bank financing by small firms. Consistent with these findings, financial sector assessments conducted by the World Bank also often point to the limited availability of leasing and factoring, two important financing products for small and medium enterprises.

If firms do not use bank finance, why don't they? Of the ones that have applied and have been rejected, what are the reasons? Box 1.6 provides some highlights from three of the largest countries for which

Banks are the most common source of finance

Figure 1.10 Sources of external finance for new investments

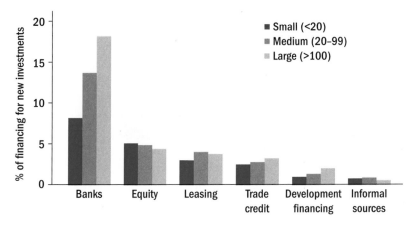

Source: ICS, covering 71 countries.
Note: Values in parentheses represent number of employees.

Box 1.6 Small firms' access to finance vs. use: firm-level surveys

ALTHOUGH BANK FINANCE IS THE MOST COMMON type of external finance, a large proportion of small firms do not have a bank loan. For example, enterprise surveys of small firms suggest that only 20 percent in China, 30 percent in Russia, and 55 percent in India have a bank loan.

Of those who do not have a loan, 85 percent in China, 95 percent in Russia, and 96 percent in India have not applied for one. So the rejection rates are 15, 5, and 4 percent, respectively.

Do these numbers reflect barriers to access or lack of need? Some of the firm surveys include questions that help shed light on this issue.

The survey results suggest that a large proportion of small firms that do not use bank loans actually do not need external finance or have been refused a loan for basic business reasons. However, in poor contractual and informational environments, the need to rely on collateral, rather than an assessment of the quality or feasibility of the project and credit history of the firm, is an important barrier for many firms. High interest rates may reflect lack of competition and infrastructure problems, in addition to other macroeconomic issues. Bank corruption is also a potential barrier deterring firms from applying for bank loans.

Why did the firm not apply for a loan?[a]

	China (%)	India (%)	Russia (%)
Does not need a loan	69	80	60
Does not think it would be approved	22	N/A	2
Application procedures are too burdensome	27	16	23
Collateral requirements are too strict	26	18	25
Interest rates are too high	17	17	35
It is necessary to make informal payments	11	N/A	6
Other	N/A	7	3

What was main reason the loan application was rejected?*

Perceived lack of profitability	18	32	11
Lack of acceptable collateral	69	N/A	56
Inadequate credit history of the firm	24	N/A	11
Incomplete application	N/A	16	11
Other	N/A	37	N/A

Source: ICS.

a. Multiple answers are allowed, and hence the percentages do not sum to 100.

surveys have offered answers to these questions. Surveys of small firms suggest that while some firms are excluded from bank finance because of high interest rates, collateral requirements, corruption in banking, cumbersome paperwork, and the like, a large proportion simply have no demand for or good projects to finance.

Smaller firms tend to face greater access barriers than do larger firms. For example, the responses to the surveys discussed in box 1.5 suggest that in Georgia, Nepal, and Uganda, the minimum SME loan amount is 20 times GDP per capita, casting doubt on whether banks in those countries can meet the borrowing needs of smaller firms. Similarly, fees on SME loans and the time it takes to process an SME loan application may represent barriers. For example, while it takes more than a month to process an application in Bangladesh, Pakistan, the Philippines, and Uruguay, the wait is less than two days in Denmark (figure 1.11). These issues are explored in much greater detail in chapter 2.

Two aggregate indicators can be created by summarizing different barriers that impede firms' and households' access to financial services. These indicators, one for access barriers for deposit services and the other for loan services, suggest an overall impression of the country characteristics that are associated with high barriers.[14]

Based on simple correlations, access barriers decline as per capita GDP rises (figure 1.12). The quality of physical infrastructure is also negatively associated with access barriers. Such relationships are not necessarily causal ones; both barriers and the country characteristics shown have common underlying structural causes. Nevertheless it is striking that indicators of competition, openness, and market orientation in the overall financial sector and economic policy are also strongly negatively correlated with access barriers at the bank level. Examples include the Heritage Foundation index of banking freedoms[15] and an index of media freedom developed by Djankov and others (2003). (Each of these has also been found to be correlated with financial depth and economic growth.)

As far as contractual and informational infrastructures are concerned, better credit registries are associated with lower access barriers, but there is no evident correlation with creditor rights, suggesting that a deficient information infrastructure may be a greater barrier to access than a deficient contractual framework. Countries that encourage market discipline by empowering market participants (through enforcement of accurate and timely information disclosure and by not distorting risk-taking incentives) also tend to have lower barriers to accessing loan services. Government ownership of banks is associated with *lower* barriers on the deposit side (as is foreign ownership of banks) but with *higher* barriers on the loan side.

Not too much should be read into these simple partial correlations. They do, however, foreshadow the characteristics that emerge again and

Smaller firms tend to face greater financial exclusion

What determines access barriers for households and enterprises?

Figure 1.11   Time to process an SME loan application

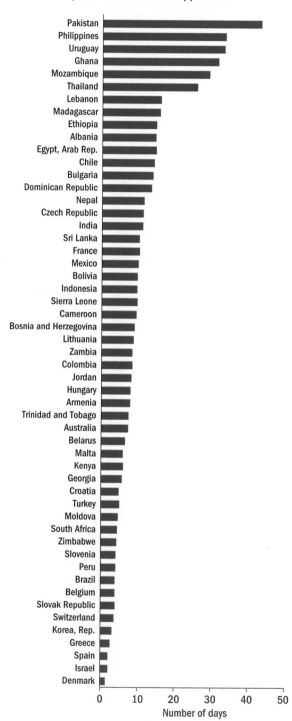

Source: Beck, Demirgüç-Kunt, and Martinez Peria (2007a).

Figure 1.12 Economic development and barriers to access

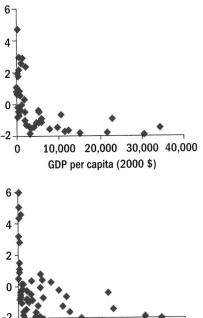

Source: Beck, Demirgüç-Kunt, and Martinez Peria (2007a).

Note: The two panels show the first principal component of the indicators of barriers to (a) loan and (b) deposit services, respectively, as discussed in box 1.5.

again in the discussions in later chapters that take a more in-depth look at access and policies to broaden it.

Conclusions

Data from financial institutions and their regulators can contribute greatly to a better understanding of the many barriers to access and usage. Ultimately, however, researchers are interested not only in measuring access to financial services and the barriers that prevent access but also in understanding the welfare impact of removing these barriers and broadening access. For this, household and firm-level surveys are necessary to distinguish between supply constraints and demand-side constraints and to determine how the removal of these different barriers would affect household welfare.

Access, and its welfare implications, can best be measured through surveys—

—and randomized field experiments have potential in evaluating impact of access

In evaluating the impact of broadening access, randomized field experiments hold promise. These experiments, which use surveys of microenterprises and households, introduce a random component to the assignment of financial products, such as subsidized fees for opening accounts or random variation in the terms of loan contracts. Continuing research in this area will shed more light on how reduced barriers and improved access affect growth and household welfare. These findings, in turn, will inform the design of policy interventions to build more inclusive financial systems, and the efforts to narrow the access indicators to track over time. We discuss these issues in more detail in the remainder of the report.

Notes

1. Conceptually, when discussing the impact of finance on growth, it is important to distinguish between two different effects (Mankiw, Romer, and Weil 1992) the impact of finance on raising income levels of developing countries and on helping countries converge in income toward advanced economies; and the impact on steady state growth rate. The second effect could result from the role of financial development in promoting innovation and accelerating the outward movement of the frontier. Empirically, there is very little evidence to distinguish between these two effects. However, see Aghion, Howitt, and Mayer-Foulkes (2005), discussed below.

2. A return to rising inequality in several advanced economies in the past couple of decades shows further shortcomings of the Kuznet's model.

3. Key contributors to this literature are Alesina and Rodrik (1994); Perotti (1992, 1993, 1996); Persson and Tabellini (1994); for a contrary view, see Forbes (2000). World Bank (2006a) and Birdsall (2007) also discuss the implications of this literature and provide further references. An interesting case study is that of the Republic of Korea and the Philippines, which looked quite similar with regard to their development in the early 1960s, except in the degree of income inequality. Over the following 30-year period, income per capita in the Philippines (the more unequal country) barely doubled, whereas fast growth in Korea resulted in a fivefold increase.

4. There are other possible channels through which higher inequality could slow growth: for example, if inequality results in less-accountable governments or if it undermines civic and social life (compare Birdsall 2007).

5. Also see the discussion in Demirgüç-Kunt and Levine (2007) and many references therein.

6. See for example, Aghion and Bolton (1997); Aghion, Caroli, and Garcia-Penalosa (1999).

7. See Beck, Demirgüç-Kunt, and Levine (2007); Honohan (2004).

8. Of course, some netting of interinstitutional accounts is still needed.

9. For a general review of issues around data collection in this area, see Honohan (2005b).

10. The focus on individuals rather than households raises issues of comparability with other surveys: use of financial services can differ considerably between different household members, and it would be a mistake to assume that one household member's use is representative of the access of the other members. Surveys that randomly question individuals in a household are a less-promising basis for welfare analysis, which requires good-quality data at the household level.

11. In the context of the Year of Microcredit 2005, a coordinated effort was also started by World Bank, UN Capital Development Fund (UNCDF) and the U.K. Department for International Development to implement a consistent, stand-alone household survey instrument across developing countries to measure access to and use of financial services. Currently, the Research Department of the World Bank and UNCDF are planning to move forward with this effort, which should allow consistent cross-country comparison of finance-related questions and derivation of the share of households that use different financial services from different providers.

12. Genesis (2005a) examines the costs of using bank accounts in seven countries: Brazil, India, Kenya, Malaysia, Mexico, Nigeria, and South Africa. According to Genesis (2005b), the 2 percent limit is based on unpublished research by the South African Universal Services Agency in the context of a mandated rolling-out of telecommunications service to lower-income families. As both financial transaction accounts and telecom service can be considered network products, similar assumptions on affordability for both services seem reasonable.

13. Surveys are now being designed to reach informal firms also; see http://www.enterprisesurveys.org.

14. The aggregate indicators are the principal component indicator of the underlying indicators for deposit and loan services, respectively. Beck, Demirgüç-Kunt, and Martinez Peria (2007a) use a data set of 209 banks in 62 countries and regress these aggregate indicators of barriers on bank-level controls and one country-level variable at a time, such as the quality of physical and information infrastructures, protection of creditor rights, bank and media freedoms, and government ownership of banks.

15. This index takes into account government involvement and ownership, existence of directed lending and controls, quality of regulation and supervision, and the ability of foreign institutions to operate freely.

CHAPTER TWO

Firms' Access to Finance: Entry, Growth, and Productivity

IT IS BY PROVIDING FINANCIAL SERVICES TO ANY AND ALL FIRMS WITH good growth opportunities that the financial sector helps developing economies to grow and to converge on the high-income levels of advanced economies. This is not just a matter of the overall volume of lending: it matters crucially which firms get finance and on what terms, that is, on whether creditworthy firms of all sizes, both incumbent ones and those that seek entry, have broad access to finance at reasonable costs. Improving access to external sources of funding is undoubtedly the main challenge for firm finance in developing countries, and that fact alone justifies the attention it receives. Naturally, it is also the area of finance that has received the most econometric research attention. Other dimensions of finance also matter, such as cash management and payments services, risk management, and insurance, and they deserve further research attention.

This chapter looks at how firms finance themselves in developing countries and explores the barriers to improved contracting between firms and the providers of funds. It discusses the channels through which finance affects firm performance and the relative importance of financing obstacles as a constraint to firm growth compared with other obstacles in the business environment. Firms finance their operations and growth in many different ways, reflecting both the preferences of management and the options that are available to them. Availability of external financing for firms depends on the wider institutional environment, and lack of availability is one of the more important business obstacles firms have to overcome. Better access to finance can help new firm entry and growth, which in turn promotes growth at the aggregate level.

This chapter examines the impact of financial barriers on firms—

—and on economic structures in general—

The chapter documents how improvements in the functioning of the formal financial sector can be expected to reduce financing constraints more for small firms and others who have difficulty in self-financing or in finding private or informal sources of funding. As a result, the effectiveness of finance has a significant impact on the ownership structure, the dynamism, and the resilience of the economy at large. Finance does not just raise aggregate firm performance uniformly but also transforms the structure of the economy by affecting different types of firms in different ways. The removal of financial barriers appears to be especially beneficial for small firms—which embody much of an economy's latent dynamism. Removal or reduction of financial barriers can thus broaden the sectoral range of the economy and reduce its vulnerability to sector-specific shocks. The institutional environment can also influence patterns of ownership—for example, well-functioning financial and legal systems can lead more firms to incorporate and result in more diffuse patterns of firm ownership.

—identifies firms' sources of finance—

Finally, the chapter examines the ability of firms, especially small firms, to access finance from different sources, including banks and other intermediaries, securities markets, and foreign investment. Special attention within this section is given to the much discussed issue of foreign-owned banks and their contribution to improving access. The debate about whether banks or markets do a better job no longer excites much interest: each has its place in ensuring that finance reaches a wide clientele. Creating the infrastructures that let both markets and institutions reach their optimal level is likely to be the best policy. Relationship lending, which relies on personal interaction between borrower and lender and is based on an understanding of the borrower's business and not just on collateral or on mechanical credit scoring systems, is costly for the lender and thus requires either high spreads or large volumes to be viable. However, if the customer's creditworthiness is hard to evaluate, then there may be no alternative to relationship lending—although this may lead to discrimination against certain groups. The modern trend to transactional lending—whether based on assets or, for example, on automated credit appraisal using improved data—is clearly the way of the future. Credit registries are an important tool for the expansion of transactions-based lending technologies.

—and considers the role of foreign banks—

Foreign banks bring with them capital, technology, know-how, and a degree of independence from the local business elite. However, the role of foreign banks in improving access has always been controversial, partly for political reasons. Foreign banks have a comparative advantage in transactional lending, which raises concerns about their contribution to credit access for countries where relationship lending is still needed. The entry of foreign banks has directly benefited larger firms, and in many countries this improved credit access has extended directly or indirectly to smaller firms. Nevertheless there are also some indications that the arrival of foreign banks has not always been good for small firm access to credit, at least at first.

Nonbank finance remains much less important than bank finance in most developing countries, but this can be expected to change. The corporate bond market and organized securities markets are chiefly of relevance to larger firms, although by broadening the range of firms that have access to long-term funding, these markets do make a contribution to access. Foreign direct investment offers a partial substitute for local finance and is an alternative that has proved important in some countries. FDI appears to have eased financing constraints—although again the benefits are most apparent for larger firms.

—and the growth of nonbank finance

Access to Finance: Determinants and Implications

Firms finance their operations and growth in many different ways. Their financing choices are influenced by the preferences of each firm's entrepreneurs and, more important, by the options that are available to them. In what form, from whom, how successfully, and at what cost firms are financed thus depends on a wide range of factors both internal and external to the firm. The internal financial resources available to the firm's entrepreneurs and other insiders are of course important. Not only are these the basis for most start-ups, but they can help leverage external finance, that is, finance from outsiders. But given information and agency problems (discussed in chapter 1, box 1.2), external financing also depends on the firm entrepreneurs' own ability to project a credible financing proposal, their willingness to share control, the nature of their business plan, and the uncertainties and risks involved in implementing it. The credibility of the proposal depends not only on the substance of the business plan, but on how the firm is governed and on the transparency of its operations and financial condition.

Circumstances external to the firm are also important. Availability of external financing depends not only on the firm's situation, but on the wider policy and institutional environment supporting the enforceability and liquidity of the contracts that are involved in financing firms. And it depends on the existence and effectiveness of a variety of intermediaries and ancillary financial firms that help bring providers and users of funds together in the market, not least by helping overcome information and agency problems (Tirole 2006).

As countries differ in their financial contracting environments, so too the extent and pattern of firm financing tend to differ. Most important, these background conditions affect the extent to which *firms as a whole* face financing constraints in different countries (and even within countries across different states or provinces; see Laeven and Woodruff 2007). As noted in chapter 1, access to finance is among the aspects of the business environment most frequently cited by surveyed enterprises in the developing world as an important obstacle to their growth.[1]

Moreover, investigations of the impact of financing obstacles on firm growth reveal that firms' complaints are valid—their growth is significantly constrained by lack of access. One nice piece of evidence on this comes—somewhat ironically, given the policy recommendations of this report—from a study of a directed credit program in India. Banerjee and Duflo (2004) studied detailed loan information on 253 small and medium-size borrowers from a bank in India both before and after they became newly eligible for the program. Specifically, the size definition of the program was changed in 1998, which enabled a new group of medium-size firms to obtain loans at subsidized interest rates. Naturally these firms began to borrow under this favored program, but instead of simply substituting subsidized credit for more costly financing, they expanded their sales proportionally to the additional loan resources, which suggests that these firms must have previously been credit constrained.

Moreover, as shown in figure 2.1, the new beneficiaries experienced significantly higher costs and profits, while there was no significant effect for other firms.[2] The reader should not, of course, jump to the conclusion that directed credit is the best—or even a good—solution to the existence of credit constraints. As discussed in chapter 4, not all such programs even reach their intended target groups or result in increased output for the eligible firms, let alone their impact on the rest of the economy.

More extensive cross-country evidence comes from the responses of some 10,000 firms in 80 countries to the World Business Environment

Barriers to finance are a constraint to firm growth—

—indeed, the major constraint to firm growth, according to surveys of managers

Figure 2.1   Response of beneficiaries under a credit scheme

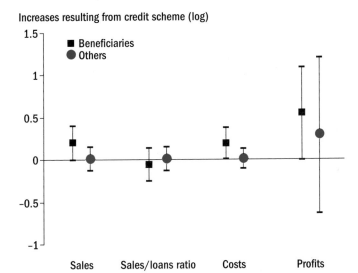

Source: Based on Banerjee and Duflo (2004).

Note: This figure shows estimated logarithmic increase in sales, costs, and profits for beneficiaries and nonbeneficiaries of the credit scheme. Error bars indicate 95 percent confidence intervals.

Survey of 1999–2000. It turns out that respondents who identify finance as a constraint are more likely to experience slow output growth (Beck, Demirgüç-Kunt, and Maksimovic 2005).[3] Among the three constraints these authors focus on—corruption, legal, and finance—financing constraints lead to the greatest reduction in firm growth (figure 2.2). While other business environment obstacles are also important, they are

Figure 2.2   Impact of self-reported obstacles on growth of firm sales

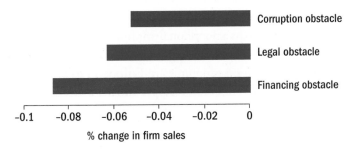

Source: Beck, Demirgüç-Kunt, and Maksimovic (2005).

Note: The figure shows the estimated reduction in the rate of firm sales growth for a firm reporting the given obstacle (calculated at the average value of the obstacle).

often related to finance, and even when these interactions are controlled for as well as they can be in a cross-section, access to finance seems to emerge consistently as one of the most important and robust underlying factors that constrain firm growth (Ayyagari, Demirgüç-Kunt, and Maksimovic 2006a).

Both cross-country and case-study evidence thus points to the existence of financing constraints and shows how access to and use of credit can alleviate these constraints.

The Channels of Impact: Micro and Macro Evidence

The next issue is to identify the channels through which easier access to external finance increases firm growth and ultimately economic growth. There are numerous *potential* channels, and recent research shows that finance is associated with all of them.

- The availability of external finance is positively associated with the number of *start-ups*—an important indicator of entrepreneurship—as well as with firm dynamism and *innovation*.
- Finance is also needed if existing firms are to be able to exploit *growth* and *investment* opportunities and to achieve a larger equilibrium size.
- Firms can safely acquire a more efficient productive asset portfolio where the infrastructures of finance are in place,[4] and they are also able to choose more efficient organizational forms such as incorporation.

Better access to finance can promote new firm entry and growth

To get a flavor of the nature of the empirical evidence researchers use in detecting these effects, look, for example, at the evidence on start-ups and their subsequent growth. Klapper, Laeven, and Rajan (2006) extracted data on more than 3 million firms from the Amadeus database (which assembles information mainly from national company registries in advanced and transition economies in Europe). From inspection of the reported age of each company, Klapper and her colleagues were able to compute the entry rate for each of eleven two-digit sector groups and thus assess the effect of entry and other regulations on the degree of new firm entry and firm growth. Figure 2.3 shows striking differences, even between two developed economies such as Italy and the United Kingdom, in such dimensions as the rate of firm entry (higher in the

Figure 2.3 Italy vs. U.K.: firm size at entry and over time

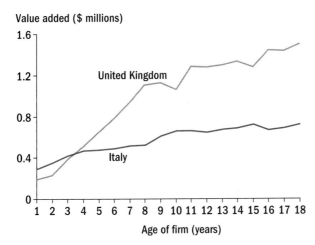

Source: Klapper, Laeven, and Rajan (2006).

United Kingdom), initial firm size at start-up (higher in Italy), and more rapid growth (higher in the United Kingdom).

The econometrics shows that such differences are in part related to firm registration costs (more than six times as high in Italy as in the United Kingdom), as well as to easier access to external finance in the United Kingdom. The authors also dig deeper and test the conjecture that, within countries, entry regulations would have the greatest effect in industries that—in a lightly regulated economy like that of the United States—would be most likely to have a high entry rate. Indeed, this proves to be so, providing a more convincing case for the importance of avoiding unnecessarily burdensome regulation. But not all types of regulations hinder: it turns out that the kinds of regulation needed for well-functioning finance (such as accounting standards and property rights) have a *positive* effect on entry.[5]

The wealth of information generated on a cross-country basis by the Investment Climate Surveys can be used to examine the role of finance in influencing a range of enterprise characteristics. For example, Ayyagari, Demirgüç-Kunt, and Maksimovic (2007a) exploited the responses of some 17,000 firms in 47 countries to the questions on enterprise innovation.[6] Taking an average of each firm's responses to the innovation-related questions, these authors assembled a range of country- and firm-level variables likely to be associated with firm innovation, including

Use of external finance is associated with more innovation by firms

61

Box 2.1 Are cross-country regression results credible?

ECONOMETRIC STUDIES PURPORTING TO EXPLAIN cross-country differences in economic growth rates and other country characteristics have proliferated in recent years. Not all of these studies have been equally convincing. Numerous published papers did not take adequate account of the formidable problems of making valid inferences from such data. The most widespread problems include heterogeneity of effects across countries, measurement errors, omission of relevant explanatory variables, and endogeneity, all of which tend to bias the estimated effect of the included variables. These problems are not limited to cross-country regressions, but they seem especially prominent in this area. Of these, endogeneity is the most intractable. It arises when the common effect of an omitted factor or disturbance on two variables is misinterpreted as a causal link between them. Econometric theory offers a number of possible solutions, but most of them call (in one way or another) for what are known as instrumental variables. These are not always available or credible, given that their validity and effectiveness depends on the instrument being correlated with the explanatory variables, but (crucially) not otherwise correlated with the dependent variable. The second criterion for validity—the so-called exclusion restriction—is difficult to verify.

The cross-country studies cited in this report have all made plausible efforts to deal with these problems, sometimes by painstaking collection of data on ingeniously chosen instrumental variables; indeed, the literature has relied heavily on just a handful of such instruments (compare Pande and Udry 2006). Since they cannot logically have satis-fied the exclusion restrictions required to ensure their validity for all of the applications, in at least some applications they must have been invalid.

Sometimes, a more direct approach can be taken using micro data and making use of sectoral or firm-level differences. For example, instead of just looking at country aggregates, it may be plausible to assume that the effect being measured, if present at all, is stronger in some sectors, or for some types of firms, than others; in other words, some sectors or firms are more *susceptible* to the causal factor being examined (for example, financial sector development). Even if the causal factor varies only across countries, its impact can then be more precisely measured if data is available at the firm or sector level.[a]

The additional information obtained by working with cross-country firm- or sector-level data may not be as great as at first appears, however; the different firms in any given country are likely affected by common disturbances, which, if neglected, can result in overestimating the precision of coefficient estimates. Dropping the cross-country dimension often allows researchers to take explicit account of special circumstances and to exploit more detailed data, such as data across different states or regions of a country. The quality of the data is more likely to be uniform for observations within a single country. But omitting cross-country variation comes at the cost of narrowing the range of variation in the phenomena being studied—indeed, some causal factors of interest may not vary at all within a country. All in all, it is through an accumulation of evidence using different methodologies that the complete picture can be progressively filled in.

a. Several of the papers discussed in this chapter employ this assumption, using the product of the causal variable and the supposed sectoral or firm-level susceptibility as the explanatory variable. This approach was first applied in the financial access literature by Demirgüç-Kunt and Maksimovic (1998) and by Rajan and Zingales (1998). Using firm-level data from 8,500 large companies in 30 countries, the former used a financial planning model to calculate how fast those firms could be expected to grow if they had no access to external finance. The extent to which firms were able to grow faster than this internally financed growth rate represented the firm's growth susceptibility to good finance. In countries with greater financial depth, stock market development, and legal enforcement, a higher proportion of firms were able to grow at rates that are possible only with access to external finance. Rajan and Zingales worked with data on 36 sectors in 41 countries and assumed that each sector's susceptibility to financial development would be correlated across countries with the degree to which large firms in the same sector in the United States relied on external financing. This statistical technique is also referred to as a form of "difference-in-differences" estimation.

information about the structure of each firm's financing. Despite the inclusion of the other control variables and even after controlling for reverse causality by using instrumental variable techniques, they found that firms' use of external finance was associated with more innovation. This finding was even more strongly evident when access to finance was from foreign banks.

The results of this firm-level, cross-country evidence are pretty unambiguous. Access to and use of finance, and the institutional underpinnings that are associated with better financial access, favorably affect firm performance along a number of different channels. If entry, growth, innovation, equilibrium size, and risk reduction are all helped by access to and use of finance, it is almost inescapable that aggregate economic performance will also be improved by having stronger financial systems.

Indeed, this result is likely a glimpse of the main underlying mechanism behind the now relatively long-established finding that a significant fraction of the differences across countries in economic growth in the latter half of the 20th century can be explained by variations in their level of financial development (Levine 2005; World Bank 2001). The finance and growth literature typically measures financial development by the ratio of bank credit to the private sector to GDP, an inevitably crude measure that captures only two aspects of financial development, namely, the ability of banks to mobilize resources, and the degree to which they channel these resources to the private sector. Indeed, researchers' extensive use of this banking-depth variable to summarize financial development occurs primarily because—unlike other measures—it is available for many countries over a long period of time. Among the dimensions not explicitly captured by this measure are the ability and success of banks in making good credit appraisal and monitoring decisions and in maintaining operational efficiency; the measure also does not capture the operation of nonbank aspects of the financial sector, including the market for equities. Given the imperfections of this measure, it is all the more striking that such a strong statistical cross-country correlation between financial development and growth was detected and proved robust to the application of instrumental variables to take account of endogeneity. Indeed, when the adjustment for endogeneity is made, it *increases* the estimated impact of finance on growth, which underscores that credit depth is only a proxy for the true degree of financial development.[7]

Broader access to finance also promotes growth at the aggregate level

Overall banking depth (not just private credit) is also correlated across countries with overall economic growth, but less robustly: it does seem that restricting attention to private credit, as opposed to all bank intermediation, is correct. Look, for example, at China (a country that is excluded from most econometric studies, not least because of the difficulty of reliably measuring private credit, due to the ambiguity of firm ownership in the process of China's transition from the planned economy system). Interprovincial differences in growth rates in China are highly correlated with banking depth—but *negatively* (Boyreau-Debray 2003; Boyreau-Debray and Wei 2005). Mobilizing huge amounts of funds to pour into the declining parts of the Chinese state enterprise system, as the main Chinese banks were doing during the last decades of the 20th century, does not appear, on this evidence, an effective way of employing the financial system in the interests of economic growth. China has continued to grow rapidly, as more workers shift from subsistence agriculture and other low-productivity activities into the modern sector. But the Chinese banking system, despite being one of the deepest in the world, has not been a major contributor to this growth (figure 2.4).[8] The finance and growth link is thus better seen as one that operates by enabling privately owned firms to reach their potential.[9] Likewise, the aggregate evidence on long-term growth shows that finance has its influence through productivity gains rather than simply through an increase in the volume of investment (Beck, Levine, and Loayza 2000; Love 2003); finance also plays an important role in reallocating investments across sectors as demand shifts (Wurgler 2000).[10]

Rapid growth of the banking sector can be potentially destabilizing

Banking systems can grow too quickly—with the boom inevitably followed by a bust—and in some countries the huge size of the banking system reflects policy distortions that are inhibiting the emergence and growth of complementary segments of finance. Perhaps therefore it is not so surprising that the econometric link between banking depth and aggregate economic growth has weakened in recent years, in particular when the data set includes the 1997–98 East Asia financial crisis (Rousseau and Wachtel 2005).

There also seems to be a threshold effect at the other end of the scale: below a certain level of financial development, small differences do not seem to help growth.[11] In these countries, financial development may boost income but not the long-run growth rate. Indeed, Aghion, Howitt, and Mayer-Foulkes (2005) suggest that it is lack of access to finance that prevents entrepreneurs in poor countries with undeveloped financial

Figure 2.4   Finance and growth across Chinese provinces

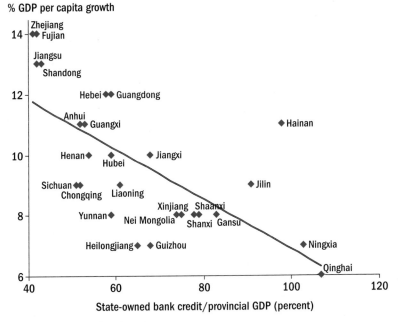

Source: Boyreau-Debray (2003).
Note: This figure plots credit by state-owned banks relative to provincial GDP against GDP per capita growth.

systems from catching up. Without access to finance at a reasonable cost, and lacking sufficient personal wealth, these entrepreneurs cannot afford to make the needed investments in innovation. The theoretical access-based model of Aghion, Howitt, and Mayer-Foulkes implies that low-income countries with low financial development will continue to fall behind the rest, whereas those reaching the financial development threshold will converge and, up to a certain point, will do so faster the higher the level of financial development. Comparing average long-term economic growth rates for a cross-section of about 70 countries, they find—consistent with their theory—that financial development helps an economy converge faster but that there is no effect on steady-state growth.

Summarizing, access to credit supports firm growth and ultimately national growth through a variety of different channels. Providing access to credit to the most efficient and innovative enterprises is behind the well-documented causal relationship between financial depth and national growth. But who benefits the most from financial deepening

Box 2.2   External vs. internal and formal vs. informal finance

TWO ASSUMPTIONS, EXPLICIT OR IMPLICIT, IN much of the literature on financial access are that availability of external finance and greater formality in finance are both improvements over internal and informal finance.

The idea that availability of external finance represents an improvement comes from two rather different perspectives. First is the idea that a latent pool of enterprise and innovation exists in an economy that, absent external finance, can be made effective only if the entrepreneurs happen to begin with sufficient wealth either themselves or through associates (Rajan and Zingales 2003). Second (and in a sense the opposite problem) is the question of agency: a firm that generates too much free cash may find its insiders making poor investments and relaxing cost control efforts (Jensen 1988; Stulz 1990). If that happens in enough firms in a rapidly growing and profitable enterprise sector, excess free cash could actually weaken the growth process compared with a situation where the enterprise sector has to rely more on external finance provided by an efficient

and competitive financial system. The contemporary case of profitable state-owned companies in China provides an interesting case for this last point, as discussed by Kuijs (2005).

The argument that informal financial systems may substitute for formal financial systems has been canvassed for the case of China by Allen, Qian, and Qian (2005, 2008). But their story takes as given obstacles to formal financial development such as restrictions on entry and pervasive state ownership of banks. Even if informal finance works in such conditions, it is just a second-best solution. Besides, informal sources of finance vary widely in their effectiveness. Ayyagari, Demirgüç-Kunt, and Maksimovic (2007b) provide evidence from China that, on average for the firms in their sample, access to formal finance was associated with faster firm growth. More generally, informality and relationship lending survive where the institutions needed to support modern technologies of credit appraisal and monitoring are not present.

and better access? What impact does financial deepening and broadening have on the economy's structure? We turn to these questions next.

Transforming the Economy: Differences in Impact

Finance does not just raise aggregate firm performance uniformly; it also transforms the structure of the economy by affecting different types of firms in different ways. As already discussed, some categories of firms—the small and the new, for example—have more difficulty obtaining external finance than others. But as financial access conditions improve in an economy, those that were formerly shut out have an opportunity to expand. In this way, financial sector development has consequences for the composition and performance of the enterprise sector in terms both of size and of ownership.

The size distribution of firms can be affected by the availability of external finance: financial development aids entry of small firms much more than that of large ones, but small firms usually struggle more to get finance when the environment is weak.[12] The size and success of sectors in which small firms have a natural advantage, or those in which firms generally rely more on external finance (including export-oriented firms),[13] are also particularly dependent on financial sector development.

Not only do small firms report higher financing obstacles than do large firms; they are also more severely affected when they encounter these obstacles. Survey findings suggest that financing obstacles loom much more for small firms than for large firms (figure 2.5). Specifically, Beck, Demirgüç-Kunt, and Maksimovic (2005) find that financing constraints reduce firm growth by 6 percentage points, on average, for large firms but by 10 percentage firms in the case of small firms. This difference between small and large firms is as big or even bigger for some of the specific financing obstacles reported in the World Business Environment Survey, such as collateral requirements, bank paperwork,

Lowering financial barriers is especially beneficial for small firms—

Figure 2.5 The effect of financing constraints on growth: small vs. large firms

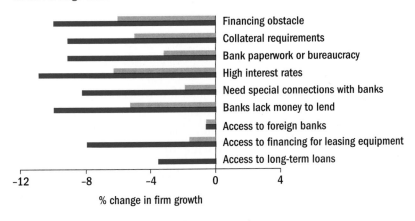

% change in firm growth

Source: Beck, Demirgüç-Kunt, and Maksimovic (2005).
Note: This graph shows the effect of different financing obstacles on firm growth for small and large firms, measured at the average constraint for the two size groups.

interest rate payments, the need for special connections, and banks' lack of lending resources. In addition, the lack of access to specific forms of financing such as export, leasing, and long-term finance is significantly more constraining for small firms (Beck, Demirgüç-Kunt, and Maksimovic 2005).

To the extent that small firms embody much of an economy's latent dynamism, a weaker financial system, by constraining such firms, may condemn a country to a much slower growth path. More generally, the economy as a whole may lose out on the potential for wealth creation in sectors that might give the economy a comparative advantage were it not for the sector's difficulty in accessing needed financial services.[14] With a narrower range of healthy sectors, the economy's resilience to sector-specific shocks is also likely to be weakened.

—which in turn can widen an economy's sectoral range and dynamism

While lack of financial access tends to hurt small firms the most in countries with underlying weaknesses in their institutional environment, empirical evidence also suggests that small firms benefit disproportionately—in terms of seeing their constraints relaxed—as financial systems develop (Beck, Demirgüç-Kunt, and Maksimovic 2005; Beck and others 2005). Hence it is those who were previously constrained—not those who were already getting finance—that benefit most from financial development. This effect also shows up when studying episodes of financial liberalization. Laeven (2003) shows that small firms' financing constraints decrease following financial liberalization (including interest rate liberalization, elimination of credit controls, privatization, and foreign bank entry), while large firms' financing constraints actually increase (perhaps reflecting the loss of preferential access to finance by large and politically well-connected firms).

Financial development influences ownership patterns

Perhaps even more important, ownership patterns depend on financial sector development, both because firm entrepreneurs choose ownership structures in large part to ensure adequate financing, and because finance tends to go to firms with conducive ownership structures—the selection effect. Specifically, background conditions in the financial sector influence the degree to which the producing firms choose to incorporate or remain controlled by a closed group of family members.

For example, Demirgüç-Kunt, Love, and Maksimovic (2006) use survey data from 52 developed and developing countries to investigate the drivers of the decision to incorporate and the gains for the enterprise from incorporation They find that firms are more likely to incorporate in countries with better-developed financial and legal systems, strong creditor and shareholder rights, and effective bankruptcy processes. While incorporated firms do not necessarily report lower financial barriers to their operation and growth in an average country, financial and institutional development does seem to lower obstacles more for incorporated than unincorporated firms. Similarly, incorporated firms grow faster than unincorporated firms only in countries with higher levels of institutional development. These results suggest that the costs and benefits of the legal form of enterprises is endogenous to a country's institutions: incorporated firms have a comparative advantage in countries with institutions that support formal contracting, while unincorporated firms are more adapted to operate in countries with less-developed formal institutions where firms have to rely on informal institutions and reputation.

The institutional environment can also affect other dimensions of ownership. Family firms, even large ones, are still remarkably common, as are interrelated multifirm business groups. Ownership concentration is prevalent in countries with weak minority shareholder rights, suggesting that the inability to share control and profits with nonmanagement shareholders might very well result in limiting the opportunities for raising external equity (La Porta, Lopez-Silanes, and Shleifer 1999). The prevalence of interrelated business groups in many developing countries is similarly attributed to the lack of functioning financial markets, forcing firms to look for alternatives in the form of internal capital markets of large business groups.

Financial development and easier access to external finance thus allows incorporated, self-standing, and independent enterprises with widely spread ownership to flourish. This has a range of broader implications for the identity and concentration of ownership in the economy at large. For one thing, a developed financial sector also tends to be associated with a greater degree of competition in the nonfinancial enterprise sector. More broadly, ownership structures in the enterprise sector can influence political economy performance (Rajan and Zingales 2003).

Summarizing, financial development that improves access to external finance by firms has a deep impact on the sectoral and industrial structure of an economy. What institutions and markets matter most for broader access to external finance, particularly for small firms? We address this question in the next section.

Increased shareholder rights can broaden the ownership base

What Aspects of Financial Sector Development Matter for Access?

We now examine different sources of access to finance. This section looks first at the old "banks versus markets" debate, before turning to a more detailed look at the role of banks (especially foreign banks), nonbank debt markets, and equities. Other dimensions of finance, such as cash management, payments, and insurance, are not specifically discussed, reflecting the state of the literature. In particular, the role of domestic and foreign financial intermediaries (including insurance firms) in helping to manage risk for firms in developing countries is an area deserving much more formal econometric research to add to a sizable practitioner literature.

The main message of these subsections can be briefly summarized. On the debate between banks and markets, the suggestion that one type of system is clearly better than the other no longer has much support in the literature, whether for access or for financial sector development. Instead, creating the infrastructures that let both markets and institutions reach their optimal level is likely to be the best policy.

Making credit from banks and other intermediaries that provide debt finance more widely accessible calls for two complementary approaches. On the one hand, the modern trend to transactional lending, whether based on assets or on automated credit appraisal such as credit registries, for example, is clearly the way of the future. On the other hand, neglect of relationship lending can mean that large parts of the market are underserved where infrastructures are weak and economic activity more informal. The role of foreign banks in improving access has always been controversial, partly for political reasons. We look in some detail at the evidence here, and conclude on balance that opening to foreign banks is likely over time to improve access for small and medium enterprises, even if the foreign banks confine their own lending primarily to large firms and governments.

The corporate bond market and organized securities markets are chiefly of relevance to larger firms, though by broadening the range of firms that have access to long-term funding, they do make a contribution to access. Indeed, the spillover effects of greater access for large firms may be significant for smaller firms because they often rely on trade credit, another area that deserves more research. Opening up the equity market to foreign investors improves access for the larger firms. The market for private equity (including through inward foreign direct investment) can also reach medium-size firms, and its development depends on adequate shareholder protections and accounting and other information.

Banks versus Markets

As mentioned, much of the early econometric evidence on cross-country differences used broad measures of financial development such as banking depth. That was largely a matter of convenient availability of data, and it certainly does not imply that nonbank finance is of lesser concern. Even a deep banking sector can hinder access if it lacks competition, mainly serves incumbents at high cost (something that has often been observed with state-owned banking systems), or operates without regard to prudential standards. In contrast, a liquid securities market can contribute an additional valuable dimension to financial access (albeit mainly for larger firms).

Following a vigorous debate about the relative merits of bank-dominated systems and those oriented to the securities market, the proponents of each seem to have fought themselves to a standstill. There are good reasons for thinking that each has its sphere of comparative advantage (Allen and Gale 2000). For instance, banks can be effective in financing ventures and firms active in sectors where there is little dispute over the sector's prospects and where firms can be relied upon to pay back loans provided they maintain cost control and productive efficiency. Even though just a few banks may control most of the loanable funds, that need not result in exclusion of creditworthy borrowers. In contrast, where an entrepreneur seeks external financing for a venture about whose prospects there is considerable disagreement, the securities markets can help: even if majority opinion is against the scheme, the entrepreneur can find financing if a sufficiently well-financed minority of investors likes the project.

But when it comes to aggregate economic growth, the research evidence shows that it does not matter for long-term economic growth whether a financial system is primarily bank-based or market-based. What does matter is the level of overall financial development of banks and markets (Demirgüç-Kunt and Levine 2001; Levine 2002).

The same is true at the sectoral level: there seems to be no tendency for sectors especially reliant on external finance to grow more (or less) quickly in a bank-dominated system than in a market-based system

Both banks and markets have a role to play—

—although markets may be better at providing long-term finance

(Beck and Levine 2002). The growth in the number of firms in the sector, or in the average size of firms, is likewise insensitive to the relative size of the banking and securities sectors.[15] There is a hint, however, in the results obtained by Demirgüç-Kunt and Maksimovic (2002), that firms' ability to obtain financing may be affected in different ways by the two systems, especially at lower levels of financial development.[16] While development of both banks and markets improves access to external finance, a relatively larger securities market may be associated with relatively better access of firms to long-term financing, with banking development more associated with availability of short-term financing. Hence differences in the contracting environments and their impact on relative development of banks versus markets may have important implications for which firms and projects have access to finance, despite our inability to observe an impact on growth using aggregate data. More recent analysis helps shed light on some of the underlying aspects of financial sector development in broadening access.[17]

Access to Debt Finance

Debt finance is the major source of external funding for firms of all sizes

Debt finance is typically the major source of external funding for firms of all sizes, no matter how small.[18] Diverse lending technologies are employed for reaching different types of client in contrasting environments, especially where clients do not have conventional collateral or where collection of collateral is not secure.[19] Conventional practice distinguishes between transactions lending, based primarily on "hard" quantitative data (such as a credible set of borrower financial accounts) or secured on assets, and relationship lending, based significantly on "soft" qualitative information. In practice, however, the menu is much broader (as Berger and Udell 2006 emphasize).

Because of the time and effort involved in understanding the borrower's business and financial needs, relationship lending is costly for the lender and therefore requires either high spreads or large volumes to be viable. If the customer's creditworthiness is hard to evaluate, then there may be no alternative to relationship lending. In a broad sense, relationship lending is at the core of the banking business, continuing to give banks a comparative advantage over markets and nonbank financial institutions, even in developed countries (Boot and Schmeits 2005). Indeed, limited access to credit in some difficult environments may be attributable to the reluctance of existing intermediaries to engage in relationship lending on a small scale (Honohan and Beck 2007).[20] For lenders willing to put in the effort, however, relationship lending can be profitable.

Credit networks that employ and sustain a form of social capital through relationship lending have long been observed in different parts of the world. These networks are often characterized by a common ethnicity of the participants, although ethnic group membership does not automatically convey membership in the credit network.[21] Biggs and Shah (2006) describe credit networks observed in the responses to enterprise surveys in a sample of African countries in the 1990s.[22] They show that a common ethnicity greatly increases the likelihood of a trade credit relationship between any two firms, and that a lengthy specific relationship history between the two firms involved in the credit transaction is not required: network membership itself seems to be sufficient. Credit between firms from different networks is much less likely and does require a lengthy trading relationship. As a result, firms that are not in the dominant networks are effectively shut out of credit, resulting in ethnically biased financial access. For example, enterprises that form part of a network of European-owned or Asian-owned firms enter at a larger size, show higher productivity, and grow faster compared with other African enterprises.[23] To overcome the de facto exclusion of the latter from these networks based on relationship lending, it would be desirable to build the infrastructures that allow a move towards the greater formality and anonymity of modern transaction-based lending.

Corruption in India and the strong pro-state orientation of formal finance in China mean that relationship lending has had to assume an important role in supporting the recent fast growth of firms in those countries, as documented by Allen, Qian, and Qian (2005, 2008) and by Allen and others (2006). For the firms that responded to their survey in India, informal governance mechanisms, such as those based on reputation, trust, and relationships, are more important than formal mechanisms, such as courts, in resolving disputes, overcoming corruption, and supporting growth. Apparently, the pervasiveness of petty corruption more than offsets the advantages of inheriting the common law legal origin in India, inhibiting the growth of transactional lending. Despite the need to rely on relationship lending, however, the Indian economy has managed to grow at a rapid rate, showing the potential for these mechanisms to substitute at least partially for more formal finance in a very poor country. Likewise in China, the fast growth of private

> **Informal relationship lending discriminates against firms outside the credit networks—**

> **—though informal finance has filled some of the gaps left by constrained formal systems**

firms in some coastal provinces seems to depend a lot on relationship lending (facilitated by Confucian ethics), including from unlicensed private financial intermediaries, as well as on relationships built on social capital and shared interests with local government officials. (See box 2.2, however, for a somewhat different perspective).

Other forms of lending can provide financial access

But even where standard types of transactional lending based on transparent financial accounts are not available, other forms of transaction lending may be possible, as Berger and Udell (2006) stress. Provided the relevant laws are in place, asset-based lending such as factoring, fixed-asset lending, trade finance, and leasing are technologies that can release sizable financing flows even for small and nontransparent firms to finance the relevant assets. To be sure, factoring does require a degree of creditworthiness but not necessarily of the "borrower," but rather its customers. That may often be the case, as where a major exporter buys on credit from smaller suppliers. As a result, factoring is found to be more prevalent where credit information is good, though it does not seem to require a high degree of property rights protection (Klapper 2006).

It is striking that some of these techniques have not been more widely used in developing countries. Leasing, for example, constitutes only a few percentage points of fixed investment in the typical developing country, while it reaches up to 20 percent in many developed countries. Similarly, factoring in the United Kingdom reaches 7 percent of GDP, whereas it constitutes less than 1 percent of GDP in most developing countries (Klapper 2006). The limited role of leasing and other nonstandard debt financing is also illustrated by the financing patterns reported in chapter 1 and potentially reflects the shortcomings of the underlying legal, informational, and institutional environment, as is discussed later.

Credit registries and credit scoring can expand access for small firms—

Credit registries are important tools for the expansion of transactions-based lending technologies (Miller 2003; Love and Mylenko 2003; Brown, Jappelli, and Pagano 2006; Powell and others 2004). Credit registries ease for the lender the routine task of verifying aspects of the repayment record (and sometimes the outstanding indebtedness) of the applicant borrower and increase the cost of delinquency, thereby reducing moral hazard. They also help build a database that the lender can use to generate credit scores predicting repayment on the basis of borrower characteristics. This technology is quite mature in the United States, where, as shown by Berger, Frame, and Miller (2005), the use of credit-scoring technology for small business loans has led to an expansion in the availability of loans to small and riskier firms, even by larger banks that would hitherto have shied away from this segment. The use of credit scoring for small business lending, often based on data collected for credit registry purposes, is growing in developing countries as well (De la Torre, Martinez Peria, and Schmukler 2007), although it has yet to reach many countries: this is banking at what is currently a very active frontier.

The more information is stored in the credit registry, the more useful it is in selecting out the risky borrowers without reducing overall access to credit. For instance, Powell and others (2004) use the actual data in the public Argentine credit registry to show that availability of systemwide registry information can substantially improve the precision of credit decisions even for a large bank (figure 2.6). In addition, they show that availability of positive information (for example, history of borrowings, not just defaults) could enable a lender to lower the default rate from 3.8 percent to 2.9 percent while still lending to 60 percent of the sample borrowers.

—by helping to identify risky loans

It is not just the lenders who benefit from better credit information sharing. Using firm-level survey data across 24 transition economies, Brown, Jappelli, and Pagano (2006) find a positive association between the quality of the credit registry and the ease of external financing (figure 2.7). This relationship was confirmed using panel data over time for a limited set of countries.

Figure 2.6 Credit information sharing and loan losses

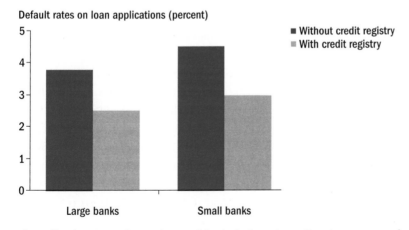

Default rates on loan applications (percent)

■ Without credit registry
■ With credit registry

Large banks   Small banks

Source: Based on an experiment using actual data in the Argentine credit registry, as processed by Powell and others (2004).

Note: Default rate is computed for banks that are targeting a 60 percent acceptance rate of loan applications and optimizing use of a credit registry where available.

Figure 2.7 Credit information sharing and firms' financing constraints

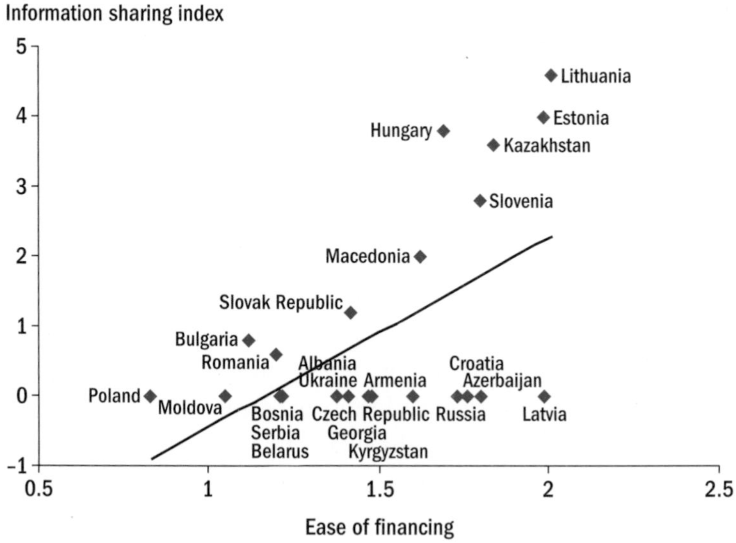

Source: Brown, Jappelli, and Pagano (2006).
Note: This figure plots the quality of credit information sharing against the across 24 transition countries. Ease of financing ranges from 0 to 3, with higher values meaning lower obstacles to financing.

While public credit registries may have some potential advantages, such as the power to compel lenders to share positive information, the experience has been that most public registries do not make as much of the information at their disposal as they might. Increasingly public credit registries are being complemented, where they exist, by private credit bureaus.

With more countries considering the move to Basel II, which can make use of private credit rating agencies, the credit information industry is likely to see considerable expansion in the years ahead.[24] And the more sophisticated the statistical analyses of loan loss probabilities, the more small borrowers can benefit through cheaper access to bank loans. For instance, using data from the Chilean public credit registry, Adasme, Majnoni, and Uribe (2006) have shown that the distribution of loan losses from small loans (equivalent to less than $20,000) is much less skewed than that for large loans (figure 2.8).[25]

The implication is that, while banks making small loans do have to set aside larger *provisions* against the higher expected losses from small loans—and therefore they need to charge higher rates of interest to cover

Figure 2.8 Credit loss distribution for portfolios of large and small loans

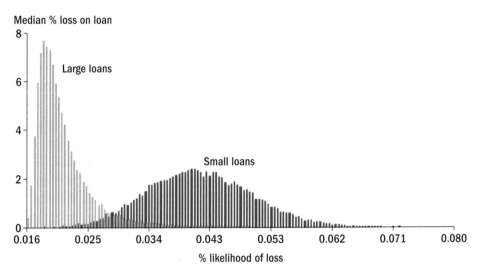

Source: Adasme, Majnoni, and Uribe (2006).
Note: This figure shows the loan loss distribution for portfolios of large and small loans based on data from Chile. Although the probability of loss on small loans is higher, the median percent loss on large loans is much higher and there are far more very high losses for large loans.

these provisions—they need relatively less *capital* to cover the upper tail of the distribution, that is, to support the risk that losses will exceed their expected value (such losses are sometimes known as "unexpected" loan losses). It is important that in making regulatory arrangements, such as those of Basel II, policy makers do not neglect such findings and unnecessarily penalize small borrowers.

The Role of Foreign Banks

The growing market share of foreign-owned banks in developing and transition economies has resulted from a number of forces, including the privatization of long-established state-owned banks (in response to their disappointing financial and economic performance) and the aftermath of banking crises, when distressed banks were put up for sale, often after being financially restructured at the expense of the host country government. Foreign banks were often the successful acquirers, transforming the ownership structure, especially in many parts of Latin America, Eastern Europe, and Africa. Foreign banks have also entered de novo, although typically remaining relatively small in that case. In addition to the big international banks, foreign entry has come from regionally specialized banks or those from a neighboring country often exploiting close business or cultural ties (Claessens and van Horen 2007).

A growing market share for foreign-owned banks excites controversy

Foreign owners bring capital, technology, know-how, and a degree of independence from the local business elite. It has been suggested that they can help stabilize the banking system and the macroeconomy, and they have tended to be more efficient and profitable than incumbent banks in developing countries. But have they improved access? This is a highly contested issue. Most foreign banks are relatively large (at least in their global operations) and may struggle to understand aspects of the local business culture. It is a commonplace observation in advanced countries that large banks have a comparative advantage in transactions banking based on "hard" information, whereas the comparative advantage for relationship lending to small or otherwise opaque firms lies with small, thus local, banks. The progressive extension of credit information will tend to erode these differences over time, but there is no doubt that the credit environment in developing countries tends to be considerably more opaque than in advanced economies. Could it therefore be that in countries relying heavily on foreign banks, the SME sector will experience more limited access to credit? Indeed, many foreign banks do not concentrate on SME lending but stick mainly to the banking needs of larger firms and high-net-worth individuals.[26] Foreign banks are more efficient and can undercut the local banks in their targeted segments. But that does not imply that foreign entry will result in lower system-wide availability of credit for SMEs. Instead, the increased competition for large customers can drive other banks to focus more on providing profitable services to segments they had formerly neglected.[27]

The evidence suggest foreign banks benefit firms of all sizes—

Ultimately this is an empirical issue, and one on which much recent evidence from developing countries has accumulated, although with somewhat contrasting results across different regions. Overall, foreign bank entry has been a welcome improvement for larger firms, and this improved credit access has in many countries extended to smaller firms. Nevertheless there are also some indications that the arrival of foreign banks has not always been good for small firm access to credit, at least at first.[28]

The evidence on the impact of foreign banks comes from a myriad of different types of analysis on different types of data sources; some international, some (more fine-grained) at the national or subnational level.

The benchmark research finding on the relation between financial access and foreign bank presence comes from a reanalysis of the responses to access questions in the WBES surveys. In a very direct approach that yielded striking results, Clarke, Cull, and Martinez Peria (2006) found that respondent firms were less likely to rate high interest rates and access to long-term loans as major obstacles in countries with sizable foreign bank shares. The effect was stronger for larger firms but was present even for small firms (figure 2.9).[29]

Figure 2.9 Foreign bank participation and financing obstacles

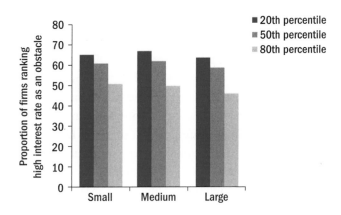

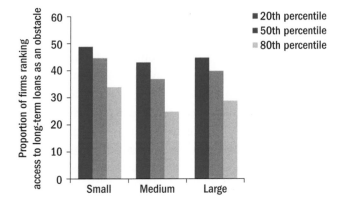

Source: Clarke, Cull, and Martinez Peria (2006), table 3.

Note: This figure shows the likelihood that small, medium, and large enterprises rank high interest rates and lack of access to long-term loans as the major obstacles in developing countries at the 20th, 50th, and 80th percentile of foreign bank ownership, holding other firm and country characteristics constant. Small firms are defined as those with 5–50 employees, medium firms as those with 51–500 employees, and large firms as those with 500 or more employees.

—although the impact
of foreign banks has not
always been positive—

One contrary suggestion that a larger share of foreign bank ownership might not always be so good for financial development or access comes from broad-brush aggregate cross-country data. Confining themselves to low-income countries (the poorest 60 or so) Detragiache, Gupta, and Tressel (2006) found that a higher share of foreign-owned banks is significantly and negatively correlated with private credit growth, even after controlling for some other national variables. This somewhat surprising result does not hold for middle- and upper-income countries and may reflect the more cautious approach that foreign banks take in countries with deficient legal and information infrastructures.

Greater richness of evidence is obtained if bank-by-bank data for locally owned and foreign-owned banks is available for comparing behavior between the two groups and also to see whether more entry by foreign banks affects the behavior of local banks. Among recent studies taking this approach, Clarke and others (2005) collected data from bank supervisory entities in Argentina, Chile, Colombia, and Peru for the late 1990s, a period in which there was substantial foreign entry in that region. The data included each bank's origin (and, if foreign, its mode of entry; distinguishing between de novo, by acquisition, or long-established), and the share of its lending portfolio going to SMEs. Controlling for the bank's size, age, and financial performance, they find that, as expected, foreign banks lend less to SMEs, but that the differential is largely associated with small banks. There is little difference between the share of small business lending in the portfolio of medium and large foreign-owned and domestic banks—with foreign banks even nudging ahead in Chile and Colombia.[30]

—especially for smaller firms
in the short term

This bank-level evidence is partly confirmed by firm-level evidence from transition economies, which have also seen rapid foreign bank entry over the past 15 years, with foreign-owned banks accounting for over 90 percent of total credit in several countries. Examination of firm-level data (from the Amadeus database) on medium and large firms in that region shows that the process of foreign bank entry has been associated with more rapid sales growth and total assets of large firms, and an increase in both firm entry and exit rates. Using 60,000 firm-year observations covering the period 1993–2002,[31] Giannetti and Ongena (2005) also found that these effects were stronger for firms in sectors that are more bank-susceptible (in the sense explained above). However, they also found that foreign bank entry was negatively associated with the growth of the smaller firms in their sample. It remains to be seen to what extent this experience proves to be a transitional one, both in the sense of being specific to the rapid structural changes that were happening in Eastern Europe in those years—indications are that firms established from 1989 through 2003 did not benefit so much from foreign bank entry—and in the sense of evolving over time as the foreign banks' behavior matures. Foreign bank managers in Eastern Europe themselves report an evolution in their strategy toward a focus on smaller firms as the lending environment becomes both more competitive and more transparent.

The arrival or expansion of foreign banks, however, can also be disruptive, generating extensive changes in economic behavior. A study in India by Gormley (2004) is highly instructive in this regard. He shows that the state-owned development banks reduced the volume of long-term lending in districts where foreign banks had entered. The newcomers took up only some of the slack. While they gave some firms more credit than these firms had before—in effect skimming the cream of the best clients—they did not take on all of the clients dropped by the state-owned development banks, regardless of profitability. Many of those firms that thus lost access to long-term bank finance were able to make up the deficiency, however, because they were part of an industrial group. Gormley was unable to detect any adverse consequences of the refocusing of bank lending in sales or bankruptcies.[32]

Foreign banks can generate extensive changes in economic behavior

Gormley notes that in the years following entry the foreign banks seem to have expanded the clientele to whom they would lend, but even though the liberalization that triggered entry started in 1994, he suggests that it is still too early to determine the scale of long-term effects. Also, as observers of the Indian scene will be aware, foreign entry was not the only source of heightened competition in India; bank privatization also contributed to increased competition.

Mian's (2006) study of 80,000 bank loans in Pakistan during the period 1996–2002 throws light on the possible limitations of many international banks when it comes to lending in developing countries. He finds that foreign-owned banks were more conservative, shying away from soft-information loans; this was true even for foreign banks that had been present in Pakistan for a very long time. Specifically, they were less likely to lend to small firms, domestically owned firms, firms that were not part of a business group (that is, groups of firms with overlapping directorships), or those without other banking relationships (figure 2.10). Mian also compares foreign banks of different nationalities and finds

Foreign banks tend to avoid relationship lending

Figure 2.10   Bank ownership and borrower characteristics in Pakistan

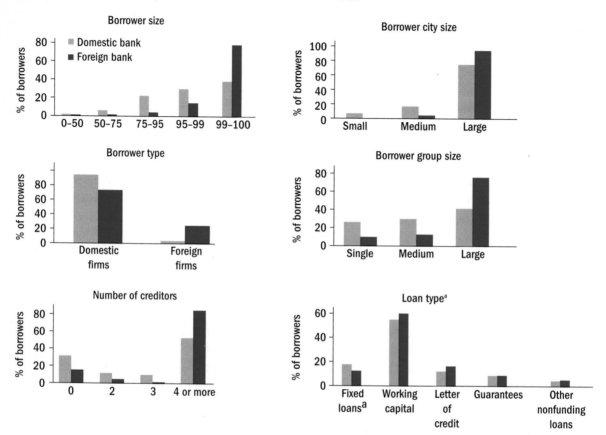

Source: Mian (2006).

a. All loan types are short-term loans except fixed loans, which have a maturity of more than two years.

that non-Asian foreign banks were less likely than Asian banks to lend to Pakistani firms. Second, despite being such conservative lenders, foreign banks did not have lower default rates in Pakistan and were less likely to renegotiate and recover after default. It is not as if all the good borrowers were being served by existing locally owned banks: Mian found that during the period under review, private domestic banks established new branches from which they served new, soft-information costumers rather than existing customers from other banks.[33]

Foreign bank entry can also influence the degree of concentration in a country's banking system (although it is only one contributory factor;

large state-owned banks, for example are another contributing factor). On the one hand, the arrival of foreign banks injects a degree of competition for the rest; on the other hand, the foreign banks tend to be large and their entry might displace others (Claessens, Demirgüç-Kunt, and Huizinga 2001; Bonin, Hasan, and Wachtel 2004).[34] The competitive structure of banking can also affect the degree to which firms have access, but the effect seems to be highly dependent on other characteristics of the business environment for banking. Greater concentration is often equated with greater monopoly power, but this may not be the case in banking if the various market segments are vulnerable to new entrants (Berger and others 2004). Other indicators of monopoly power are also needed.[35] Nevertheless, big banks almost inevitably enjoy a degree of monopoly power; indeed the logic of modern banking increasingly entails exploiting economies of scale and diversification.[36]

Some scholars have suggested that a degree of monopoly power for banks might even be good for small borrowers' access to credit. They argue that the investment in relationship banking required to determine whether a small borrower is creditworthy is likely to be rewarded by a stream of profits only in an uncompetitive market.[37] If so, only banks with monopoly power will make the effort to build the relationship. However the responses of firms to the WBES survey provide little evidence to support the idea that a more concentrated banking system is good for access. Adverse effects of concentration can be found only in low-income countries or in those countries with weak credit information or tight restrictions on the scope of banking (Beck, Demirgüç-Kunt, and Maksimovic 2004). Although small, low-income countries may stand to benefit most from greater banking competition, it is precisely in these that achieving a sufficient number of well-capitalized and qualified bankers is problematic.

A balanced overall statement of the available empirical evidence is that opening to foreign banks has the potential to convey net benefits by introducing competition and increasing efficiency and independence of local political processes and that these benefits are likely to be greater as time goes on and the entrants learn more about local conditions. The benefits are also likely to be greater in host countries that have the necessary information and contractual frameworks and incentive structures in place that facilitate foreign banks doing what they are best at, namely, automated transactions lending. While foreign entry generally generates more competition for the incumbents, the end result may not always be

Foreign banks may increase banking concentration—and competition

The benefits of foreign banks are more apparent in the longer term

an increase in competition if entry happens through acquisition, especially in a small market. Given the little empirical support for the theory that increased monopoly power improves the access of small borrowers, such entry may not necessarily lead to greater access. There are indications that foreign entry tends to make domestic financial institutions seek out nontraditional businesses, including services for previously excluded segments of the population, as these institutions find their traditional businesses coming under competition. Hence, locally managed banks with a business model focused on addressing opportunities in the local business community have the potential to survive foreign entry, adding value by broadening access, especially to the SME sector.

Access to Nonbank Debt Finance

A poor business environment can inhibit long-term bank financing

Where long-term finance is available, the evidence is that it makes a positive contribution to firm growth (Demirgüç-Kunt and Maksimovic 1999). But there are numerous barriers to availability of long-term finance. It is not just that banks need to maintain liquidity, an aspect that is often stressed. In reality, well-run banks with a stable deposit base can and do lend at maturities well beyond the nominal maturity of their deposits. Indeed this maturity transformation is one of the key contributions of banking to the wider economic system. Other factors at both the national and firm-level also impose barriers to long-term finance. At the aggregate level, macroeconomic risks loom large in the decision to make a long-term loan, as do weaknesses in the credit information environment and contract enforcement.[38] In dealing with riskier and more opaque borrowers (for example, small or new firms, or those with an adverse credit history), banks prefer to use shorter-term loans, which can be renewed or renegotiated, so that they can maintain control over the lending relationship and retain the possibility to influence firm management during the course of the relationship.[39]

For long-term lending, the role for bond financing is potentially larger, can provide competition for banks, and can serve as a spare tire to be employed in the event of a banking crisis. The potential here should not be exaggerated, however, as Gormley, Johnson, and Rhee (2006), for example, point out in their study of the Korean financial crisis of 1997–98. When that crisis triggered a freeze in bank lending, a private bond market easily sprang to life, capturing households' savings and channeling them to corporations. But it was the largest corporations, the *chaebols*, that received the financing, and the public was willing to invest in bonds because it perceived them as a safe investment, assuming that the *chaebols* would be regarded by the authorities as too big to fail. This public perception was proved correct by the bailout of bond investors after the 1999 collapse of the large *chaebol* Daewoo. Smaller firms, despite their often better corporate governance structures, were unable to access the bond market even after banks stopped lending.

Private bonds can provide a competitive alternative to banks, but banks can also use bonds to exploit their credit appraisal capacity while economizing on capital and liquidity by packaging residential mortgages and other small or medium-size loans into larger units that then can be sold to pension funds and other institutional investors. Mortgage-backed bonds issued by banks perform a similar function and can work in less sophisticated financial systems. The legal, accounting, and other requirements to make this kind of financial engineering effective,

Bond financing can provide competition for banks

Box 2.3   When access can be too tempting: risks and use of foreign currency borrowing by firms

ONE MAJOR RISK THAT CAN ARISE FROM FINANCIAL globalization is the assumption by financial, and especially nonfinancial, firms of much greater foreign exchange risk than is prudent. The temptation to do so often arises when macroeconomic and exchange rate policy results in high and volatile nominal interest rates for borrowings in local currency, whereas creditworthy borrowers may access foreign currency borrowing either from locally based or foreign banks at much lower nominal interest rates, but accepting the exchange risk.[a] The combination of availability of foreign capital and high domestic interest rates has often been associated with a policy of fixing the exchange rate at what seems an undervalued rate: promoting an export and profit boom as well as capital inflows caused by expectations of a nominal currency appreciation. The combination greatly

heightens the risks, and a reversal of investor sentiment can mean very large currency movements and an economic crisis, as has been seen in such disparate cases as Chile in 1982–83 and Indonesia in 1997–98. It is not a simple task to calculate even approximately what a prudent foreign exchange exposure would be for a firm whose nonfinancial business has an international component. (South African Airlines recently incurred heavy losses as a result of treasury policies that could be characterized as overhedging of foreign exchange.) The scale of onshore dollarization of bank deposits and international fixed-interest lending has surged several times in the past couple of decades (De Nicoló, Honohan, and Ize 2005; Goldstein and Turner 2004), making currency exchange risk a problem that is likely to recur.

a. See Allayannis, Brown, and Klapper (2003) for a study of firms' strategies to hedge foreign exchange rate exposure in East Asia before and after the crisis.

including the role of independent credit-rating firms to help investors price these bonds, are considerable and beyond the reach of smaller or less advanced markets, but the details need not concern us here. Where bond financing is possible, it can improve the price and availability of longer-term credit to smaller borrowers.

Access to External Equity

Even start-up firms need equity to finance working capital; entrepreneurs everywhere have recourse to relatives and friends for initial equity to supplement their own resources. The quantitative importance of internal financing from retained earnings to help support the growth process has already been discussed. As firms grow, so too does the importance of having access to sources of external equity. Bank loans cannot perform this function. In most countries there are individuals and firms who, in one way or another, arrange private equity for some of the most promising growth firms, but a wider investor clientele can be tapped through a listing on an organized stock exchange.

Stock market development requires a sound regulatory environment

The development of shareholder capitalism depends on strong *investor rights* and on adequately enforced public disclosure of the financial condition of public companies (Morck and Steier 2005). Reliance on disclosure and private enforcement mechanisms seems more effective than public enforcement policies and restrictions imposed by authorities (La Porta, Lopez-de-Silanes, and Shleifer 2006). In many countries, information and investor protection are not adequate to allow the stock market to fulfill its full potential in establishing the full price of each equity stock. As Morck, Yeung, and Yu (2000) and Jin and Myers (2006) show, stock prices of different firms move closely together in the stock exchanges of many countries and especially in countries with weak shareholder rights and lack of firm transparency (figure 2.11).[40] This contrasts to the situation in advanced economies, where the correlation of individual stock prices with the average of the market tends to be rather low. The strong co-movement of stock prices may mean that little firm-specific information comes into the public arena. As a result, individual firm equity is not, on average, fully priced, and the discount is likely to be greater, the greater the firm's growth prospects. It is not surprising, then, that most of the largest firms in the corporate sector of such countries tend to be controlled by a small elite group of families, as outsiders doubt they will benefit from holding shares—with reason,

Figure 2.11   Stock price synchronicity with disclosure and governance

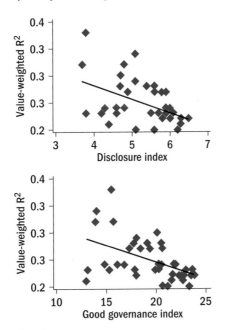

Source: Jin and Myers (2006).
Note: This figure compares the degree to which stock prices tend to move together in each of 40 stock exchanges with indicators of disclosure and governance.

as Desai and Moel (2007) document in several spectacular cases. The consequences can be lower investment than optimal.[41]

Investor rights and transparency might not be enough to foster liquid equity markets. Rather, a critical mass of issues, issuers, and investors seems to be necessary (De la Torre and Schmukler 2007). The recent merger wave among the stock exchanges of developed countries and the deepening of a rather limited set of emerging stock exchanges raise questions about the extent to which smaller emerging countries will have the critical mass to support national stock exchanges or will need to rely on regional or foreign exchanges for firms' funding needs.

These findings confirm the importance of shareholder protection and information for ensuring that the stock market makes external capital available to firms with growth prospects. However, making reforms is not an easy matter. Controlling families often do not seem interested in increasing the transparency of the market or in boosting the rights of minorities (even though such actions could make cheaper capital available). Indeed, they seem to be effective in blocking, through their

Small economies may benefit from regional exchanges

rent-seeking activities, a strengthening of the financial system for fear that a stronger system would allow the emergence of challengers to their incumbency.[42] Venture capital is also more effective when underlying legal protections are present (Cumming, Schmidt, and Walz 2006).

External listing by larger firms might not be good for equity access of smaller firms

Opening up equity markets to the outside world has made a big contribution to improving access and cost of equity finance for larger local firms.[43] A listing (or ADR[44]) in a foreign market by such firms improves their access to equity by increasing the share price and making them more attractive for institutional investors, thus generating an incentive for firms to expand (Aggarwal, Klapper, and Wysocki 2005; Levine and Schmukler 2007a). Such listings can import corporate governance (Coffee 2002), although this finding is not reflected in any sustained increase in the market value of the firm (Levine and Schmukler 2007a). These gains, however, might be partly offset by loss of liquidity in local markets, potentially limiting access to outside equity for smaller firms (Levine and Schmukler 2007b). The net overall impact on the access of small firms is not clear; after all, improved access by large firms may spill over to small ones through trade credit. Furthermore, as larger firms have greater access to, and substitute, these alternative sources of funding for bank finance, banks are likely to become more interested in serving smaller clients.

FDI may ease financing constraints—

Foreign direct investment offers a partial substitute for local finance, a fact that has proved important in some countries, where it appears to have eased financing constraints, at least for large, publicly listed firms.[45] To be sure, foreign investors likely choose some of the best-performing local firms in which to invest, so this selection bias needs to be taken into account (Weiss and Nikitin 2004). However, FDI transactions in which firms in advanced economies have acquired listed firms in developing countries have been associated with sizable stock market gains for both acquirer and target. That finding implies consequential gains in profitability over time, according to a study by Chari, Ouimet, and Tesar (2005) of 1,629 acquisitions in Argentina, Brazil, Chile, Indonesia, Republic of Korea, Malaysia, Mexico, the Philippines, and Thailand (figure 2.12).

—and improve firm management and use of technology

The mode of entry can be influential in determining how productive the investment will be. A particular issue is whether insisting on joint ventures rather than allowing foreign control of the enterprise is better for the host country overall. Moran (2005) has observed that target companies that have been integrated into the foreign acquirer's worldwide

Figure 2.12 Returns to shareholders in acquiring and target firms around the date of FDI announcement

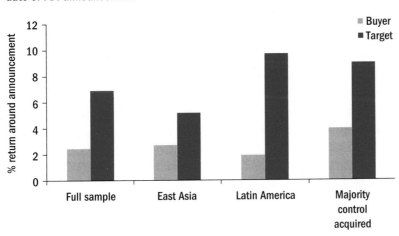

Source: Chari, Ouimet, and Teas (2005).

operations tend to be larger, better managed, and more technologically advanced than those whose purpose is to serve protected domestic markets in the host country. Many of the most effective FDI transactions, therefore, go well beyond providing financial access to the target firms, which instead are swallowed up.

With the emergence of large private equity firms in the advanced economies temporarily taking majority stakes in firms in the developing world (such as banks in Korea, following the crisis of 1997–98), the dividing line between FDI and other equity investment has become somewhat blurred. At the same time, locally controlled private equity funds, often affiliated with banks or other financial service providers, have also been created in numerous countries. One way or another, venture capital and private equity (including venture capital for near start-ups) have been an increasingly important source of finance for certain categories of firms in developing countries, although such investment has been subject to waves of enthusiasm (the mid-1990s, for example) followed by valley periods. These transactions are not very fully documented in available data, so they have not been subjected to the same kinds of econometric analysis discussed in this chapter.[46] A half-dozen large emerging economies currently receive most of the flow of FDI—Brazil, China (including Taiwan), India, Korea, Russia, and South Africa. This geographic concentration is likely to persist, because of the size of these economies, the availability (in some of them) of large, capital-hungry, natural resource–based projects for foreigners to invest in, and the perceived quality of the overall investment environment, including the availability of local currency debt financing to complete the package and a market on which the equity stake can be floated in due course (Rubenstein 2006). Nevertheless, private equity firms have been looking at most countries with increasing interest since 2003, and, while there may be interruptions, private equity may become an increasingly important source of financing for larger firms with growth potential.

Conclusions

Barriers to finance are a major obstacle, especially for new and small firms

Availability of external financing for firms depends on the wider institutional environment; lack of availability does constrain firm growth, and it is one of the more important business obstacles firms have to overcome. Access to finance contributes to firm entry, growth, and innovation, among other things. Small and new firms are affected the most by financing constraints. Yet they also benefit the most as financial systems develop and financing constraints consequently ease. Empirical evidence suggests that it is through improving access for enterprises that financial sector development makes an important contribution to economic growth.

Foreign banks improve access to finance, especially in the longer term

While relationship lending remains important in many parts of the world, the modern trend is increasingly toward transactional lending. In this regard, good credit registries can be a powerful force for expanding the reach of lenders. Not least because international banks have a comparative advantage in transactional lending, their arrival or expansion in a country can cause natural apprehension about their possible effect on broad access to credit. However, the balance of a large body of evidence is that even where foreign entrants are highly selective in their target credit market, access to credit from the system as a whole usually improves. And it is increasingly likely to do so as time goes on. In contrast, the performance of state-owned banks in this dimension has tended to be poor.

Nonbank finance has a growing role to play

Nonbank finance remains much less important in most developing countries, but that too can be expected to change. Bond finance is an increasingly important alternative to bank finance, mainly for large firms. Access to external equity requires strong investor rights; where these are present, opening to capital inflows can greatly improve access and lower the cost of capital. That is true both for portfolio equity investments and for foreign direct investment and private equity, which are likely to become increasingly important. While bond and equity markets are most directly relevant for improving access to finance for larger firms, these markets are also likely to have an indirect effect on access for small firms, as trade credit represents an important source of external finance for many small firms.

Notes

1. There is a large empirical literature on financing constraints that arise because of information asymmetries and on the resulting agency problems between lenders and borrowers (see surveys by Schiantarelli 1995; Blundell, Bond, and Meghir 1996; Hubbard 1998; and Bond and Van Reenen 1999). While most of this literature has tried to infer financing constraints indirectly from investment–cash flow correlations or deviations from optimal investment patterns, studies highlighted in this chapter use more direct measures. Also see Beck and others (2006), who use the WBES survey data discussed in the text and show that self-reported financing constraints are robustly correlated with firm size, age, and ownership (domestic or foreign).

2. The increase in sales was proportional to the increase in bank credit, another piece of evidence to support the authors' hypothesis that credit constraints were at work. While the increase in profits might be partly explained by the subsidized interest on directed lending, the magnitude seems too large to be the sole factor.

3. Surveyed businesses in the WBES were asked (among other things) to rate financing, legal, and corruption obstacles, as well as others, on a scale from 1 (no obstacle) to 4 (major obstacle), to reflect the extent to which these obstacles affected the growth of their business. Regressing firm sales growth on financing, corruption, and legal obstacles, while controlling for firm and country characteristics, shows that all three obstacles significantly constrain firm growth. If all three obstacles are entered in the regression, financing and legal obstacles still remain negative and significant, while the corruption obstacle loses its significance.

4. This is evidenced for example by the increased willingness of firms to diversify by acquiring intangible assets in countries where property rights are secure (Claessens and Laeven 2003).

5. Using household survey data from Bosnia and Herzegovina, Demirgüç-Kunt, Klapper, and Panos (2007) study determinants of self-employment for

individuals. They find that personal wealth predicts the choice of becoming an entrepreneur, as does receiving remittances (although negatively). However, access to bank finance predicts survival as an entrepreneur beyond the first year.

6. Specifically, respondents were asked whether they had (i) developed a major new product line; (ii) upgraded an existing product line; (iii) introduced new technology that has substantially changed the way that the main product is produced; (iv) discontinued at least one product (not production) line; (v) opened a new plant; (vi) closed at least one existing plant or outlet; (vii) agreed to a new joint venture with a foreign partner; (viii) obtained a new licensing agreement; (ix) outsourced a major production activity that was previously conducted in-house; or (x) brought in-house a major production activity that was previously outsourced.

7. Measurement error in a causal variable tends to bias the OLS (ordinary least squares) estimates downward, whereas reverse causality or an unobserved common causal factor would tend to bias the OLS estimates upward. This downward bias has been noted in econometric studies of other supposed causes of growth as well (Pande and Udry 2006). Note however that this interpretation depends on the use of valid instruments in the attempt to adjust for endogeneity. Using an invalid instrument (for example, one that should really be included in the equation as an explanatory variable) will bias the adjusted (instrumental variables) estimate.

8. The supposed inefficiency of Chinese bank lending should not be overstated, though, especially for recent years. Using firm-level survey data, Cull and Xu (2000, 2003) find that bank finance was associated with higher subsequent firm productivity in the 1980s, while government transfers were not. This relationship, however, weakened in the 1990s. Drawing on a sample of mostly small and medium Chinese firms, which account for the most dynamic part of the Chinese economy, Ayyagari, Demirgüç-Kunt, and Maksimovic (2007b) show that those receiving bank credit around 2002 did tend to grow more quickly than the average firm, whereas those receiving funds from informal sources did not. This suggests that even if the bulk of Chinese bank credit has not been directed to financing the most productive firms, credit decisions of Chinese banks regarding smaller enterprises have been associated with faster firm growth, and the formal financial system is still better than the informal one in picking the best performers.

9. That Vietnam has also seen perverse flows of credit is argued by Malesky and Taussig (2005), who find that despite rapid increases in both bank deposits and credit in recent years, suggestive of financial development, this additional credit does not seem to have found its way into the provinces where it is most needed, that is, provinces with the highest share of private entrepreneurs. Private entrepreneurs seem to be crowded out systematically by state-owned enterprises. Connection to the government and the party, in contrast, seem to

help private entrepreneurs gain access to credit. These authors also find a negative relationship between access to credit and investment growth. Simply put, firms receiving bank finance in Vietnam are not the engines of growth. At the same time, expanding private firms seem to rely mostly on retained earnings and personal savings to finance investment. There is one positive exception to this disappointing picture: in more competitive provinces, that is, in those where there are more private entrepreneurs per capita competing for credit, easier access to credit is positively related to investment growth. Overall, these results point to a misallocation of banking credit to connected firms in less competitive regions of the country.

10. Also, Rajan and Zingales (1998) find the growth effect of finance only on industries that need it most, and not on all industries, suggesting that it is the efficiency of financial intermediation that matters, not simply capital accumulation.

11. See, for example, Rioja and Valev (2004a, b).

12. Noting that most enterprises need some initial wealth, Aghion, Fally, and Scarpetta (2006) see the financial system as allowing entrepreneurs to leverage this initial wealth—the better developed the financial system, the higher the leverage, a phenomenon that allows efficient newcomers to displace even well-financed but inefficient incumbents. Working with data on more than 10,000 firms drawn mainly from national business registries and administrative records in 16 countries, including 7 developing or transition economies (and using the susceptibility measure of Rajan and Zingales, mentioned in box 2.1), they find that national policies that restrict credit availability tend to limit entry and growth of small firms to a much larger extent than do labor market regulations. On the other hand, large firm entry is not affected by financial development.

13. Given that exporting firms face fixed costs and might therefore depend more on external finance than other firms, Becker and Greenberg (2005) conjectured that countries with higher levels of financial development should have higher exports. And indeed—using bilateral trade data and controlling for other variables in a gravity regression—they find that countries with higher levels of financial development export more. This effect is stronger in industries in which exporters potentially face higher fixed costs, as proxied by the lack of standardization, or for exports to nonneighboring countries or countries with a different language.

14. Using the Rajan and Zingales methodology, Beck (2003) shows countries with better-developed financial systems have a comparative advantage in industries relying more on external finance.

15. These results are reported by Beck and Levine (2002), who used the same sectoral data source for 42 countries as Rajan and Zingales (1998) (see

box 2.1), but added measures of the relative size or activity of the securities markets and the banking system.

16. Specifically, Demirgüç-Kunt and Maksimovic (2002) found no additional explanatory power when they added a variable indicating the relative size of securities markets and banks to their analysis of the proportion of each county's firms that were growing faster than could be achieved solely with internal resources. But the equations, containing both banking depth and stock market turnover as independent explanatory variables in quadratic form, did suggest that stock market development might be more important than bank development in allowing firm growth that required long-term financing. (For their dependent variable, they counted the number of firms—out of a total of more than 10,000 from 32 countries—that were expanding sales faster than would seem supportable from internal resources or short-term borrowing, as modeled by a standard financial planning model. (This study built on a paper they published in 1998; see box 2.1).

17. Of course the dichotomy between banks and markets is also too simplistic. Many nonbank institutions, including nondepository mortgage lenders, leasing, and factoring companies, are involved in specialized forms of asset-based finance. And important channels of equity finance—venture capital, business angel finance, and other forms of private equity—can operate without much use of organized securities exchanges. Institutional investors too are important providers of several forms of financing. The bank-market distinction is nevertheless a useful handle: much of what can be said about bank finance applies to nonbank lenders; much of what is important for securities markets is also relevant for private equity.

18. There are good theoretical reasons for debt finance to be the major source of external finance, not least because, relative to other forms of sharing the returns on a project, the debt contract economizes on precise monitoring of project performance (Diamond 1984).

19. De la Torre, Martinez Peria, and Schmukler (2007) show that banks in two very different institutional environments (Argentina and Chile) adapt to lend to SMEs and overcome institutional weaknesses. Banks do so by lending short term, collateralizing their loans, or securing their loans in some other forms.

20. It is perhaps worth emphasizing the difference between relationship lending and *related-party lending,* which is a form of self-dealing. Although banks often resort to related-party lending where information about other borrowers or contract enforcement is lacking, such lending can ultimately impose social costs, as is well illustrated in the discussion by Maurer and Haber (2004) of Mexico's experience in the early 1900s and by La Porta, Lopez-de-Silanes, and Zamarripa (2003) of the more recent experiences in East Asia in the 1990s.

21. A classic account of the Jewish Maghribi traders' network in the late Middle Ages is in Greif (1993).

22. These Regional Program on Enterprise Development surveys were carried out in five African countries during the 1990s. For a book-length discussion of the findings, see Fafchamps (2004).

23. Fisman (2003) controls more carefully for unobserved firm quality and still finds that firms are more than twice as likely to receive trade credit from within their ethnic community than from outside. However, he also finds that these ethnic ties account for only 15 percent of the overall preferential credit access enjoyed by entrepreneurs of non-African descent.

24. Ensuring that the growth of this industry is based on trustworthy rating agency firms is a nonnegligible challenge (Honohan 2001).

25. Bebczuk (2007) undertook a similar exercise using Argentine data and reported similar findings.

26. In some countries foreign banks have entered the SME lending market themselves (De la Torre, Martinez Peria, and Schmukler 2007). This does not only imply relying on the transaction-lending techniques mentioned above, but it does imply a learning process for foreign banks. Similarly, bank-survey evidence from transition economies has shown that many foreign banks are taking advantage of the improving contractual and information frameworks in these countries and are applying business models from their mostly West European home countries and (de Haas and Naaborg 2005). Some banks in transition countries also have been expanding intraregionally and moving beyond a traditional focus on large corporations to provide more financial services geared to SMEs in host countries. In Sub-Saharan Africa, where foreign banks have long been criticized for neglecting all but the large, international borrowers, a more differentiated picture has been emerging in recent years (Honohan and Beck 2007).

27. In most cases, an important market segment typically remains to be served by locally owned and smaller banks. Indeed, cross-country evidence (Berger, Hassan, and Klapper 2004) suggests that where smaller non-state-owned local banks have a higher market share, economic growth is stronger, although it has not proved possible to establish that this growth is attributable to more SME lending.

28. The Mexican case, where foreign banks spent $30 billion between 1997 and 2004 and increased the foreign ownership of the Mexican banking system from 11 to 83 percent, provides an interesting illustration of the fact that large-scale foreign entry is not a panacea even for a highly distressed banking system. Tracking each bank in Mexico, Schulz (2006) shows that, over the period 1997–2004, bank capital strengthened, the quality of the loan portfolio

improved, and there appears to have been a modest increase in productivity (the latter always hard to measure in banking because of its multiple joint outputs). During this period, bank lending to the private sector continued the slump that had begun with the crisis of 1994; there has since been a recovery. But Haber and Musachio (2005) find it impossible to detect any indication in the data that foreign acquisition slowed credit granting by a bank, although the foreign banks did effectively screen out problem borrowers and were ahead of the others in achieving reduced loan losses.

29. Of course one might get such results if foreign banks tend to be attracted to countries where the financial market works well anyway. To control for this, Clarke, Cull, and Martinez Peria (2006) also looked at firms' opinions about access to nonbank finance. It turns out that the presence of foreign banks has no significant impact on the responses to the control question.

30. It is not so easy to draw conclusions about the interest rates charged. For example, using the same basic data sources, Martinez Peria and Mody (2004) found that whether bank entry was by merger, acquisition, or de novo, foreign-owned banks charge narrower margins, by 50 basis points on average, than domestic banks; and the difference is even larger for de novo foreign banks. Of course, with interest rates differing widely between customer types, it is difficult to be sure that the control variables are adequate to reveal a true price differential, rather than a reflection, for example, of foreign banks lending to low-risk, low-spread borrowers, and funding on wholesale terms.

31. And using instruments that predict foreign bank entry, but not firm growth, in a convincing attempt to ensure that the measured effects were not attributable to a common hidden cause.

32. Even firms outside a formal group structure can indirectly access bank credit if they are granted increased trade credit from firms with growing bank borrowings. Trade credit in effect offers credit access to an additional layer of firms, exploiting information and other bilateral relationships (Fisman and Love, 2003; Love, Preve, and Sarria-Allende 2007; Burkart, Ellingsen, and Gianetti; 2004; Omiccioli 2005).

33. But the same database from Pakistan has also thrown light on the potential deficiencies of state-owned banks and specifically on the nexus between politicians and state-owned banks (see chapter 4).

34. Levy Yeyati and Micco (2007) argue that the extensive foreign bank entry in Latin America in the 1990s resulted in a less competitive banking system overall, although this contention is not undisputed. Their evidence comes from showing that bank revenues became less sensitive to variations in input costs, as happens with a monopolist charging "what the market will bear," in contrast to a competitive system that effectively fully passes on changes in input prices to the customer.

35. For example Demirgüç-Kunt, Laeven, and Levine (2004) show that restrictions on bank entry, measured by the fraction of entry applications rejected by the regulatory agency, are more closely correlated with interest margins than with concentration. Using data on net interest margins of some 1,165 banks from 47 countries, they find that countries that restrict foreign bank entry end up with higher bank margins.

36. It seems that transactions costs, including those of acquiring information, are strongly related to distance, resulting in a degree of monopoly power for local banks. Very convincing evidence on this point comes from a market as developed as Belgium, for which Degryse and Ongena (2005) document how the lending rates charged by one bank vary according to the physical distance between the customer and the nearest competitor bank.

37. Studies of this proposition for the United States and other advanced economies show that its applicability is context specific, with few simple lessons directly applicable to all developing countries. For instance, Cetorelli and Strahan (2004) show that new entrants found it more difficult to get finance in U.S. states with less competitive banking markets, but Zarutskie (2005), using data based on corporation tax returns, finds less investment (as indicated by higher rates of return) and less external financing for small firms following increases in competition resulting from the liberalization of U.S. interstate banking. Using data from different Italian regions, Bonaccorsi di Patti and Dell'Ariccia (2004) find that bank concentration can have a positive effect on firm entry where information is opaque. Bertrand, Schoar, and Thesmar (2007) show that the far-reaching French banking liberalization of the 1980s did not uniformly increase credit availability but made it more sensitive to borrowers' business prospects.

38. Using data on 27,000 publicly listed firms in 27 developed economies and 18 developing economies, Sorge and Zhang (2006) find that countries with better quality of credit information (broader coverage of public and especially private credit registries as well as better accounting standards) are characterized by a higher share of long-term debt as a proportion of total corporate debt.

39. Based on an extensive U.S. survey of small business finance, Ortiz-Molina and Penas (2006) provide evidence that loan maturity is positively correlated with firm size and age and with the amount of collateral posted—though personal guarantees do not have this effect. Firms that have had a loan delinquency in the previous three years had shorter maturities.

40. The Jin and Myers (2006) results are based on data from 40 stock exchanges and use a variety of measures of opacity, including the diversity of analysts' forecasts, accounting completeness, and auditing activity.

41. Himmelberg, Hubbard, and Love (2002) examine the return on capital for a panel of more than 6,000 listed firms on 38 stock exchanges and detect

a strong and sizable positive relationship between the share of stock held by insiders and the accounting return on capital, suggesting underinvestment in the most closely held firms. With such a high return, they "should" have invested more. The degree of ownership concentration is also strongly correlated with an index of shareholder protection (measuring, for example, whether voting is proportional to shareholding, use of proxy voting, and the right of minority shareholders to challenge oppressive majority decisions in court). See also Burkart, Panunzi, and Shleifer (2003) and Nenova (2003).

42. For a review of these and other issues related to family control, see Morck and Yeung (2003).

43. See overviews by Bekaert, Harvey, and Lundblad (2005) and Gupta and Yuan (2005).

44. An American Depository Receipt (ADR) is, in effect, a repackaging of a non-U.S. equity into a convenient form for U.S. investors to trade in U.S. stock markets. Depository receipts are also traded in the securities markets of some other advanced economies.

45. This, at least, was the finding of Harrison, Love, and McMillan (2004), who took data for 7,000 firms from 40 countries and estimated the sensitivity of each firm's investment decisions to its available cash. The authors were exploiting the idea that if a firm has easy access to finance, it should be able to finance profitable investment opportunities regardless of the immediate availability of cash balances. In practice, firms' investments do tend to be sensitive to their cash holdings. But this sensitivity proves to be lower for firms in countries with high inward FDI. Contrary, then, to the fears of some that inward FDI would tap local capital markets, diverting funds from incumbent firms, it seems that FDI does brings its own funding with it. In specific cases, though, borrowing from banks by foreign-owned firms could crowd out local firm financing. Another paper by Harrison and McMillan (2003) finds this crowding-out effect for Cote d'Ivoire, which the authors conjecture may result from the existence of interest ceilings and the links between many of the foreign-owned firms with the French parents of the local banks.

46. An interesting study by Da Rin, Nicodano, and Sembenelli (2004) shows the way. It uses information on the size of private equity investments in 14 European countries. The authors track the impact of policy and other variables on the division of these funds between early stage (seed and venture capital) and late stage, and between high-tech and other sectors.

CHAPTER THREE

Household Access to Finance: Poverty Alleviation and Risk Mitigation

OVER THE LONG TERM, ECONOMIC GROWTH HELPS REDUCE POVERTY and can be expected to lift the welfare of most households. This chapter returns to the questions first raised in chapter 1: Well-functioning financial systems contribute to growth, but do poor households benefit proportionately from financial reforms that strengthen the economy generally? To what extent is an emphasis on financial sector development as a driver of growth consistent with a pro-poor approach to development? Or could the deepening of financial systems lead to a widening of income inequalities? Must poor households and microentrepreneurs have direct access to financial services for there to be meaningful poverty reduction? What techniques are most effective in ensuring sustainable provision of credit and other financial services on a small scale?

This chapter reviews the findings of recent research on these questions. Although several theoretical models have highlighted the risk that selectively increased access to credit could worsen inequality, the empirical evidence does not seem to bear out this risk. Instead, available evidence suggests that a more developed financial system tends to reduce inequality in the long run. That is not simply because microfinance could help the poor directly—indeed the evidence from microstudies of favorable impacts from direct access of the poor to credit is not especially strong. The conclusions of studies using calibrated general equilibrium models, specific policy experiments, and econometric analysis of cross-country data tend to be more positive than are those of the microstudies.

These studies alert us to the likely importance of indirect effects in explaining the relationship between financial development and income inequality. These effects are well tracked in the general equilibrium models discussed below, which show that better financial access for

> The empirical evidence suggests that financial sector development is consistent with a pro-poor approach to development—

> —but some of the most important links may be indirect

nonpoor entrepreneurial households has a strongly favorable, indirect effect on the poor. These findings imply that for financial development to have maximum impact on pro-poor growth, the focus should be broadened from improving finance for the poor to improving finance for all. That is particularly true in many developing countries, where large segments of the middle class are still among the financially excluded, as was discussed in chapter 1.

Access can be provided by a range of institutions

Delivering broader access is the task of a growing array of financial institutions, including specialized microfinance institutions (MFIs), cooperatives, and savings banks. The techniques they use to reach a wider clientele, while controlling both risks and operating costs, are evolving, as is their use of information and communication technology. This chapter reports on recent research that has thrown much light on the relative importance of different obstacles to improved access at the micro level and on the techniques that work well, particularly given the recent trends of globalization and technological advances.

Finance, Inequality, and Poverty

At the outset, it is not immediately obvious that expanding access to financial services will reduce inequality. After all, the successful microentrepreneur who manages to get financing for her ideas will experience an increase in income that her neighbor does not. Indeed, the more successful she becomes, the wider the income gap would be. This increase in income inequality is what is predicted by some of the theories discussed in chapter 1. At the same time, giving people a wider set of growth opportunities through increased access to finance should eliminate inequities caused by barriers to such access. At the end of the day, the net result of greater financial access on measured inequality will be an empirical issue, and it is one on which there is a considerable body of recent research.

Theory suggests that greater financial access could raise income inequality in the short term—

Theoreticians have developed simple, stylized models to analyze these questions. Imagine a world in which individuals, differing in their wealth and entrepreneurial skills, must choose between subsistence farming, wage work, or entrepreneurial endeavor. Without access to external finance, the amount of investment an entrepreneur has to start is limited to her wealth. Start-up costs will often be too large to allow poorer or less-skilled individuals to become entrepreneurs, so they will remain subsistence farmers or work for a wage if it is high enough. Introducing a banking sector into such a world allows skilled entrepreneurs to borrow to finance setup costs. Although such a stylized world is far from the complex reality of even the very poor in developing countries, it offers a glimpse of the range of possible impacts on growth, inequality, and welfare that can come from increasing access to finance. But the size and even the nature of these impacts depend on the magnitude of, for example, the behavioral responses, the distribution of skills and wealth, and the productivity of labor and capital. Is it possible to derive realistic estimates of the size of these various parameters from what is known about the economic decisions of actual individuals and households? A paper by Giné and Townsend (2004) attempts to do just that. Drawing on data from a collection of surveys of Thai households, stretching from 1976 to 1996, the authors use information about wealth, wage rates, financial transactions, and occupational choices to estimate some of the model's parameters; they calibrate other parameters to help the model fit the evolution of Thai growth and savings rates. The authors then use this model to simulate how increasing the share of households with access to credit affects entrepreneurship, employment, wages, and ultimately growth and income distribution.

Giné and Townsend compare the evolution of growth and inequality in the model with the actual development in the Thai economy and show that financial liberalization and the consequent increase in access to credit services can explain the fast GDP per capita growth in the Thai economy during the period, but they also initially increase income inequality. Underlying these developments are occupational shifts from the subsistence sector into the intermediated sector, that is, the sector with access to credit and accompanying changes in wages. Net welfare benefits of increased access are found to be substantial. Although they are concentrated disproportionately on a small group of talented, low-wealth individuals, who without credit could not become entrepreneurs, a wider class of workers also benefits because eventually wage rates increase as the new entrepreneurs use their newfound access to credit to build their companies. Savers also benefit in the form of higher interest paid on their savings. But there are also losers; these are former entrepreneurs who lose because they have to pay the much higher postliberalization wage rates.[1]

When calibrated to fit Thai data on finance, growth, and inequality, the general equilibrium model analyzed by Giné and Townsend implies that the greatest quantitative impact of financial deepening and financial

—which was evident in a study of the Thai economy—

—although the biggest impact was due to higher wages, which led to lower inequality in the longer run access on income inequality comes through indirect labor market effects. Depending on initial conditions and the choice of parameters, these effects also result in a long-term decrease in income inequality that off-sets short-term increases coming from wealth gains of new entrepreneurs.

Finance and poverty—the micro evidence

Although calibrated theoretical models illuminate important aspects of the financial development process and provide illustrative quantification of these processes, their findings must be interpreted with care, because they do exclude other potentially important influences on growth and inequality.[2] A more direct approach to assessing the impact of access to finance is to zoom in on specific schemes or experiments in which some, but not all, households are eligible, and try to uncover the consequences both for beneficiaries and for those excluded. Unlike general equilibrium models and the aggregate regression methodology, discussed later, the microanalyses often focus on the direct effect of access to finance on the well-being of households with access, not always taking into account possible spillover and indirect effects that are highlighted in the general equilibrium analyses.

The benefits of microfinance may reflect selection bias—

The success stories of microfinance are well documented. But to be convinced of the overall benefit of microfinance, skeptics require careful differentiation between those changes that can be clearly attributed to financial access and those that might have happened anyway or result from other changes in the environment in which microfinance clients operate. In other words, is measurement of the true effect biased by a selection effect? For example, was it the more talented or otherwise well-endowed households that actually got the loans and might have prospered even in their absence? Or did the MFI target the village because it was particularly deprived and hence may have benefited even if its condition remains behind that of unserved villages? How specific is the impact to the village; can the same MFI scheme have the same effect in other villages? Numerous studies have attempted to find ways of answering these questions on the basis of particular features of the MFI design.

Debate surrounding even the most famous MFI, Bangladesh's Grameen Bank, illustrates how difficult this task has been. In a celebrated and very careful study of Grameen Bank and two other MFIs in Bangladesh, Pitt and Khandker (1998) exploited an exogenous eligibility criterion: to be eligible for credit from these three MFIs, households could not own more than one-half acre of land. All other things being equal, the difference in the fortunes of two households with just under and just over half an acre could be attributed to the program. The sharp cutoff of the eligibility criterion seemed to allow the researchers to avoid a selection-effect bias. Using appropriate econometric techniques to correct in this way for selection, Pitt and Khandker found small but significant and positive effects of the use of credit on household expenditures, household assets, labor supply, and the likelihood that children attend schools.[3] This effect was stronger for female program participants than for male participants. The study also found that labor supply response was surprisingly low compared with the response of assets and expenditures, suggesting that the effect of finance goes through productivity of labor, rather than the amount.

However, even this research has not gone unchallenged. For example, there is doubt that the half-acre rule was systematically and rigorously applied. If it was not, then its use to correct for selection bias is weakened. Khandker (2003), using panel data from a follow-up survey on the same group of borrowers, was able to obtain more precise estimates by controlling for unobserved, but time-invariant borrower characteristics. His results suggest a substantially lower impact of credit than the original Pitt and Khandker study found.

Another opportunity to assess the impact of access to credit while avoiding selection bias was seized by Coleman (1999), who studied microcredit borrowers in northeast Thailand. He exploited the fact that six communities had been identified as future locations for village banks, and that there was a list of self-selected villagers who wanted to apply for loans once the banks were established. By comparing these borrowers-in-waiting with actual borrowers of existing banks in other villages, Coleman could reasonably hope to have corrected for the selection bias that would have resulted from simply surveying a random group in the not-yet-served villages.[4] He found no significant impact of credit on physical assets, savings, production sales, productive expenses, labor, or expenditures on health care or education. In a similar study, Cotler and Woodruff (2007) compared small-scale retailers receiving loans from a Mexican microfinance lender with a similar group of retailers that had been selected to receive such loans in the future. They found a positive and significant effect of the microlending program on sales and profits only for the smallest retailers, but a negative effect on larger retailers' sales and profits.

A more direct way to avoid selection bias is to construct a genuine experiment in which the subjects and the control group are chosen randomly and thus create the necessary exogenous variation needed to

—and the empirical evidence is mixed

A field experiment using random selection criteria highlights the benefits of microcredit—

identify impact. Recently, Karlan and Zinman (2006a) persuaded a South African consumer lender to relax its risk assessment criteria for a randomly chosen group of barely rejected loan applicants. The random nature of the assignment of credit helps the authors to get around the problem of selection bias.[5] Comparing the group of randomly chosen borrowers with the control group of marginally rejected applicants, Karlan and Zinman found that six to twelve months after the loan application, borrowers were significantly more likely to retain wage employment, less likely to experience hunger in their household, and less likely to be impoverished.

—but more research is needed in this area

Further research, ideally using real experiments, is needed to convince the skeptics that access to microcredit really is good for the neighborhoods where it becomes established, as most well-informed observers and practitioners believe.[6] It has to be said that the current systematic statistical research evidence on the benefits of microcredit is not yet overwhelming. The studies reviewed here were undertaken in very different institutional settings and with different credit products. Individual or household welfare is notoriously difficult to measure, which biases microanalysis against finding a positive effect of access to credit. More research is needed to assert whether there is a robust and positive relationship between the use of credit and household welfare, including moving out of poverty.

Several other studies have used cross-sectional household data to assess the impact of access to finance on households' consumption patterns, income prospects, and the decision to send children to school rather than using them as laborers in the household. Most of these studies, however, use proxy measures of access to finance such as durable assets, which can be used as collateral, rather than the direct measures used by the studies mentioned above. Survey data of this type for Peru suggest that lack of access to credit reduces the likelihood that poor households send their children to school, while studies for Guatemala, India, and Tanzania point to households without financial access as being more likely than households with more assets to reduce their children's school attendance and increase their labor if they suffer transitory income shocks. Survey data for Guatemalan microentrepreneurs show a positive effect of credit use on upward class mobility, allowing them to expand their businesses. Finally, consumption patterns of Indonesian households that live closer to the nearest BRI branch, the largest MFI lender in the country, show smaller or no effects from health shocks compared with households living farther away.[7] Box 3.1 discusses the links between access to financial services and some of the Millennium Development Goals.

Box 3.1   Access to finance and the Millennium Development Goals

IN 2000, 189 NATIONS ADOPTED THE MILLENNIUM Declaration, specifying eight Millennium Development Goals, including eradicating extreme poverty by 2015. The other goals concern education (universal primary education), gender equality, health (reductions in child and maternal mortality and reversing the spread of AIDS, malaria, and other diseases), environment, and global partnerships. While access to financial services is not explicitly mentioned among these goals, both theory and numerous empirical studies, including many mentioned in this text, suggest that access to financial services is an important direct or indirect contributor to the achievement of most of the goals (Claessens and Feijen 2006; Littlefield, Morduch, and Hashemi 2003).

In the case of education and health, one important effect of access to financial services is through the income effect: better access to financial services improves incomes and therefore the possibility of obtaining health and education services, and at the same time it reduces the need to rely on children as laborers in the household. Allowing women direct access to financial services might improve their possibilities to become entrepreneurs, thus increasing their individual incomes, their chances

to become more independent, and their participation in family and community decision making. There is also an important insurance effect: better access to credit, savings, or insurance services reduces the need to use child labor as a buffer in the case of seasonal income fluctuations and transitory income shocks and allows consumption smoothing in the case of transitory income reductions resulting from health shocks. It also allows faster attention to health problems. Finally, there is an aggregate infrastructure effect, with more efficient financial institutions and markets allowing more private and public investment in the construction of schools and health facilities.

The links between access to finance and the goals of environmental stability and global partnerships might be less obvious and have not been researched very thoroughly. However, arguments can be made for such relationships, at least at the aggregate level. Ensuring environmental stability will require large investments in new technologies, and financial depth has shown to be conducive for capital reallocation across sectors. Finally, the goal of global cooperation will be hard to achieve without better functioning global financial markets.

To evaluate the effect of increasing financial access for households and microentrepreneurs, one has to look beyond the direct impact on the household or enterprise and assess the impact on the whole economy. That cannot be done through micro studies. In particular, even if the very poor do not themselves gain access to financial services, they may benefit substantially from increased employment and other opportunities resulting from the activities of less-poor microentrepreneurs whose access has improved. With large numbers of the nonpoor still excluded from access to credit, these systemic effects could include trickle-down effects for the poor from improved access for the nonpoor. However, they could also include perverse trickle-down effects: if only a subset of households in a village has access to credit or insurance to smooth consumption,

Finance, inequality and poverty—the aggregate evidence

that subset will bid up the price of nontraded goods when a negative shock hits the village, so excluded households will be worse off than if nobody had access to credit or insurance (Morduch 2006).

Financial development reduces poverty through its effect on overall growth—

Chapter 2 has already discussed the evidence for a strong causal link between financial development, as measured by financial depth, and overall national economic growth. That chapter also identified improved access to finance by firms as an important channel through which this effect works. If income growth rates of the poor remain broadly in line with those of the rest of the population, aggregate economic growth will mean a reduction in absolute poverty as more households graduate beyond the poverty threshold (Ravallion 2001). Only a sizable fall in the income share of the poor could prevent aggregate economic growth from lowering absolute poverty.[8] If growth reduces the absolute poverty count, it is said to be pro-poor in the absolute sense. Growth that reduces poverty by narrowing income differentials is said to be pro-poor in the relative sense. Recent research suggests that financial development generates pro-poor growth in both senses.

—increases the income share of the poorest quintile—

For example, Beck, Demirgüç-Kunt, and Levine (2007) look at cross-country data for varying periods during 1960–2005 to assess the relationship between financial depth and changes in both income distribution and absolute poverty. They work with a simple decomposition of the income growth of the poorest income quintile into mean per capita national income growth and the change in the share of the poorest quintile. A large body of literature has established that finance has a positive impact on GDP per capita growth; but what about the relationship between finance and changes in the income share of the lowest income quintile? The authors find a positive relationship between financial depth (as measured by the ratio of private sector credit to GDP) and the change in the share of the lowest quintile in total national personal income. Not only does a deeper financial system accelerate national growth, but it is associated with a faster increase in the income share of the poorest group. Indeed, almost half of the beneficial effect of financial deepening on average income of the poorest quintile comes from this improvement in the (relative) distribution of income.

They also obtain similar results when they look at the changes in the Gini measure of income inequality. The relationship between financial development and the growth rate of the Gini coefficient is negative, suggesting that finance reduces income inequality. Not only are these findings robust to controlling for other country characteristics associated with economic growth and changes in income inequality, but the authors also make an attempt to control for potential reverse causality, using historic variables such as national origin of the legal system to extract an exogenous component of financial development, as well as panel techniques that control for omitted variable and endogeneity bias.

Although cross-country studies are subject to the caveats discussed in box 2.1, these findings are also consistent with the findings of general equilibrium models discussed earlier, in that financial development is associated with reductions in income inequality over the long run. Further evidence is provided by cross-country studies looking at the relationship between financial development and the level of income inequality. Li, Squire, and Zou (1998) and Li, Xu, and Zou (2000) find a negative relationship between finance and the level of income inequality as measured by the Gini coefficient, a finding confirmed by Clarke, Xu, and Zhou (2006), using both cross-sectional and panel regressions and instrumental variable methods.

In some countries, far more than the bottom 20 percent are poor when measured against the international standard poverty lines of $1 or $2 a day; in other countries almost nobody is poor by these demanding standards. To look more directly at the impact of financial development on absolute poverty, Beck, Demirgüç-Kunt, and Levine (2007) also estimate the change in the share of each country's population below the international poverty line that results from financial deepening. Again, they find a robust effect of finance on poverty alleviation—countries with higher levels of financial development experienced faster reductions in the share of population living on less than $1 a day over the 1980s and 1990s (figure 3.1).

—and lowers poverty

The economic impact is strong as well, as discussed in box 3.2. The relative importance of economic growth and the distributional impact of finance vary according to initial conditions: not surprisingly, the distributional impact is strongest for countries with relatively high per capita income and a very unequal income distribution, while the growth impact is strongest in relatively poor countries with a relatively equal income distribution.

This finance-poverty evidence is consistent with the findings of Honohan (2004), who showed that even among societies with the same average income, those with deeper financial systems have lower absolute poverty. These findings all point in the same direction: policies fostering financial sector development are not only pro-growth, but also pro-poor in both relative and absolute senses.[9]

Figure 3.1   Financial depth and poverty alleviation

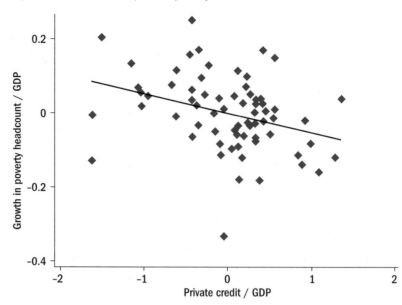

Source: Beck, Demirgüç-Kunt, and Levine (2007).

Note: This figure is a partial scatter plot of growth of poverty headcount vs. private credit to GDP, controlling for the initial level of poverty headcount, with data averaged over the period 1980–2005.

The cross-country evidence has the merit of broad coverage, but the quality of the data is uneven from country to country. Gini coefficients, quintile shares, and poverty headcounts are all subject to substantial measurement problems.[10] The shortcomings of financial depth as a measure of financial development, let alone financial access, have already been pointed out. That the results obtained with aggregate data are stronger than the results of the micro studies cited earlier may point to the potentially greater importance of spillover effects, which are not captured by micro studies. But the stronger results may also reflect the difficulty of controlling for reverse causality in cross-country regressions. It is therefore important to seek additional types of evidence for systemic effects of improved financial access. Two policy changes that can be thought of as akin to natural experiments point in the same direction.

A natural experiment from Indian regulations shows the impact of improved access—

One experiment involved the Indian government's policy on bank branching, imposed between 1977 and 1990. In those years a commercial bank in India was allowed to open one new branch in a district that already had a bank presence only after it opened four branches in areas without a bank presence. This policy led to the opening of 30,000

Box 3.2 Financial depth and poverty reduction: how big is the effect?

JUDGING FROM THE REGRESSIONS ESTIMATED BY Beck, Demirgüç-Kunt, and Levine (2007), the relation between financial depth and poverty is not only causal and statistically significant but sizable. Even after account is taken of the effect of other control variables, almost 30 percent of the cross-country variation in changing poverty rates can be attributed to cross-country variation in financial development. Consider, for example, the fact that the share of the population in deep poverty (less than $1 a day) fell by 14 percent a year in Chile between 1987 and 2000, whereas it rose at a similar rate in neighboring Peru. Chile has a much deeper financial sector (private credit is 47 percent of GDP) than Peru (private credit is 17 percent of GDP). The estimated regression implies that had Peru started with the same financial depth as Chile, its poverty headcount would have grown a full 5 percentage points more slowly, so that by 2002, just 5 percent of Peru's population would have been living on less than $1 a day instead of the actual share of 10 percent.

Such comparisons have to be interpreted with caution, though, for several reasons. The regression coefficients indicate marginal, not large, discrete changes; the variable measuring financial depth is only a proxy; omission from the equation of other unmeasured causal variables may be exaggerating the measured impact of financial depth. However, even if one is convinced that private credit is associated with faster poverty reduction, that is not an invitation to policy makers to expand credit freely: attempts to force the rate of financial deepening through lax monetary policy, for example, will not generate true financial development and will prove to be unsustainable.

new rural branches over the period, as well as to an increase in deposit and credit volume in states with initially low levels of financial development. Burgess and Pande (2005) find that as a result of this branching regulation, nonagricultural output grew faster, and poverty declined faster, in states that started the period with a lower level of financial development, while the opposite was true before and after this period of regulation. Further, wages of agricultural workers grew faster during this period, while the wages of urban factory workers do not show such a time pattern. This seems to suggest that financial development—triggered by the branching regulation—led to faster reductions in poverty. The cost-benefit calculation of this policy, though, is a different matter (see box 4.3 in chapter 4) and suggests that the macroeconomic costs might have been significant.

Another natural experiment is offered by the branching deregulation implemented by different U.S. states over a 20-year period from the mid-1970s to the mid-1990s. Following Jayaratne and Strahan (1996), a large literature has evaluated the effect that easing restrictions on intra- and interstate branching had on income growth, banking sector structure, and entrepreneurial activity. The variation in timing of the

—as does one from the U.S. experience with liberalization

deregulation over a 20-year period and the fact that the deregulation was not driven by expectations of higher growth or higher entrepreneurial activity allow researchers to perform difference-in-differences estimates, thus holding constant unobserved state-level and year effects. Beck, Levine, and Levkov (2007) exploit the same quasi-natural experiment to assess the effect of branching deregulation on income inequality; they find that states see their Gini coefficient decrease by a small but statistically significant amount in the years after deregulation relative to other states and relative to their own level before the deregulation (figure 3.2). This effect eliminated about one-sixth of the overall increase in income inequality that the United States experienced over this time period. Over three-quarters of the inequality reduction after deregulation comes from changes in the distribution of income among wage and salary earners, with less than a fifth coming from distributional changes among self-employed proprietors, suggesting that the main effect of branch deregulation on income inequality in this case is not enhanced entrepreneurship, but rather the indirect effects of higher labor demand and higher wages.

Figure 3.2 Branch deregulation across U.S. states and income inequality

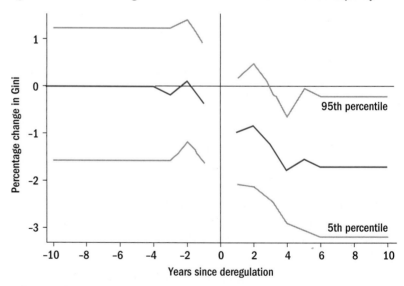

Source: Beck, Levine, and Levkov (2007).
Note: This graph illustrates a regression of the log of the Gini coefficient across U.S. states and over the years 1977 to 2003 on state and year dummies, other time-variant state characteristics and dummy variables indicating t + x years, where t is the year of branch deregulation and x goes from -10 to +10. Gray lines indicate 95 percent and 5 percent confidence intervals.

Of course care must be taken in extrapolating findings from a system as developed as that of the United States, where most households have at least some access to formal financial services, in contrast to the situation in low- and middle-income countries. Nevertheless, these results are consistent with the results obtained by Giné and Townsend (2004) for the effects of financial liberalization in Thailand.

Despite the theoretical possibility that a selective expansion of access to finance could initially worsen income inequality, and methodological challenges notwithstanding (see box 3.3 for a summary), the balance of evidence from specific quasi-experimental events, estimation of general equilibrium models, and broad cross-country regressions is that financial development and improved access to credit tends not only to accelerate economic growth but to lower household poverty and inequality.

In summary, improved access to finance reduces inequality and poverty—

Much remains to be learned about the channels through which financial development affects income inequality and poverty alleviation. Is it through providing access to credit to a larger proportion of the population or through fostering more efficient capital allocation, that is, through fostering more competitive and open markets? Is it through depth or through broader access that finance helps reduce income inequality and poverty? Given the wide differences that exist in financial inclusion across countries, to what extent do these effects depend on the initial level of financial access and economic development?

—but the nature of the transmission mechanisms is unclear—

Since the strongest evidence for a favorable finance-inequality relationship points to important labor market effects of financial deepening and broadening, one must consider whether direct provision of financial services to the very poor is the best way to use finance to help the poor. Indeed, improving access for small firms and for nonpoor entrepreneurial households can be a powerful mechanism for helping reduce poverty. It is easy to see that financing opportunities for the nonpoor in particular regions or among particular ethnic groups could help improve the functioning of labor and product markets and the efficiency of investment, leading to better employment opportunities for the poor in those regions as well.

—with evidence suggesting that the indirect effects on poverty may be more important

The discussion so far has focused exclusively on the use of credit services, since that is the financial service the literature has focused on most extensively. However, credit is rarely the first financial service priority for very poor households. Access to savings and insurance services helps cushion income shocks and smooth consumption, while access to formal

Poor households need other financial services, not just access to credit

Box 3.3 Methodological challenges in analyzing the impact of financial access

BOTH THE TECHNICAL ADVANCES IN COMPUTING power and the availability of subnational and even household data have helped researchers move beyond cross-country regression analysis to assess the relationship between finance, growth, and inequality and thus overcome problems of endogeneity, heterogeneity of the relationship between dependent and independent variables across countries, and nonlinear effects. Some of these strategies use innovative historical instruments and panel data. However, even employing firm- or household-level data, be it within or across countries, does not by itself solve the identification problem of endogeneity and spurious correlations, as the debate between Pitt and Khandker (1998) and Morduch (1998) has shown. Identifying an exogenous policy change, preferably at different times across subnational units, overcomes selection problems by utilizing a difference-in-differences estimator that holds constant other confounding effects. Two such examples, the social banking experiment in India, and the branching deregulation in the United States, are discussed in the text.

However, such quasi-natural experiments are rare, and researchers have therefore also exploited general equilibrium models and household-level micro data to calibrate them. This technique has the advantage of being thoroughly based in theory and controlling for dynamic effects, unlike regression analysis. At the same time, its application is limited by the variables included in the theoretical models and by the availability of household data. While these structural models are promising in improving the understanding of the micro foundations of growth

and inequality, it is not always clear how much the insights from these stylized models rely on specific details of how the imperfections were modeled and whether the results are robust to these choices.

Another valuable approach is the use of controlled or natural experiments in specific countries or in specific locations, such as the one undertaken by Karlan and Zinman (2006a) in South Africa and others discussed here in the context of evaluating the impact of microfinance. Of course, natural experiments are scarce, and controlled experiments can be costly to implement and their results specific to their context. In addition, they necessarily measure partial equilibrium effects and, unlike aggregate studies, do not pick up spillover and indirect effects. Furthermore, many important policy issues with implications for financial access, such as regulation and supervision of financial institutions, involve country-level variation and do not lend themselves to randomization.

Finally, laboratory experiments work with potential clients or people with similar profiles and mimic different financial contract mechanisms. Experimental games have the advantage of allowing researchers to have even more control of events, but they also have the shortcoming of being a staged setting that might or might not be consistent with real life behavior.

Given that each methodological approach has its advantages and shortcomings, a robust research philosophy would try to identify the most important policy questions and to employ appropriate and feasible methods for addressing them.

payment services is increasingly important in market-based economies. This is an area that requires future research.

Having established the importance of access to finance, the next task is to consider what is the best way of reaching out to low-income households and microentrepreneurs to foster access to and use of credit, savings, and payment services. The following section discusses institutional and product innovations to reach out to these customers traditionally excluded by the banking system.

Providing Financial Access to Households and Microentrepreneurs: How and by Whom?

The considerable success of the microfinance movement, both technically and in its ability to mobilize financial and political support, has focused attention on direct access to credit for poor people and especially for poor women. In what has been an accelerating revolution over the past few decades (Robinson 2001), specialized microfinance institutions have reached millions of clients, and many of them have achieved impressive repayment rates, especially when compared with the disappointing record of an earlier generation of development banks. Attention has also broadened to other types of financial institutions, such as savings banks, including postal savings banks, and financial cooperatives and credit unions that have also been catering to the financial needs of low-income households and microenterprises.

Now mainstream financial institutions are becoming interested in the market at the "bottom of the pyramid," to use the term popularized by Prahalad (2004). At the same time, some of the stronger MFIs have secured banking licenses and offer a wider range of services to a broader clientele. Many have graduated beyond the need for sizable subsidies to ensure their financial viability, whereas others still seek subsidies to help keep the costs to the borrower to a minimum. There has been much experimentation in lending technologies as practitioners find the various formulas with which they began unduly constraining. These techniques included the use of various forms of mutual guarantee in small or large borrower groups (joint liability), and programs of progressively larger loan sizes as loans were repaid and new loans given (dynamic incentives). To attract savings, financial institutions of all sorts are using new methodologies, such as mobile branches, deposit collectors, and cell phone technology, and developing new products, such as commitment savings products and micro-insurance policies.

Against this background, a growing number of researchers has been using formal econometric techniques to assess quantitatively some of the key operational issues that face MFIs and other providers of financial services to small-scale users. The findings—several of them striking in

The growth of microcredit has attracted new players—

their precision—have used replicable statistical evidence that has either confirmed or questioned practitioner intuition. This section reviews some of the main findings in five areas of interest: the relative importance of transaction costs and two key information barriers, moral hazard and adverse selection, for outreach to low-income borrowers; the sensitivity of the demand for microcredit to the level of the interest rate charged; the relative effectiveness of group and individual lending; the complementary role of access to noncredit services; and the link between subsidies and outreach to the poor. While most emphasis is placed on credit, the discussion also highlights the importance of depository, insurance, and especially payments services. Throughout, the discussion emphasizes the potential effects of globalization and technological advances on access to financial services. It concludes with some observations on the likely welfare implications of targeting efforts to expand household access to the very poor, noting again that access for nonpoor entrepreneurial households can have a sizable antipoverty impact.

—despite obstacles to delivering credit to the poor

As already discussed, the main problems in delivering credit are linked to risk management and the high transaction costs of processing, monitoring, and enforcing small loans, which increase break-even interest rates for these loans. The risks include those arising out of information asymmetries. These asymmetries can result from adverse selection, that is, the inability of the lender to distinguish between high- and low-risk borrowers, or from moral hazard, that is, the tendency for some borrowers to divert resources to projects that reduce their likelihood of being able to repay the loan and the inability of the lender to detect and prevent such behavior. Depending on the specific information asymmetry and the ability of potential borrowers to pledge collateral, lenders may try to use the interest rate or a combination of the interest rate and collateral as a screening and sorting mechanism (Bester 1985). If collateral is not available, lenders are forced to rely only on the interest rate, but in doing so, they risk excluding, or crowding out, safe borrowers. Indeed, under some circumstances lenders will prefer to keep the lending rate below the market-clearing level for fear of worsening adverse selection; that behavior in effect rations credit by nonprice means (Stiglitz and Weiss 1981). Even more borrowers will be rationed out if the high transaction costs of lending to them lead to break-even interest rates that are too high to make lending safe (Williamson 1987).

How relevant and important are these three factors—adverse selection, moral hazard, and high transaction costs—for credit rationing of poor households and microentrepreneurs? The existing evidence points to moral hazard as the driving factor, with a less significant role for adverse selection. Although high transaction costs can also result in high repayment burdens, there is evidence of very high rates of return to investment by microentrepreneurs, which explains why some borrowers are prepared to pay very high interest rates.

Are the interest rates on microloans too high? Much of the microfinance revolution has been built on the premise that its clients can afford to pay high interest rates given very high marginal returns on capital. But measuring these returns is challenging. Using field experiments, de Mel, McKenzie, and Woodruff (2006) and McKenzie and Woodruff (2007) estimate capital returns to investment in microenterprises in light manufacturing and commerce in Sri Lanka and Mexico, respectively. The enterprises are given cash or equipment, depending on the outcome of a lottery, and this exogenous shock is used to compute the return to capital. They find returns of 5–7 percent per month in Sri Lanka and 20 percent or more in Mexico! While these returns might seem high—even unrealistically high in the case of Mexico—they are based on grants, not loans; are measured only over the short term; and increased capital by 25 percent on average. Thus, these returns might not be replicable over the long term. Nor does it follow that the microentrepreneurs would have pursued the same strategies if they had had loans instead of cash or equipment. Nevertheless, these estimates suggest that some microentrepreneurs are indeed able to pay the high interest charged by microfinance institutions, at least where these loan resources are being invested.

That is not to deny that high interest rates are costly for borrowers, especially poor ones. In their eagerness to emphasize the importance for the development of sustainable microfinance by removing constraining interest rate ceilings, some advocates may have overstated the insensitivity of borrowers to high interest rates. In contrast, Dehejia, Montgomery, and Morduch (2005), using data from a credit cooperative in Dhaka, and Karlan and Zinman (2007), using data from a South African consumer lender, both find rather high elasticities of loan demand with respect to interest rates, that is, loan demand decreases as interest rates increase. Emran, Morshed, and Stiglitz (2006) provide a theory to reconcile these empirical findings with practitioners' oft-repeated assertions that borrowers are insensitive to interest rates. They point to imperfections in the labor market, especially for women, and suggest that it is only for as long as these imperfections prevent women from entering the

High returns allow some microentrepreneurs to pay high interest rates—

—but the demand for microcredit is interest-elastic

labor market that their demand for credit will be so interest inelastic. Curiously, the Bangladesh data suggest that the elasticity decreased (in absolute value) with the borrower's income, whereas the South African data suggest the opposite. While MFIs in Bangladesh demanding higher interest rates to compensate for higher costs and risks may face problems reaching out to poorer clients, the South African lender does not seem to face these problems. These contrasting results might reflect differences between consumer and production credit or different institutional settings. Ongoing research is trying to shed more light on the interest rate elasticity of microcredit borrowers.

Moral hazard may be more important for default rates than repayment burden

One recent experiment in which interest rates were varied among a homogenous group of borrowers suggests that the repayment burden is the least of the obstacles the borrowers faced. This experiment points to moral hazard, including the inability of the lender to enforce repayment from willful defaulters, as the driving factor limiting outreach to the poor. Karlan and Zinman (2006b) used a randomized direct mail offer by a South African consumer lender to distinguish between adverse selection, moral hazard, and repayment burden, as illustrated in figure 3.3. Specifically, customers were sent credit offers with either

Figure 3.3 Testing for credit constraints in South Africa

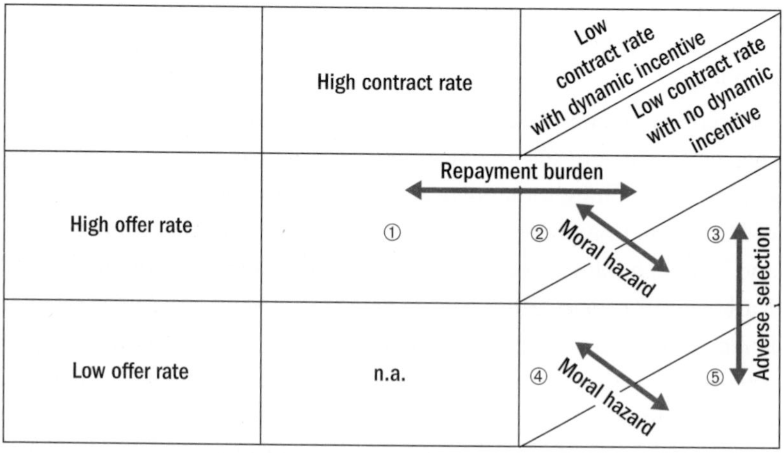

Source: Karlan and Zinman (2006b).

Note: This figure illustrates the setup of the consumer credit experiment that Karlan and Zinman ran in South Africa to distinguish between repayment burden, adverse selection, and moral hazard.

a high or a low interest rate, and the response of customers to this offer helps to identify adverse selection, that is, the difference between ex ante high-risk and low-risk customers (difference between points 3 and 5 in figure 3.3). Some of the customers with the initial high offer rate then received a lower rate when they responded favorably to the offer, and the difference between customers with the same high initial offer rate (and thus the same ex ante risk profile) but different final contract rate helps identify default due to repayment burden of high interest rates (difference between points 1 and 2 in figure 3.3). Finally, some borrowers were offered the prospect of a repeat loan if they repaid their loan in time; the comparison between borrowers with and without this dynamic incentive allows identification of moral hazard, that is, incentives to repay (difference between points 2 and 3 and between points 4 and 5 in figure 3.3). Karlan and Zinman find strong evidence for moral hazard but evidence for adverse selection only for female borrowers and borrowers who had not borrowed from this lender before. The evidence for default due to repayment burden is weak. Quantifying the effect of moral hazard, they find that between 10 and 15 percent of default is due to moral hazard, with the remainder due to observable differences in risk across borrowers.[11]

The entry of a Guatemalan MFI into a credit bureau offers another innovative experimental setup to distinguish between adverse selection and moral hazard and yields similar results to those in South Africa (de Janvry, McIntosh, and Sadoulet 2006). While this entry was initially not announced to borrowers, the subsequent staggered education of borrowers, who were organized in joint-liability groups, allowed the researchers to distinguish between moral hazard and adverse selection effects. Specifically, the initial effect on repayment of the announcement of the existence of the credit bureau helps isolate and identify moral hazard, that is, repayment incentives, as group composition is constant in the short run. Subsequent changes in group composition and the effect of those changes on repayment, on the other hand, can be attributed to adverse selection, that is, selection of lower-risk group members. The authors find that delinquency attributable to moral hazard declined 18 percent. Reductions in delinquency resulting from changes in adverse selection, that is, replacement of high-risk with low-risk group members, as measured over several loan cycles where groups can adjust their composition, are weaker, but still present. The most significant change in group composition was a large exit of women and corresponding large

Adverse selection problems might be more pronounced among female borrowers

entry of men, suggesting again that adverse selection problems might be more pronounced among female borrowers.

Summarizing, many microentrepreneurs are able to pay high interest rates given high returns on capital. Therefore, the high transaction costs associated with small loans, the resulting high interest rates, and thus the higher repayment burden do not seem to be obstacles to reaching poor households. Rather, outreach to these groups is impeded by the inability of poor borrowers to commit the use of loan resources to projects with a risk acceptable to the lender and by the inability of lenders to enforce repayment. The inability of lenders to distinguish between good and bad credit risks before making the loan is also an obstacle, but less so. The research reviewed so far, however, points to two techniques that can be used to overcome these barriers—joint-liability lending and dynamic incentives through repeat lending.

Joint-Liability Lending and Dynamic Incentives

Overcoming obstacles— joint-liability lending and dynamic incentives

The use of joint-liability groups is a traditional tool to overcome the hurdles of adverse selection, moral hazard, and monitoring and enforcement costs. Joint liability can reduce all three of these barriers to lending, but there are trade-offs (see Ghatak and Guinnane 1999 for an overview). By pooling borrowers that know each other well and making them jointly liable for each others' loan repayment, the lender effectively outsources the screening and monitoring function. Through assortative matching—safe (risky) borrowers will join with other safe (risky) borrowers—the lender can screen borrowers by the company they keep. Joint-liability lending reduces monitoring and enforcement costs and thus allows lower interest rates. These lower rates reduce the repayment burden and result in less credit rationing. Most important, lower monitoring costs and strong enforcement through social sanctions can reduce moral hazard problems in joint-liability credit contracts if borrowers decide cooperatively on project choices. However, joint-liability lending can also induce strategic default; if good borrowers see the prospect of future loans wane because other group members are not repaying their loans, they have fewer incentives to repay (Besley and Coate 1995). Further, joint-liability lending is not suitable where different members of the group have different borrowing needs.

Joint-liability lending was already being applied by German cooperatives in the 19th century. Introduced into the microfinance movement

Box 3.4 Testing impact with randomized control trials

MEASURING THE IMPACT OF NEW MICROFINANCE programs or products requires careful design because standard assessments comparing customers before and after introduction of a new program or product or a comparison between participants and nonparticipants suffer from two serious shortcomings (Goldberg and Karlan 2005). First, selection bias can occur if there is a correlation between the take-up decision of customers and other individual characteristics that explain the outcome variable. Further, dropouts can bias the comparison between program participants and nonparticipants. Second, such assessments suffer from a lack of a proper counterfactual, that is, how the same group of clients would have behaved without the new program or product.

To overcome these methodological challenges, researchers are increasingly using randomized experiments to assess new microfinance programs and products. The characteristics of these experiments can be summarized as follows. First, the evaluation has to be prospective; in other words, it has to start before the new product is introduced so that the changes induced by the product can be properly assessed. Second, to have a proper counterfactual, the evaluation should be based on comparison of a treatment and a control group, where only the first has access to the new program or product. Third, assignment to either group has to be random to

ensure that clients in both groups have the same characteristics; only then can the effects of the new program or product be isolated. Fourth, the researchers have to take into account two potential spillover effects: experiment spillover, where members of treatment and control groups find out about each other; and impact spillover, where the effects of the new program or product spread to people and areas beyond the treatment group.

Although they have limitations, carefully planned and executed impact evaluations are a powerful instrument both for individual financial institutions that want to assess the profitability and impact of new products and programs and for policy makers who want to assess which interventions are the most promising in reducing poverty. A significant shortcoming is the high costs of such evaluations, which prevent many MFIs from using them (Armendáriz de Aghion and Morduch 2005). In addition, the question of external validity—whether the results of the evaluation are applicable in different socioeconomic and institutional contexts—cannot be addressed with such experiments.

A final word of caution concerns the use of these impact evaluations for public policy or public resources. Because no counterfactual or alternative intervention is being evaluated, either in the financial sector or for nonfinancial interventions, one has to keep in mind the partial equilibrium aspect of these assessments.

in the 1980s by the Grameen Bank in Bangladesh, joint-liability lending quickly became popular with pioneer microcredit institutions. Given its limitations, however, many MFIs, including Grameen itself, have moved away from a pure joint-liability lending model and now also offer individual loans. The limitations of relying on just one lending model are also reflected in the results of recent field research, especially some studies that have made very effective use of randomized control trials (box 3.4).

How important are reductions in adverse selection, moral hazard, or monitoring and enforcement costs for the success of joint-liability lending? Giné and others (2006) find in the setting of laboratory experiments in Peru that both the screening of group members before the loan is made and the monitoring of borrowers afterward have an important role in the success of joint-liability lending.[12] However, they also find that joint liability helps reduce moral hazard only when the group forms voluntarily. Using household data across members of more than 262 Thai joint-liability groups, Ahlin and Townsend (2007) find that informal sanctioning, thus ex post reductions in moral hazard, fits the data best in poor rural areas, while ex ante screening, thus reducing the risk of adverse selection, fits the data best in more affluent areas.

Joint liability can help reduce moral hazard when social connections are strong—

The importance of moral hazard reductions through joint-liability lending is confirmed with evidence from poor rural Peru, where Karlan (2007) exploited a natural quasi-random group-building process, where members were randomly assigned to groups rather than selecting their peer group members themselves. He finds that stronger social connections between group members (as measured by geographic proximity and common ethnicity) lead to better repayment and higher savings than for groups where social connections are weaker. Given the absence of peer selection in this group-building process, Karlan concludes that the better repayment behavior is attributable to reductions in moral hazard; in other words, joint-liability groups that were more socially connected were better able to prevent their members from diverting loan funds to risky projects or other purposes.[13] He finds direct evidence that members of groups with better social connections have better knowledge of each other and are more likely to punish defaulters by cutting relationships; however, they are also more likely to forgive debt, suggesting that peers in these groups know how to distinguish between culpable or blameworthy default on the one hand, and bad luck on the other.

However, some evidence suggests that social ties can be too strong, leading to collusion and lower repayment. Ahlin and Townsend (2007) find evidence in their Thai data that stronger social ties, measured by more sharing between unrelated members of the groups and clustering of relatives, are associated with lower repayment performance. Similarly, Giné and others (2006) find in their laboratory experiment that communication between group members leads to higher default due to riskier investments.

—but group-based lending may not always be better than lending to individuals

Existing evidence thus clearly shows that group-based joint-liability lending can, but does not necessarily, lead to better repayment performance. Yet recent evidence has also shed doubt on the superiority of group-based lending vis-à-vis individual lending. In an experiment in the Philippines, some of the borrower groups were randomly converted from group liability to individual liability. Giné and Karlan (2006) found that conversion to individual liability groups does not change the repayment rate for preexisting borrowers but does attract more borrowers. Perhaps surprisingly, the new members have closer links to the other individual liability borrowers, suggesting that fear of peer pressure might have been limiting growth of existing joint-liability groups. It could also be that the joint-liability nature of the program was keeping the good-risk borrowers out of the program. Ongoing research is trying to distinguish between new microcredit clients that are randomly assigned to either individual or joint-liability lending.

Some observers have criticized MFIs for making larger loans to individuals, complaining that the MFIs are drifting from their focus on the poor. Cull, Demirgüç-Kunt, and Morduch (2007) examined data from 124 MFIs in 49 countries and find that both group- and individual-based lending institutions are able to earn profits while serving the poor, but a trade-off between profitability and outreach emerges when serving the very poor.[14] Individual-based lenders have the highest average profit levels but perform less well on measures of outreach.

To summarize, joint-liability lending can help overcome barriers to reaching poor households and microentrepreneurs and has shown its usefulness in many different settings, but it also has its limitations. As members' borrowing needs diverge over time, conversion to individual lending might be necessary. Further, diverging borrowing needs might also destroy screening and monitoring incentives and may create tension among borrowers, as those borrowing little are still liable for the larger amounts of their peers. Finally, joint liability can result in collusion and increased, rather than reduced, risk taking.

Dynamic incentives, such as the promise of repeat lending, have been another mechanism to overcome moral hazard in lending relationships with risky and high transaction cost borrowers, as shown by Karlan and Zinman (2006b) in the context of their work with a South African consumer lender. Similarly, Giné and others (2006) find that giving borrowers the prospect of repeat loans reduces both the riskiness of investment and improves repayment performance. The introduction of progressive lending, that is, increasing loan amounts over time, can further increase the opportunity costs of default for borrowers, thus reducing loan delinquency (Armendáriz de Aghion and Morduch 2005).[15] The interaction of joint liability and repeat lending, however, can also backfire; if borrowers see the prospect of future loans wane

Overcoming moral hazard through the promise of repeat lending—

121

Box 3.5   Informal finance

INFORMAL FINANCE IS NOT THE SUBJECT OF THIS report, which deals essentially with formal finance. To be sure, informal financial services still do represent a significant part of the financial dealings of poor people, especially but not only in developing countries, although reliable quantification on this point is not readily available. An extensive literature discusses this area (see Rutherford 1998).

The reason for focusing on formal finance is the underlying premise that formal, modern finance can potentially provide most of the financial services needed by poor people with greater efficiency and security than informal finance (see box 2.2). Formal finance has not yet superseded informal finance largely because the current working practices of formal financial intermediaries are not adapted to providing services in small packets at a cost that makes them affordable to the poor. Technology—financial and physical—as well as an improved overall infrastructure, can help bring costs down to realistic levels, but only if the management of formal institutions chooses to focus on the potential for doing profitable business with what C. K. Prahalad has termed the "bottom of the pyramid." Prahalad's image conveys the potential volume of small-scale business, which can make it attractive even if the setup costs (required to achieve low unit costs) are high.

At the same time, many features of informal finance convey lessons that can and have been successfully adopted and adapted by formal and semiformal intermediaries. Scholars have in particular been fascinated by the durability of rotating savings and credit associations (ROSCAs), one of the most striking forms of informal financial intermediary (see, for example, Ghatak and Guinnane 1999). Regular payments by each member and assignment of the collected resources to one member help overcome savings and credit constraints, reduce problems

of cash management and storage, and allow members to realize large investments, be they for consumption or business purposes. The use of social capital and peer pressure that holds ROSCAs together and reduces the threat of default by individual members has important parallels to the use of joint-liability lending by many MFIs. But ROSCAs cannot hope to match the scale of resources of the formal financial system, with its ability to pool risks and intermediate over extended periods and across geographic areas.

Hawala and other ethnically based international money transfer businesses have achieved astonishing efficiencies for payments along certain migration corridors. Corresponding small payments made through the banking system's procedures have generally been more costly and slower, though of course the banking system's procedures are scalable and the network of correspondents is essentially universal, as are the networks of the major formal international money transmission companies. Funeral insurance arrangements are a common product of community-based informal insurance associations, especially in AIDS-plagued Africa.

The high cost of credit from informal moneylenders is often cited as a main reason why the microfinance revolution can bring benefits to the poor (Robinson 2001). The possibility of providing alternative formal financial solutions for those who might otherwise fall into the trap of debt bondage is for many a sufficient reason to emphasize the need for improving the reach of the formal financial sector. Yet unregistered (and therefore usually) illegal moneylenders continue to operate in deprived neighborhoods of even the richest economies (as is discussed in chapter 4). The shortcomings of informal finance mean that it will fade in importance as economies and financial systems mature and improve in their outreach.

as other members fail to repay, their incentives to repay decrease. The Ecuadorian microlender Childreach is an example: as rumors of its impending failure spread, the microlender faced a rapid increase in loan delinquency (Bond and Rai 2002).

—frequent repayment schedules—

Other mechanisms linked to the microcredit movement have not been thoroughly assessed yet. Specifically, frequent (weekly, for example) and regular repayments are said to impose discipline on borrowers. On the one hand, repayment schedules that are too frequent might limit the investment opportunities of borrowers and are useful only for borrowers with several diversified income sources. Some observers even claim that frequent repayment schedules are paid out of savings rather than from returns on investment (Rutherford 1998). In those cases, providing credit services is only a second-best solution, and the first-best would be the provision of savings services for the poor. On the other hand, frequent repayment might also be a tool of MFIs to use better informed informal lenders, inasmuch as some borrowers have to rely on these moneylenders to help them make weekly payments (Jain and Mansuri 2003).

—and public repayment

Some other microlending techniques include repayment in public, forced savings, notional collateral, and targeting of women. Public repayment is said to increase social pressure and the threat of stigma, while at the same time reducing transaction costs for lenders (Armendáriz de Aghion and Morduch 2005). The requirement to keep a certain fraction of the credit as savings with the microfinance institution has often been cited as a success factor, although the practice has not yet been thoroughly evaluated. The use of assets with "notional" rather than resale or salvage value, such as refrigerators and televisions, has often been quoted as increasing the leverage of the lender over the borrower and augmenting payment discipline. Finally, the targeting of women by microlenders has been indicated as a factor for commercial success as well as enhanced social benefit (box 3.6).

Looking beyond microcredit—

Most of the microcredit movement and literature has focused on production credit for household enterprises or microenterprises. But even if lack of financing is fundamentally the only constraint for poor microentrepreneurs, as is asserted by Muhamed Yunus, founder of Grameen Bank and winner of the 2006 Nobel Peace Prize, they do also face numerous practical challenges. Hence some MFIs have decided to offer complementary extension services, such as training or health services.

Are they wise to do so? There could be economies of scope in providing these different services, but there might also be benefits of specialization.

Box 3.6   Microfinance and gender

THE MICROCREDIT MOVEMENT HAS FOCUSED on women, with some programs providing services exclusively for women and others having a majority of female borrowers. Why this focus on women?

First, women traditionally face greater access barriers to formal banking services and are thus also credit-constrained to a greater extent than men. In some countries, women are legally barred from opening accounts or applying for credit. In most of the developing world, women would not be deemed creditworthy since they do not hold formal sector jobs or the titles to their houses. Many restrictions faced by the poor in the developing world are thus even more exacerbated for women. As discussed by Emran, Moshed, and Stiglitz (2006), women also have lower opportunity costs if they do not hold formal sector jobs and are thus more likely to pay the high interest rates required for sustainable microfinance.

Second, experience has shown that repayment is higher among female borrowers, mostly due to more conservative investments and lower moral hazard risk. The lower moral hazard risk might stem from lower mobility and higher risk aversion. Given that moral hazard seems to be the constraining factor in outreach to low-income households, women might therefore be the more attractive clients. While adverse selection might be more problematic among women, the joint-liability technique can control for this risk.

Third, some practitioners stress social objectives as women seem to be more concerned about children's health and education than their husbands. As already discussed, Pitt and Khandker (1998) and Khandker (2003) find a stronger effect of Grameen Bank in Bangladesh on female than on male borrowers. For example, Khandker (2003) shows that the impact of credit on nonfood expenditures is higher among female compared to male borrowers.

Finally, focusing on women might empower them in the intrafamily decision process, as shown by Ashraf, Karlan, and Yin (2006b); use of a commitment savings product increased expenditures on female durable goods. Similarly, access to credit and the subsequent establishment of a microenterprise might give women more say in intrahousehold decisions, as Johnson and Morduch (2007) illustrates with some anecdotes from Bangladesh, Sierra Leone, and Zambia. Providing access to financial services for female savers and borrowers might thus directly contribute to the Millennium Development Goal of gender equality (box 3.1). For a detailed discussion of gender and credit, see Armendáriz de Aghion and Morduch (2005, chapter 7).

Karlan and Valdivia (2006), and Ashraf, Giné and, Karlan (2007) find that MFIs that offer extension services have higher client retention and better repayment performance than MFIs that do not offer such services. Their clients also have better business outcomes.

Even the limited focus on production credit might be mistaken. Recent analysis of survey data from Indonesia suggests MFI clients use credit as much for consumption as for investment purposes (Johnston and Morduch 2007). This finding applies not only to households that do not run microenterprises but even to a quarter of microentrepreneur households (figure 3.4). As discussed earlier, consumer credit is also the

Figure 3.4   Use of microcredit for consumption purposes

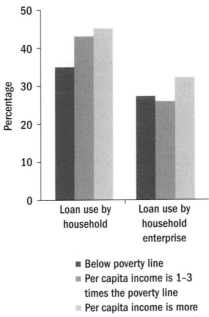

Source: Johnston and Morduch (2007).
Note: This figure shows the percentage of surveyed Bank Rakyat Indonesia customers at different income levels in Indonesia that indicated they used the credit for consumption purposes.

only credit type shown to be robustly linked with higher household welfare (Karlan and Zinman 2006b). This is not a negative outcome, but it does suggest a very different vision of microfinance from the original.

In addition to the reluctance of traditional lenders to reach out to low-income households and microentrepreneurs, risk-averse producers might be reluctant to take up loans. While credit-financed microenterprise might increase the level of income, it might also increase its variation. Indeed, in their survey Johnston and Morduch (2007) find a large group of households that do not want credit although they are deemed creditworthy by officials of a microcredit institution.

While research on a randomly chosen sample of entrepreneurs in Sri Lanka finds credit constraints are the main reason for the lack of expanding business, not missing insurance markets (de Mel, McKenzie, and Woodruff 2006), take-up of credit might be increased if coupled with a proper insurance mechanism. This might be especially true for agricultural producers who are subject to high price and yield volatility.

—to microinsurance—

Insurance products with or without credit might thus help these farmers expand without taking on too much additional risk. Traditional insurance to farmers to protect them against climatic and other shocks has proved costly and unmarketable because of high moral hazard risk from misreporting. As an alternative, insurers have developed weather index insurance, which compensates farmers according to objectively verifiable benchmarks likely to be correlated with the actual damage the farmer has suffered.

How successful are such insurance schemes? Giné, Townsend, and Vickery (2007) assess the introduction of a rainfall insurance product, first designed by a large insurance company in southern India in 2004 and marketed by a microfinance institution. In villages where policies were sold, the authors find that less than 5 percent of the targeted population buys the insurance product and less than 3 percent of the purchasers change their production patterns. Why such low uptake of the product? The most common reason given for not buying the insurance, according to Giné, Townsend, and Vickery (2007), is lack of understanding of the product. The cost of insurance combined with credit constraints constitute another powerful factor explaining the lack of take-up. Lack of trust that the insurer would pay claims promptly or at all if the insurable event occurs is likely also a factor—not unwarranted given the experience with many financial innovations in low-income environments in the past. Overall, it seems the insurance product did not reach the most vulnerable households that would benefit most from it.

In a similar experiment in Malawi, farmers were randomly offered the choice between a simple credit contract or one that combined credit with insurance (Giné and Yang 2007). The latter is effectively a contingent credit contract, that is, a loan that has to be repaid only in good times. Surprisingly, the take-up of the credit-insurance contract was significantly lower than the take-up of the credit contract, and the difference cannot be explained by the cost of including insurance. Unlike microcredit, microinsurance products are still in their infancy, so it is too early to draw definite conclusions. But this research shows the substantial barriers that providers have to overcome to market the product effectively to the target population.

Rainfall insurance is only one of the microinsurance products that have been developed over the past years. Life and health insurance policies are increasingly offered by both commercial and nongovernmental organization (NGO) insurance institutions. For such policies to be viable for a commercial insurer, there needs to be a delivery channel with which potential clients are familiar, such as an MFI or an NGO (as in the two cases discussed). While a large practitioners' literature discusses these different products and delivery mechanisms, rigorous research assessing their impact is still to be conducted.[16]

To what extent do poor households really need credit? In the absence of credit, the poor might simply accumulate savings over time before investing and thus overcome credit constraints. If they are too poor to accumulate savings, access to credit can improve their incomes, although poor households might run the risk of overindebtedness. Dale Adams and others argue that better savings vehicles, not what they call "microdebt," are the financial service most needed by most of the poor: rotating savings and credit associations (ROSCAs) and microcredit are thus seen as imperfect tools to address savings constraints (Adams and von Pischke 1992; Rutherford 1998). This school also argues that despite popular beliefs to the contrary, the fact that the poor are capable of weekly repayments shows that the poor are capable of saving, even if it is only in small amounts (Rutherford 1998).

Why are poor households less likely to save in monetary forms, that is, through the banking system, than other households? One constraint is certainly the geographic distance to bank outlets. A large share of the poor population in many developing countries is still concentrated in rural areas, and banking systems in developing countries typically concentrate their branch network in urban areas. That geographic access can matter for monetary savings is shown by the analysis of a pseudo-natural experiment in Mexico. Specifically, Aportela (1999) analyzed the results of the expansion of a government-owned Mexican savings institute in the early 1990s. This expansion happened only in some states, and there seems to be no significant correlation of state characteristics with the expansion programs. Computing savings rates of low-income households from survey responses before and after the expansion started, Aportela shows that the expansion increased the savings rate of low-income households—the ones targeted by the expansion in the first place—but had no effect on high-income households. In addition, the increased financial savings did not seem to crowd out other informal ways of savings: there was a positive net effect on the overall savings of the typical household.

The importance of geographic proximity points to local savings banks and post office networks as important tools for attracting savings

—and microsavings

Geographic distance is an important barrier to savings for many households

by low-income households. In 19th century Germany, municipalities established local savings banks to do just that. The fact that almost all adults in most countries in continental western Europe have checking or savings accounts is often attributed to the dense networks of savings and cooperative banks. Similarly, postal savings banks have traditionally played an important role in the rural and more remote areas of many developed and developing countries, despite their often weak financial structure and suboptimal service provision.

Commitment devices may encourage savings

Lack of geographic access is not the only impediment to saving in monetary form, however. Time inconsistency problems—short-run impatience (high discount factors in the near future) and long-run patience (low discount factors in the far future)—could explain why many individuals often regret how little they have saved. Conflicts within households over savings can also result in undersaving. In developing countries as in developed, a variety of commitment devices are used to help overcome such problems. Indeed, some of the practices of the informal ROSCAs can be rationalized in this way. Microfinance institutions around the world offer a wide variety of savings commitment devices for their clients (Ashraf, Karlan, and Yin 2003). But do these commitment devices work in increasing savings? Do they influence intrahousehold decision processes and consumption-savings patterns? Several recent papers assess these questions.

Ashraf, Karlan, and Yin (2006b, c) assess the effect of a commitment product where savers commit to forgo their access to savings accounts until a specific date or until they have reached a precommitted balance. Specifically, the authors conducted an experiment by randomly giving half of 1,800 existing or former clients of a rural Philippine bank the option to save through a commitment savings account (a locked box) that allowed them access to the funds only after they reached a self-set date or a self-set amount of savings. Only 28 percent of clients decided to take up this product, but Ashraf, Karlan, and Yin find an increase of 81 percent in average savings balances of account holders who participated in the scheme over a 12-month period. This effect was not sustained, however; after 30 months the average balance was only 33 percent higher than the average balance of nonparticipants and the difference was no longer significant; many clients stopped saving with the commitment product after an initial period. At the same time, this commitment device led to a shift in the power of decision making by women, which was seen in higher investment in durable goods associated with women, such as washing and sewing machines and kitchen appliances.

Ashraf, Karlan, and Yin (2006a) assess the effect of another technique to attract savings, designed to overcome both the problem of geographic distance and the lack of commitment, namely, door-to-door collection of savings. Among those who did take up this service, savings increased by 25 percent over a 15-month period, while borrowing went down; it is possible that savings, rather than borrowing, were thus used for consumption smoothing. Households accepting this service lived farther away from the nearest bank branch, thus indicating the importance of travel costs; and they were more likely to be married, again showing the importance of intrahousehold conflicts in the savings decision. The fact that the offer of a convenient savings instrument reduced borrowing is yet more evidence for those who interpret microcredit take-up as a surrogate solution in the absence of savings opportunities.

Geographic impediments and intrahousehold conflicts are only some of the barriers poor people face in accessing savings services offered by financial institutions, as discussed in chapter 1. Continuing research in Indonesia is exploring other dimensions such as barriers related to affordability and financial literacy.

While access to financial services, such as credit or savings services, has received a great deal of attention in recent years, access to payments services has generated even more attention. Increased globalization has heightened demand for these services. International remittances, funds earned by migrants abroad and sent to their families in developing countries, have grown so dramatically in recent years that they have become the second largest source of external finance for developing countries after foreign direct investment (figure 3.5).[17] Moreover, a large share of the population in developing countries receives remittances. Relative to private capital flows, remittance flows tend to be relatively stable and countercyclical, that is, they increase in times of crisis. Technological advances have also become important for remittance flows, as the increasing trend to send remittances through ATMs and cell phones shows.

Remittances sent through formal channels are commonly subject to high costs. These high costs drive many remittance senders to informal remittance agencies. Furthermore, the costs of sending remittances have important implications for the amount of remittances sent. Yang (2007) shows that Philippine migrants sent lower remittances in foreign currency when the Philippine peso depreciated, suggesting that they want their families to receive a fixed amount in pesos. Gibson, McKenzie, and Rohorua (2006) show a negative cost elasticity for Tonga of 0.22;

Demand for payments services has increased

Figure 3.5 Remittance flows across countries

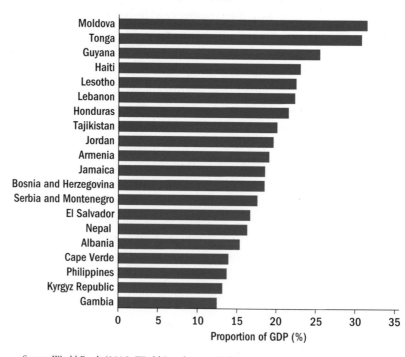

Source: World Bank (2005, *World Development Indicators*).
Note: This figure shows remittance flows through official channels as a proportion of GDP for 20 countries with the largest remittance inflows, based on national balance of payments data.

if the cost of sending the remittances were reduced to levels in more competitive markets around the world, they compute an increase of 28 percent in remittances—an amount that would constitute 4 percent of Tonga's GDP.

The high costs of sending formal remittances—

A lack of bank competition and financial underdevelopment seem to explain the high costs of formal remittances. The typical remittance fee is priced as a two-part tariff, consisting of a fixed fee regardless of the amount sent, and a variable fee arising from the exchange rate commission. As a result, the average fee for sending remittances decreases as the remittance amount increases, so the small amounts that are typically sent are subject to high costs. But remittance costs vary significantly across corridors. The decrease in fees in the U.S.-Mexico corridor, for example, has been attributed to a higher degree of competition in the remittance market (Hernandez-Coss 2005). In the Tonga-New Zealand corridor, where competition is minimal and migrants lack information about available options, the fees are three times as high as in the U.S.-Mexico corridor (box 3.7). The example of Tonga also illustrates an important factor explaining high remittance costs: lack of bank penetration not only reduces competition but also makes remittances more expensive if the alternative money transfer operators have only indirect access (through banks) to the payment system.

Tonga provides just one example of how expanded access to modern technologies can help. Technology can make business processes more efficient for financial institutions as well as increase access possibilities for customers. Technological advances can reduce the costs of banking, effectively enabling outreach further down the income pyramid to customers with demand for smaller transaction amounts.[18] For example, payment systems based on electronic fund transfers rather than checks can substantially reduce the costs of payment transfers. Cell-phone-based financial transactions (also referred to as m-banking or m-finance, with the *m* standing for mobile phone) have gained prominence in recent years. There are more cell-phone users in Sub-Saharan Africa than holders of bank accounts, and the use of cell phones for financial transactions has increased rapidly in recent years. How far this technology can go in pushing out the access frontier is still subject to debate, however. Porteous (2006) finds that use of m-banking services in South Africa is predominantly concentrated among existing bank customers, with only a few providers targeting those without accounts.

Technology can also affect customers directly. The introduction of ATMs has not only increased accessibility of accounts to 24 hours a day, thus improving convenience, but has also expanded the range of customers. Financial institutions in several Sub-Saharan African countries have introduced transaction accounts that are purely ATM based; customers do not have to enter banking halls, a cultural barrier for many Africans without bank accounts. Providing financial services through ATMs is also cheaper for the financial institution. And by encouraging channeling of payments such as remittances through the formal banking system, technological advances may broaden the deposit base of banks, allowing them to intermediate more funds to the private sector. If the banks can learn over time about their clients and their creditworthiness, including remittance recipients in the formal banking system as depositors, at least some of those customers may become borrowers. Receiving remittances through the formal banking system thus might enable recipients to gain access to other financial services as well. Two recent studies show that remittance flows pull new

—can be overcome with technology

Technology can also expand the customer base

Box 3.7 Why don't migrants use the cheapest methods? Evidence from Tongan migrants in New Zealand

REMITTANCES ARE EXTRAORDINARILY important in Tonga, where they constitute more than 30 percent of GDP and account for 20 percent of monetary household income (Gibson, McKenzie, and Rohorua 2006) Despite their importance, the transaction costs of sending remittances to Tonga by the most widely used methods are high. Typical transactions costs average 15–20 percent of the remittance amount for bank drafts, telegraphic transfers through banks, transactions through Western Union, and transactions through Melie mei Langi, a church-based money transfer operation. In contrast, transferring money through an ATM card linked to a New Zealand bank account set up by the sender costs less than 5 percent, but this method is not widely used. The cost spread between the more popular methods and ATMs means a potential loss for Tonga equivalent to 4 percent of GDP.

What accounts for the underuse of ATMs? Gibson and others (2006) use a survey among Tongan immigrants in New Zealand to explore this puzzle. First, the immigrants seem to lack knowledge: only

2 percent of those surveyed knew how to use an ATM to send money, and few knew of the hidden exchange rate premiums that increase the cost of other methods. Second, distance of recipients from an ATM in Tonga outside the capital city of Nuku'alofa limits access to this method. The figure below shows the coverage areas of ATM machines and Western Union outlets on the main island of Tongatapu. Although there are more ATMs than Western Union outlets, the ATMs are concentrated in Nuku'alofa, and cover only 77 percent of the population within a 10 kilometer radius, whereas Western Union reaches 97 percent of that population. Finally, three-quarters of respondents indicated they would not use ATMs as a method of remitting because they did not trust them, fearing unauthorized withdrawals and card skimming among other things.

This analysis suggests several ways for financial sector policy to improve both the demand for and supply of newer and cheaper remittance technologies. In particular, more attention needs to be given to improving the financial literacy of migrants and

customers into the formal banking system. Combining municipality-level and household survey data for Mexico, Demirgüç-Kunt and others (2007) find a positive relationship between the share of households in a municipality that receives remittances and total deposits to GDP, deposit accounts per capita, and branches per capita, but no significant relationship with total credit to GDP. Using household survey data for El Salvador, Demirgüç-Kunt and Martinez Peria (2007) find evidence that channeling remittances through the banking system increases banking outreach; the likelihood that the recipient has a bank account is twice as high if the remittances are received through the banking system than if they are received through informal channels, although there is no effect on the credit side.[19]

Box 3.7 *(continued)*

providing them with clear and accurate information about the alternatives available for remitting. Community newspapers and associations could play an important role in disseminating this information.

Second, expansion of access to modern technologies in the remittance-receiving country is needed to match the convenience and service offered by traditional money transfer operators.

Service areas of ATMs and Western Union on Tongatapu, Tonga

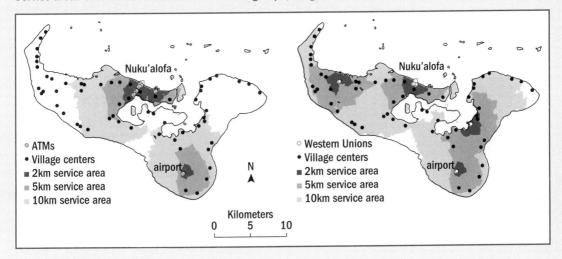

Source: Gibson and others (2006).

Reaching Out to the Poor or to the Excluded?

Thirty years after the establishment of Grameen Bank, the microfinance movement has attained a certain maturity. Microfinance increases access to financial services for those participating in the program, and, because of lower staff salaries and lack of posh banking halls, it does so at lower operating costs than commercial banks can. Nonetheless, most microfinance programs still incur high unit costs because of the small size of loans. As a result, a large proportion of the institutions—albeit mostly the smaller ones—are dependent on subsidies (Robinson 2001; Armendáriz de Aghion and Morduch 2005), and there is a continuing discussion about the financial sustainability of microcredit, regarding both its feasibility and desirability. Cull, Demirgüç-Kunt, and Morduch

Many microfinance institutions require subsidies—

(2007) looked at a sample of 124 MFIs in 49 countries representing around 50 percent of all microfinance clients around the globe, most likely, the more profitable and cost-efficient institutions. The authors find that even in this select group, only half of the institutions were profitable and financially self-sustainable, generating sufficient revenue to cover their costs (figure 3.6).

—raising questions about sustainability

One of the reasons for this lack of self-sustainability might be the lack of scale; only in eight countries do microfinance borrowers account for more than 2 percent of the population (Honohan 2004, figure 3.7), and most individual MFIs seem to be too small to reap the necessary scale economies to become financially sustainable (figure 3.8). At the same time, as MFIs grow and mature, they seem to focus less on the poor (Cull, Demirgüç-Kunt, and Morduch 2007), which could be interpreted either as a success story for their borrowers or as mission drift.

Microfinance also suffers from another important limitation: for many MFIs, scaling up to nonpoor customers will be difficult, as will be the ability of MFIs to accompany their customers as they grow richer. Joint-liability lending relies on groups of borrowers with similar borrowing needs, and the profitability of the approach relies on large numbers of

Figure 3.6 Financial self-sufficiency and subsidy dependence

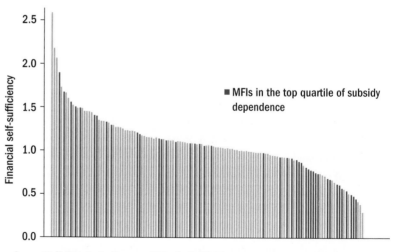

Source: Cull, Demirgüç-Kunt, and Morduch (2007).

Note: This figure shows the financial self-sustainability (ability to generate sufficient revenue to cover costs) of 124 MFIs across 49 countries, with the blue bars indicating MFIs in the top 25th percentiles in subsidy dependence (given by share of subsidies as a proportion of total liabilities plus equity).

Figure 3.7 Microfinance penetration across countries

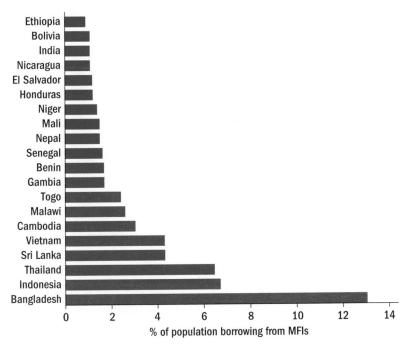

Source: Honohan (2004).
Note: This figure shows the ratio of borrowing clients to total population for the 20 countries with the highest microfinance penetration.

Figure 3.8 Distribution of MFIs by size of outreach

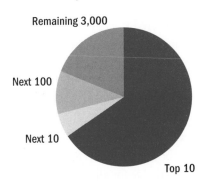

Source: Updated from Honohan (2004).
Note: This figure shows that the top 10 MFIs reporting to the Microcredit Summit (Daley-Harris, 2006) accounted for 66 percent of the total number of MFI customers in the world. At the other extreme, nearly 3,000 of the 3,133 reporting MFIs had fewer than 15,000 clients each.

borrowers and groups. The higher borrowers are on the income ladder and the larger the size of the enterprise, however, the more divergent are borrower characteristics and borrowing needs. Not surprisingly, loans made by individual-based microlending institutions are larger on average than loans made by MFIs using joint-liability lending. Furthermore, larger average loan sizes also imply lower costs (Cull, Demirgüç-Kunt, and Morduch 2007).

MFIs often are unable to meet the needs of the excluded nonpoor

MFIs in most cases do not have sufficient resources to fulfill the borrowing needs of larger microenterprises. And microenterprises might no longer be willing and able to pay the higher MFI interest rates as they expand. MFIs are constrained by the lack of savings mobilization and their reliance on donor resources. Especially in developing countries, only the formal banking system has sufficient resources to fulfill the borrowing needs of their economies' private sectors. The obvious solution—linking the microcredit sector with the banking sector—has therefore become an increasingly popular solution. In several countries, such as Bolivia and Uganda, MFIs have been given the opportunity to convert into microbanks and collect deposits from the general public. Some of the leading microfinance institutions have received equity funding from institutional investors, and links between banks and MFIs in numerous countries have provided MFIs with the necessary funding from banks, while maintaining their business and credit model to target low-income clients.[20]

Many MFIs, even with subsidies, have had trouble reaching the very poor. And, as mentioned, some MFIs have been moving upscale with their successful clients. Should policymakers worry about an apparent drift in the emphasis of many MFIs, and of the MFI industry as a whole, away from focusing on credit access for the very poor? Considering the indications that improving access for not-so-poor entrepreneurial households can have powerfully favorable indirect implications for the poor, such worries may be overstated.

A narrow focus on the poor may be counterproductive—

Focusing on finance for the very poor shifts the attention to subsidies and charity, which can hurt the quality of services. There are also good political economy reasons why the focus should not be on the poor or on how microfinance can be made more viable, but instead on how financial services can be made available for all.[21] The poor lack the political clout to demand better services, and subsidies may spoil the credit culture, that is, the willingness to repay loans since they are perceived as grants. Defining the issue more broadly to include the middle class, who often also lack access, would make it more likely that policy makers would make financial access a priority. Hence shifting the focus to building inclusive financial systems and improving access for all underserved groups is likely to have greater impact on development outcomes.

As a result, the development community has shifted its attention to building inclusive financial systems focusing not only on specialized microcredit institutions, but on an array of other financial institutions, such as postal savings banks, consumer credit institutions, and, most important, the banking system. This broader approach can lead to overall financial system efficiency and outreach to the whole population.

The recent expansion in banking services across Latin America, for example, has been driven by consumer credit, provided mostly by utility and other nonfinancial companies, such as large department stores. Although no firm data exist, anecdotal evidence suggests that this credit expansion is based on credit scoring and risk diversification through the law of large numbers. Postal networks have come to play an increasingly important role, such as in Brazil, where the postal service linked with a private commercial bank through an agency agreement, thus effectively increasing geographic access to banking services to all municipalities. Private commercial banks have taken the lead in reaching out to low-income households and microenterprises with new techniques and products, often driven by a combination of profit and social objectives.

The broader focus on an inclusive financial system raises again the question of how to ensure that financial institutions will expand outreach. How can governments and donors best help reduce transaction costs and risk that often impede commercially oriented financial institutions from reaching out to the poor and near poor? Should donors subsidize microfinance institutions so they can reach out to the very poor? Should the government subsidize financial institutions so they reach out to rural and remote areas? Several ideas and questions arise in this context.[22]

First, subsidies in the financial sector have to be assessed in a rigorous manner to compare costs and benefits with subsidies in other areas, such as education or infrastructure. Any subsidy has the opportunity costs of forgone government intervention in other sectors and areas. Second, a distinction has to be made between credit services, on the one hand, and savings and payments services, on the other hand. More of a case might be made for subsidies in payment services, because such services are considered necessary for participation in a modern market economy. Further, payment services can be seen as a network good whose

—highlighting the need to foster the development of a range of financial institutions—

—and carefully assess whether subsidies could more effectively be used in other areas benefits increase as a larger proportion of the population has access to and uses them (Claessens and others 2003). Third, subsidies should focus on overcoming the barriers to access rather than distorting prices, such as interest rates. Finally, technological advances have the potential to revolutionize access for the poor, shifting attention from subsidies to establishing an environment conducive to technological innovations that may help overcome many of the restrictions. However, these technological advances, such as m-finance, also pose important regulatory questions. To what extent should electronic and m-finance providers be considered financial institutions and thus be subject to the heavier regulatory and supervisory framework? This issue is discussed further in chapter 4.

The simple point is that access to finance is lacking not only for the poor but for vast portions of the population in many low-income economies. If attempts to ensure that the poor do get credit result in distorting subsidies that damage the incentives for the microfinance industry, and the financial sector more generally, to innovate in providing access for the nonpoor, then their net effect on the poor could be counterproductive.

Conclusions

The direct provision of credit to the poor may not be the most important channel

While still far from conclusive, the bulk of the evidence suggests financial development and improved access to finance is likely not only to accelerate economic growth but also to reduce income inequality and poverty. The channels through which finance works to produce this impact are less clear, but the evidence from cross-country research, natural experiments, and general equilibrium models suggests that direct provision of credit to the poor may not be the most important channel. Hence fostering more efficient capital allocation through competitive and open markets has always been and still remains an important policy goal.

More than just the poor face financial exclusion

In most countries around the world, however, fewer than half the households have even basic financial access; many nonpoor and small and medium enterprises are effectively excluded from the financial system. For the most part, then, improving efficiency without broadening access is likely to be insufficient because it is likely to leave untapped the talents and innovative capacity of large segments of the population. Improving access for all of the excluded, not just the very poor, is therefore also likely to be an important policy goal for most developing countries.

Reaching out to low-income households and microentrepreneurs is quite challenging however, since issues of risk management, monitoring, and transaction costs tend to increase break-even interest rates and often lead to credit rationing. Here, innovative techniques and products developed by MFIs have helped overcome these information barriers. Nevertheless, microfinance services are costly to deliver, and they typically require extensive subsidies. While a focus on improving access to the excluded does not need to involve subsidies, reaching out to the very poor does. Should such access be subsidized? Encouraging and taking advantage of technological advances, which are becoming more widespread and fast-paced due to globalization, may be more promising in broadening access for the poor than providing subsidies, as well as shifting the focus of policy to establishing an environment conducive to the adaptation of the new technologies and to the entry of providers that bring them in. These issues are discussed more fully in the next chapter, which concerns governments' role in broadening access.

Innovative techniques and products can improve financial access

Notes

1. Introducing fixed transaction costs into a general equilibrium model and thus endogenizing the size of the intermediated sector, Townsend and Ueda (2006) conclude that restrictive financial sector policies in Thailand might have slowed the growth of financial intermediation below the endogenous growth rate that would have resulted from increasing per capita income, as predicted by Greenwood and Jovanovic (1990).

2. General equilibrium models have limited power to mimic the real world, as shown by Jeong and Townsend (2003). They compare the fit of the two models with exogenous and endogenous financial intermediation, the two models later used by Giné and Townsend (2004) and Townsend and Ueda (2006), respectively, and find that while both models fit the data well, they both exaggerate the movement between low- and high-income groups and underestimate the movements within different income groups. While general equilibrium models fit the long-term trends in the data reasonably well, Jeong and Townsend conclude that they cannot account for business cycle effects.

3. Reanalyzing the same data with a different econometric technique, Morduch (1998) failed to find any significant impact of microcredit on borrowers' income, though he did find an effect on consumption smoothing.

4. This technique was later named "pipeline matching" (Goldberg and Karlan 2005)

5. It is worth noting that such a design picks up the effect of credit for the marginal borrower. Assuming heterogeneity across agents, the effect might be lower or zero for those borrowers who easily got credit, since they may have plenty of close substitutes, while the effect could be even bigger for those who were denied credit by a bigger margin.

6. In particular, it is not only the sceptics who find much of the less rigorous literature unconvincing. Coleman (1999) notes: "Most existing impact studies are nonacademic project evaluations that are of a descriptive nature or suffer from the selection bias problem." In a useful survey of microfinance impact studies confined to those that tried "to select control groups whose observed characteristics were comparable except for their participation in microfinance," Littlefield, Morduch, and Hashemi (2003, p. 2) conclude that while "the general pattern of results sheds valid light on the question of impact, . . . few studies include fully rigorous controls for selection biases." Armendáriz de Aghion and Morduch (2005, p. 199–200) write that the differences between anecdotes and statistical evidence "should not be surprising: the anecdotes are culled to show the potential of microfinance, while the statistical analyses are designed to show typical impact across the board."

7. For evidence on the relation between durable-asset holding, education, and child labor, see Jacoby (1994); Guarcello, Mealli, and Rosati (2003); Jacoby and Skoufias (1997); and Beegle, Dehejia, and Gatti (2007). Several cross-country studies also assess the relationship between financial development, education, and incidence of child labor; see Flug, Spilimbergo, and Wachtenheim (1998) and Beegle, Dehejia, and Gatti (2007). For evidence on access to credit and upward mobility, see Wydick (1999). For evidence on geographic proximity to bank branches and health, see Gertler, Levine, and Moretti (2003).

8. For a detailed discussion, see Ravallion (2004).

9. Cross-country regressions using other poverty-related measures also point to a favorable impact. For example, Claessens and Feijen (2007) find a significant impact of financial sector development on the incidence of undernourishment. One of the channels through which this relationship works seems to be financial development enhancing the level and growth rate of agricultural productivity, which in turn leads to higher output and lower prices, which helps reduce the incidence of undernourishment. However, as is the case with many cross-country studies, identification issues remain.

10. The distribution data are notoriously difficult to compare across countries for several reasons, including the fact that they are based on different welfare measures (consumption versus income), different measures of income (gross versus net), and different units of observation (households versus individuals), and adjustments for these differences are imperfect (Dollar and Kraay 2002; Deaton 2005). While these differences in measurement introduce an error into the regressions run by Beck, Demirgüç-Kunt, and Levine (2007), this error should bias their estimations against finding a significant relationship

between finance and changes in income distribution. Further, the regressions of changes in headcount on finance are less subject to this concern as the headcount measures are based on a set of consistent household surveys (Chen and Ravallion 2004).

11. Using Thai data and testing a structural model with moral hazard and limited liability due to high enforcement costs, Paulson, Townsend, and Karaivanov (2006) confirm that moral hazard is the dominant source of financing constraints. In the case of poorer households, however, they cannot reject the hypothesis that limited liability also plays a role. Giné (2005) distinguishes between transaction costs incurred by borrowers and enforcement costs incurred by lenders and shows that enforcement costs limit outreach more than transaction costs do in the context of rural finance in Thailand.

12. To tease out the trade-off in group-based lending in comparison with individual lending, Giné and others (2006) created an experimental economics laboratory in a large, urban market in Lima, Peru, and conducted difference games with microentrepreneurs and potential microfinance clients.

13. Undertaking experimental games with a group of microfinance clients in Peru, Karlan (2005) finds that cultural similarity and geographic proximity predict trust and trustworthiness.

14. This could also reflect that a disproportionate number of those MFIs that concentrate on the very poor are charitable concerns willing to channel subsidies to the poor rather than aiming at profitability.

15. However, because of imperfections in the labor market, the poor women borrowers in the model of Emran, Morshed, and Stiglitz (2006) will not be interested in expanding their operation beyond a certain scale.

16. See Roth, McCord, and Liber (2007) for an overview of microinsurance products and delivery mechanisms.

17. Official data on remittance flows—mostly from balance-of-payment statistics—underestimate their true extent because a large proportion of remittances is sent through informal channels. In addition, in many cases, remittances sent through money transfer providers that do not settle through banks are not recorded in official data either (de Luna Martinez 2005). A large share of remittances is thus misclassified as net errors and omission in balance-of-payment statistics. Using cost data on sending remittances through formal channels and assuming that use of these channels, but not the amount of remittances, is elastic to the cost of sending the remittances. Freund and Spatafora (2005) estimate that informal remittance flows equal 35–75 percent of formal remittance flows.

18. See Firpo (2005) for a discussion on the role of technology in reducing costs in microfinance.

19. Recent research also shows that remittance flows can affect financial development in the recipient countries, increasing access indirectly. For example, Aggarwal, Demirgüç-Kunt, and Martinez Peria (2006) find that formal remittance flows, as captured by balance-of-payments statistics, have a positive impact on financial intermediary development.

20. Microfinance institutions face another challenge as the industry matures—competition. During the initial stages of microfinance, most institutions compete only against informal moneylenders; their monopoly position allows them to use dynamic incentives such as repeat and progressive lending, as borrowers do not have any alternatives. However, as MFI sectors mature, as in Bangladesh, Bolivia, and Uganda, MFIs start competing directly against each other in certain regions of the country, with negative implications for borrowers, who may become overindebted and receive less favorable loan terms, but also for lenders who encounter worse repayment performance. Effective information sharing among lenders is one way of overcoming these difficulties. For example, in the already-discussed Guatemalan case, Luoto, McIntosh, and Wydick (2007) calculated that the introduction of a credit information system allowed MFIs to improve their loan appraisal to the extent of lowering their break-even interest rate by more than 2.5 percentage points.

21. Rajan (2006b) argues "let's not kill the microfinance movement with kindness. If we want it to become more than a fad . . . it has to follow the clear and unsentimental path of adding value and making money. On that path lies the possibility of a true and large-scale escape from poverty."

22. See also the discussion in Armendáriz de Aghion and Morduch (2005, chapter 9), focusing on subsidies for MFIs.

CHAPTER FOUR

Government's Role in Facilitating Access

GIVEN THE EVIDENCE THAT FINANCIAL ACCESS VARIES WIDELY around the world, and that expanding access remains an important challenge even in advanced economies, it is clear that there is much for policy to do. It is not enough to say that the market will provide. Market failures related to information gaps, the need for coordination on collective action, and concentrations of power mean that governments everywhere have an extensive role in supporting, regulating, and sometimes directly intervening in the provision of financial services.

Not all government action is equally effective, however, and some policies can be counterproductive. Complex system responses can make well-intentioned policies misfire, so successful policy design must be context specific. Governance issues are important: policy success can depend on institutional quality. Measures that are effective in environments that already enjoy strong institutions may fail elsewhere. At the same time, a well-functioning financial system itself is likely to contribute to strengthening national governance.

Previous chapters have already mentioned some individual policy issues. This chapter takes a broad view of the role of policy in improving access. It draws as much as possible on findings from formal quantitative research to throw light on a few of the more difficult choices that arise. Implementation of policy requires complementing the results of research analysis with practitioner experience, which this study does not attempt to summarize. Nontheless, the analysis presented in this chapter provides a base for sound policy advice. The treatment is necessarily selective but illustrates how other issues can be approached.

Government action is necessary to correct market failures, but some policies can be ineffective or counterproductive

Policies to improve financial access and financial development are not always the same

Many of the policies often recommended to enhance overall development of the financial sector—including the legal and information underpinnings needed to lower the cost of services for large enterprises, governmental entities, and wealthy individuals, and to improve the innovative capacity of the financial sector—will also help increase access to those now excluded from, or poorly served by, the financial sector. That reduces the number of difficult trade-offs that have to be made. But the overlap and alignment of the goals are not perfect. A policy reform package for the financial sector that does not explicitly prioritize access will tend to make different choices from one that does. For example, certain regulatory prudential measures aimed at financial stability can restrict the degree to which banks can serve small borrowers. Concentrating institution-building efforts on developing an offshore financial center to export efficient wholesale financial services could result in the neglect of the infrastructures needed to help onshore financial intermediaries reach small, local producers. A reform approach to financial sector policy that explicitly recognizes the importance of access can help ensure that financial development also makes financial systems more inclusive.

It is important to set realistic goals

In prioritizing access policy, it is important to recognize the limitations of even a very efficient financial system supported by a strong contractual and information infrastructure. Not all would-be borrowers are creditworthy, and there are numerous examples of overly relaxed credit policies that have reduced national welfare. Indeed, prudential regulation of banks in developing countries is largely concerned with ensuring that loss-making credit decisions are, on average, avoided. It is also important not to undermine market discipline by adopting rules or regulations (such as mispriced deposit insurance) that may distort the risk-taking or monitoring incentives of market participants. Access to other formal financial services can approach universality as economies develop—indeed the presumption that everyone should be entitled to some form of account at a financial intermediary has gained ground in advanced economies and is essentially a reality in several European countries. The fixed costs of service provision, however, have made it very difficult for traditional financial service providers to reach customers whose need is only for tiny payment and savings transactions or who are located in small and remote markets. Over time, technological and organizational innovations should begin to overcome these barriers, and entry and other regulatory policies should be designed so that such innovation is not inadvertently blocked. More generally, the challenge for policy is to help build the necessary infrastructures and to ensure that the financial system is one in which service providers are delivering as widely as is possible, given existing infrastructures, and are not hampered by inappropriate regulatory or other policies or by coordination failures (Beck and de la Torre 2007).

This chapter begins by discussing some overall market development issues concerning general measures for improving the contractual, information, and other infrastructures needed to support an effective financial system with good outreach. It highlights recent findings that address the question of which institutional reforms should be prioritized. For example, in low-income countries, improving information infrastructures seems to yield more immediate access benefits than undertaking legal reforms. But legal reforms are also important, and among those, there is evidence that other aspects of contract enforcement may be more important for access than protection of property rights against the state. It also notes that intermediaries can be helped to work around hard-to-remedy institutional deficiencies.

This chapter starts with an examination of institutions and infrastructure—

The chapter then turns to specific enabling policy actions to boost the capacity of market intermediaries to deliver financial access. It reviews the many supportive measures that need to be addressed. These range from specific legislation to underpin payments technologies that use the Internet and mobile phones, to ensuring that anti-money-laundering regulations do not choke household access, to securities markets regulation that is not so costly as to prevent listings by medium-size firms.

—and then turns to intermediaries—

The chapter then moves to a discussion of regulatory structure. Much of the needed regulatory structure for finance is designed to improve competition and efficiency while restraining excesses, including imprudent or exploitative behavior. The chapter focuses in particular on the potential for positive policy action to mandate access-enhancing product development, contrasting this with the usually counterproductive effect of unrealistic usury ceilings. It also describes recent evidence showing that market discipline can complement official prudential regulation but needs an appropriate policy environment to be effective.

Next the chapter addresses the controversial question of whether government should enter directly into the access business through ownership or subsidy of financial service providers. Here it looks in some detail at state-sponsored credit guarantee schemes (showing how some of these appear to be as costly as many old-fashioned state-lending programs,

—and the tricky issues of government ownership—

with little clear benefit, while potential improvements in scheme design have often been ignored).

—and political economy

Before concluding, the chapter turns to the links between politics and access. Financial sector reform delivering outreach is not politically unproblematic. Elites in closed-access societies may lose in the short run by policies that open access to finance and thereby to wider economic opportunities.

Expanding Access: Importance of Long-Term Institution Building

There is little disagreement that the ability of financial service providers to reach a broad clientele is highly dependent on macroeconomic environment and on the overall state of the contractual and information infrastructure.

Macroeconomic stability can foster financial sector development—

Theoretical and empirical research has confirmed that macroeconomic instability is an important obstacle to effective intertemporal contracting.[1] Fiscal imbalances in particular generate high and variable inflation, often making the future value of money so uncertain (and difficult to hedge) for both suppliers and demanders that long-term financial contracts simply do not exist. Households will not give up control over their savings for longer time-periods in unstable macroeconomic environments, and financial institutions will not commit beyond short-term contracts given funding uncertainties. Unsustainable macroeconomic and fiscal policies have often been the prelude to financial instability and crises; the fear of macroeconomic and financial instability also inhibits financial innovation that can promote access. In addition, the scale of borrowing by free-spending governments tends to crowd out other borrowers, including (perhaps especially) small firms.

—as can a positive business environment—

There is thus clear scope for positive government action in the areas of macroeconomic stability and general institution building that supports greater financial access. Policies not specifically addressed to financial sector needs but designed to improve the general business environment (communication, transportation, and energy infrastructure) in which financial institutions operate, as well as the general security situation, are also of evident importance.

—supported by well functioning institutions

The emphasis in recent literature on the importance of institutions— the "rules of the game"—for economic development, and on the parallel role these institutions are thought to play in financial development, suggests that the mechanisms of finance are at the heart of the complex processes that lead to accelerated economic growth in a way that is still far from being fully understood (Beinhocker 2006). As such, adjusting institutions in directions that clearly help improve the functioning of finance is likely to be a highly effective pro-growth strategy. Even if the claims that finance plays the chief causal role in economic growth were to be proved false, and instead all of the causality came from the underlying institutional framework, emphasis on ensuring financial performance is likely to select growth-effective institutions.

Building these institutions is typically a long-term and diffuse endeavor, and it necessarily involves a key role for government. Government is the natural—in many cases the only—provider of some of the key organizations that support good institutions, such as efficient, speedy, and fair courts. Government may also need to provide some or all of the needed registries of credit information, liens, and property ownership. Legislation that defines the rights and responsibilities of companies, financial entities, and other financial market participants, avoiding uncertainty or ambiguity in contracts, is also a valuable part of the financial infrastructure provided by government. First and foremost, then, governments can broaden access by making and encouraging infrastructure improvements needed for market development.[2]

Institution building requires a long-term commitment

For the policy maker, or the adviser on policy matters, the range of institutional reforms demanded can seem overwhelming, as can the difficulty of implementing even a subset of them. What then are the priorities and how best can the obstacles to implementation be overcome? These are questions to which researchers are only beginning to find solutions.

This is not the place for a handbook of good practice in institution building. For one thing, much of what is held to be good practice in this regard still amounts to a transplant of models that have been successful in advanced economies and otherwise lacks systematic evidential foundations from across the world.[3] Yet, there are some interesting lessons from recent research findings that speak to the priorities and likely successes in institutional reform.

The first wave of cross-country empirical literature on law and finance (La Porta and others 1997, 1998) established the strong role of institutions in boosting financial market depth and economic growth, including financial access.[4] To take one dimension of this, although most will agree

Evidence that legal institutions matter

that enforcement of investor and creditor rights is important for access, there has been less agreement on the nature of the legal systems that are best adapted to financial development. As with financial depth and other aggregate measures of financial development, there appear to be fewer barriers to financial access in countries with a common law legal tradition than in those whose legal origins spring from civil codes.[5] But perhaps it is not so much legal origin per se, but rather a degree of adaptability in legal institutions that is essential to ensure that contract enforcement can keep pace with changing financial technologies. In analyzing the World Business Environment Survey data, Beck, Demirgüç-Kunt, and Levine (2005) also use measures of judicial independence and adaptability to look more closely at whether the style of law in effect has an impact on access as reported in these surveys. Their regressions suggest that firms in civil code countries face larger obstacles to accessing external finance than do firms in common law countries, especially in the dimensions of collateral requirements, long-term loans, and paperwork and bureaucracy. Based on the performance of the other legal variables in the study, the authors suggest that these obstacles are more likely to result from the lack of adaptability in many civil code legal systems rather than from a lack of judicial independence from political pressures.[6]

Arguably the most important institutions to put into place to achieve economic growth are those that reliably constrain the state from compromising private property rights. North, Wallis, and Weingast (2006) argue persuasively—in their ambitious, albeit not fully elaborated or proved, thesis—that the most fundamental distinction between types of organized societies is that between open access societies and those that limit access to economic resources. The course of history suggests that the former have proved to be far and away the more successful, especially in recent times. According to the authors, social order in an open access society is maintained by competition, not rent creation, and competition requires a political system that does not depend on creating and capturing rents for a limited elite.

The risk of expropriation can be a major threat to financial sector development

This proposition finds some confirmation in econometric analysis of the cross-country data that is available on various aspects of national institutions relevant to financial sector performance. In particular, Acemoglu and Johnson (2005) have looked carefully at the different types of institutional variables found in cross-country studies to influence financial sector development and economic growth. They distinguish between those legal and political institutions that mainly underpin the security of contracting between economic agents on the one hand and those that ensure the security of private property rights vis-à-vis the state on the other. Security of contracting includes measures of legal complexity and formalism in debt recovery; security of property rights includes measures of the constitutional constraints on the political executive and the degree of protection against risk of expropriation. All of these variables are strongly correlated with financial development and economic growth (and with each other).

To eliminate the likely feedback or reverse causality from growth to institutional performance, Acemoglu and Johnson employ as instruments not only legal origin, but also the mortality of colonial settlers,[7] with the interesting twist that legal origin proves to be a predictor only of the contracting institutions and settler mortality to be a predictor of the institutions related to private property rights. Indeed, they show that legal origin is also strongly correlated with enterprise survey responses on the quality of the courts and the functioning of the judicial system, but not with survey responses on official corruption and predictability of regulation, whereas exactly the opposite is true of settler mortality. Using these instruments, it is the private property rights institutions, rather than the contracting institutions, that prove to be most strongly associated with banking depth and GDP per capita.[8]

If the econometric findings of Acemoglu and Johnson are to be taken at face value, they have some clear implications: a "grabbing state" is a major threat to financial sector development (and thus to economic growth); without institutions that restrain the state from preying on private property, the financial route to economic prosperity is severely constrained.

A conjectural synthesis of these results with those of Beck, Demirgüç-Kunt, and Levine (2005) on judicial adaptability would say that protection of private property against the state is key for the *depth* of financial sector development, but that more specific protections of contracts between private agents are important for determining *access*.[9]

The nature of the 19th century European colonial engagement is of course not the only determinant of modern institutions in countries that were formerly colonized, but the long-lasting influence of that engagement has far-reaching implications for the needed institutional reforms along this dimension. Whether a country has been a settler colony (with the settlers ensuring that they would be relatively free of arbitrary exactions by the state) or an extractive colony (seen by the colonizing

A potentially difficult transition to open societies

country as merely a source of rent through primary production) seems to have had an enduring effect. As North, Wallis, and Weingast (2006) have stressed, only a few countries have successfully made the transition from a rent-creating, limited-access society to an open society where private property accumulation is relatively secure against expropriation by government. And researchers are a long way from understanding how, when, and why countries are transformed from closed to open access. Yet this transformation is what is called for.

What should the institutional priorities be?

Pending success in reforming these most important—but intractable—institutions, it may be easier, and less politically contentious, to make progress on other dimensions. For example, within the category of legal institutions that support private contracting, Haselmann, Pistor, and Vig (2006) have distinguished between those that chiefly enable the individual lender to recover on a debt (for example, institutions relating to collateral) and those that are mainly concerned with resolving conflicts between different claimants (for example, bankruptcy codes). Basing their analysis on evidence from the transition economies of Central and Eastern Europe—which adopted relevant legal reforms at different times after the collapse of the planned economy system—these authors are able to show that bank lending is more sensitive to the institutions that govern individual claims than to those that resolve conflicts between multiple claimants.[10] Given the relative complexity of bankruptcy codes compared with laws and procedures related to collateral, this finding—which matches practitioner experience—is good news for governments overwhelmed with institutional reform challenges.[11]

While it is well accepted that, in addition to *legal* infrastructures, *information* infrastructures are also key for both financial depth and access, it is not so clear which of the two classes of infrastructure matter most for developing countries.

Information infrastructure appears to be especially important for poorer countries

A recent contribution by Djankov, McLiesh, and Shleifer (2007) in this area has uncovered systematic differences in the relative importance of these two dimensions of financial infrastructure to the growth of private credit. Based on a panel of aggregate data for 129 countries over 25 years, they confirm that creditor rights and the existence of credit registries, whether public or private, are both associated with a higher ratio of private credit depth to GDP, whether measured in levels or in terms of change. Interestingly, creditor rights (especially strong in countries that inherited the common law system) prove to be particularly important for private credit in the richer countries, whereas the information infrastructure (in the form of credit registries) seems to matter more in the poorer countries. Given that it is arguably easier to build credit registries and other elements of the credit information infrastructure in low-income countries than to make lasting improvements in the enforcement of creditor rights, this is a finding of considerable importance and practical value.

The private sector does, of course, have a number of ways of working around dysfunctional institutions. De la Torre and Schmukler (2004) discuss how U.S. dollar contracts (rather than local currency contracts), short maturities with rollover clauses, and contracting under foreign jurisdiction are mechanisms that cope with systemic risk arising from institutional deficiencies in developing countries. Using a remarkably detailed data set on the interest rate, collateral, and maturity of some 60,000 large bank loans in 21 countries, Qian and Strahan (2007) show how banks adapt to an environment of official corruption and defective property rights by shortening maturities and increasing collateral (thereby facilitating timely action to intervene and recover on debts that begin to look doubtful). These findings reinforce the point that even if protection of property rights is the key institution to get right, the collateral regime does act as a kind of substitute. If so, an improvement in the security of contracts can help the financial system work around the other deficiencies. Qian and Strahan note two other interesting points. Where the procedural costs of enforcing collateral are high, local banks hold a higher share of lending to unrated firms (including SMEs); foreign banks, which have to rely more on collateral, stay away. In addition, only the interest rate on secured loans to rated firms varies with the cost of enforcement—lenders have little intention of pursuing their claims on unrated firms through the courts.

Differences in the efficiency of legal systems can also affect the sectoral structure of lending. Haselmann and Wachtel (2006) show that banks in transition economies whose managers have more trust in the country's legal system also provide more SME and mortgage lending and less lending to consumers, large enterprises, and government. In Brazil banks provided payroll loans—loans whose repayment is deducted directly from the borrower's payroll check—at significantly lower rates than regular consumer loans, which were subject to the slow and inefficient recovery procedures of the Brazilian legal system (Costa and de Mello 2006).

These findings well illustrate the ability of financial intermediaries to adapt and work around *some* of the constraints and environmental deficiencies that they face.[12] This may explain why some reforms have

The private sector can adapt to weak institutions

Some reforms may require others to affect access significantly

disappointing results. For example, especially since the work of Hernando de Soto, it is commonly observed in the literature that, given the importance of collateral, and the fact that secure land titles can often be the best collateral available to a borrower, effective land titling programs should be a good way of enhancing access to credit. Yet, when individual land titling experiments in specific countries are examined—as reviewed, for example, in a recent paper by Pande and Udry (2006)—the estimated impact on credit has often been negligible and statistically insignificant. Evidently, in these cases lenders had already substantially worked around the lack of land as collateral, or repossessing the land was not possible despite the title, or the cumulative effect of other obstacles to the functioning of the credit market remained severe. In any event, the single reform of titling has in these documented cases not had the impact anticipated in the literature. Sometimes a comprehensive set of policy reforms is needed.[13]

One example of the kind of shortcut that governments can take to improve the functioning of the credit market is illustrated by the introduction in India in the 1990s of a new expedited mechanism for loan contract enforcement. As Visaria (2006) has shown, this new procedure bypassed dysfunctional court procedures and resulted in a considerable increase in loan recoveries. Furthermore, interest rates on new loans contracted after the introduction of the new mechanism were 1–2 percentage points lower because of compositional changes in banks' portfolios. Visaria is able to establish this from an econometric study exploiting the facts that only loan contracts above 1 million rupees fall under this new procedure (thus generating cross-firm variation for the analysis) and that political resistance and a court injunction had prevented simultaneous introduction of the new institution across all Indian states (thus allowing cross-time and cross-state variation and the use of the difference-in-differences estimator discussed in box 2.1).[14]

Specific Policies to Facilitate Financial Access

Policies to complement the long-term process of institution building

While indispensable for long-term sustainable broadening and deepening of financial systems, broad institution building is a long-term process. The government can achieve additional impact in the short to medium term by taking action specifically directed at facilitating financial market activity that helps access. Beyond the overall legal structure and its protections, an important practical question is the extent to which contract enforcement in finance needs to be supplemented by specific laws restricting and clarifying, and thereby offering more reliable protection to, certain types of financial contracts or financial business more generally. The trend worldwide has been to expand greatly the degree to which the law is tightly defined by statute rather than relying on judicial precedent in areas such as accountancy, banking, securities markets, unit trusts, leasing, payments, and so on. Indeed, the experience of practitioners in developing countries has been that many financial contracts simply do not happen without the presence of an adequate explicit law to clarify that the contract will have the protection of the courts. But it is possible that law and regulation can become too intrusive, to the point where they are counterproductive for access; two such areas—prudential regulation and anti-money-laundering—are touched on later.

Some of these measures for facilitating financial market activity are generally unproblematic from a policy point of view, and their implementation is constrained only by government capacity. These measures include putting in place the legislation, taxation, and other rules needed for specific financing tools and institutions such as leasing and factoring that are particularly suited to small and medium enterprises. So long as the tax arrangements are not unduly generous, these improvements will be uncontroversial.[15] Improved financial literacy might also help if it can be provided at a low cost. The capacity of individuals and entrepreneurs to take advantage of available financial services (and to avoid pitfalls) depends to some degree on adequate financial education. Other policies can be more controversial, either because they involve trade-offs between the goal of achieving enhanced access and other accepted goals of public policy, or because the improvement in access is ambiguous.

As discussed in previous chapters, credit registries—through which lenders share information about their clients' repayment records—are an established way of enhancing the ability of borrowers to signal a good credit record. Such registries have emerged in the private sector in numerous countries, but the public sector has also taken a leading or complementary role in many others (Miller 2003). Even where the operation and ownership of registries is left to the private sector, government action strongly influences the ability of registries to function. For example, given that privacy laws may severely constrain information sharing, the design of credit registries is highly relevant. Sharing of credit information strengthens the competitive environment in the credit

Credit registries can increase access by establishing a good credit record for some—

market. Incumbent banks, however, might not be interested in sharing positive information, as that increases competitive pressure from possible entrants. So the government may have to consider making information sharing mandatory, either through legislation or by regulation of licensed intermediaries. At a more prosaic level, measures such as giving every individual a national identification number can dramatically improve the ease and effectiveness of the operation of the credit information industry with regard to individual or microfinance borrowers.

—but also exclude high-risk borrowers

Some have argued that credit registries have drawbacks. While better credit information gives lenders the confidence to expand their customer base, it also enables them to identify and screen out some high-risk borrowers who might have received credit in a low-information environment. If so the improvement in access may not be uniform and may result in some groups being left even further behind. Evidence for this kind of effect comes from the so-called "home credit" market in the United Kingdom, where more refined information and credit scoring systems have resulted in the main mortgage lenders withdrawing from some geographical segments.[16] On balance, though, the indications are that the number of losers is small compared with the number of winners, and besides the losers are likely to be the least creditworthy and most prone to overindebtedness (U.K. Competition Commission 2006).

Some observers have also questioned the degree to which compulsory sharing of credit information undermines the profitability of relationship lending, thereby discouraging lenders from investing in such relationships and possibly reducing access in some market conditions (Semenova 2006). Errors and abuses in the maintenance of credit records can be damaging for individuals; regulations need to guard against such errors and to ensure that the collection and sharing of credit information does not in practice represent an unwarranted invasion of borrowers' privacy. Even the establishment of national identity numbers has been controversial from a civil liberties perspective in some countries.

Difficulties in repossessing collateral may lead to higher interest rates and reduced access

Reducing costs and increasing the certainty of registering and repossessing collateral in the event of a default is also crucial. In Brazil, for example, legal and enforcement obstacles facing lenders trying to repossess property have kept mortgage rates too high to be affordable for the poor (Kumar 2005). Residential mortgage lending remains small in scale and accessible mainly to upper-income groups, although there are a growing number of experiments in microlending for housing. Some specific legislation and other policy measures are typically called for to support developments here. For example, practitioners discuss the question of special policies to promote a market in mortgage securities that would help expand the supply and lengthen the maturity of housing loans (Chiquier, Hassler, and Lea 2004). Of course policy efforts to improve housing for a wider group go well beyond issues of housing finance.[17]

The rapidly evolving technologies based on the Internet (e-finance) and cell phones (mobile phones, or m-finance) can be powerful engines of access (Porteous 2006).[18] But a lack of legal clarity may impede the adaptation of these technologies. Government needs to keep legislation up to date not only to ensure contracting parties that what they intend will be unambiguously enforceable but also to prevent legislation from blocking new innovations. Even though most of the technical problems seem to have been readily soluble, and despite the huge potential market—probably more individuals have mobile phones than are connected to the electricity power grid in many low-income countries—m-finance has been slow to take off. A major early success was in the Philippines, where two companies signed up a total of 4 million customers. South Africa was also an early adopter of m-finance, and it has been followed in Africa by the Democratic Republic of Congo, Kenya, and Zambia, illustrating the potential for this technology (with its low marginal costs) to overcome the problem of high unit costs that shut out low-income customers in countries with relatively weak infrastructures.

But when it comes to policy design as it relates to m-finance, some unresolved problems have emerged. Defining and updating the legislation that gives participants in the market (especially providers) full legal protection for the diverse electronic transactions that are involved is a costly and difficult undertaking for low-income countries. From this point of view, providers have had to take a leap of faith to enter this market. There is also the question of regulatory barriers to entry. From a technical and financial point of view, telephone companies can provide small-scale payments services without having to draw on the services of a licensed bank. But regulation may insist that such services are provided only by a bank (as is the case in South Africa), and if so the compliance costs can be a major barrier to entry (Porteous 2006).[19] A contrasting example is Kenya, where the regulatory regime has been more open to initiatives of the phone companies, and innovation is beginning to be rewarded by relatively rapid consumer take-up.

Any payments system can entail risks of money laundering and terrorism financing, potentially justifying the imposition of AML-CFT

Legislation must adapt to new technologies—

—including m-finance

(anti-money-laundering and combating of financial terrorism) regulations. This too can become a barrier to the establishment of m-finance facilities, even though a risk-based approach would show that almost all of the m-finance customers pose negligible risks of this type.[20]

Even more controversial is the design of regulation for *securities markets*. While general principles have been agreed under the auspices of the International Organization of Securities Commissions, these can be implemented with varying degrees of formality. More formality means higher fixed costs of establishing and maintaining a stock market listing, and the result can be a crowding out of smaller issuers. Low-formality models, such as London's innovative Alternative Investment Market, rely heavily on the reputation of intermediaries known as "nominated advisers" to ensure that the issuer complies with the relevant principles. Because of its lower cost, this model has attracted a large number of issuers. This system has been criticized for not doing enough to protect investors. There is little systematic empirical evidence on this topic; however, some practitioners argue that by lowering entry costs, this kind of approach could yield substantial benefits of greater access for medium-sized issuers, especially in low-income countries (Grose and Friedman 2006).[21]

Policies to Promote Competition and Stability

The literature on the functioning of policies for financial intermediary competition, prudential regulation and supervision, and protection of the poor against abusive lending is vast; here we can only mention a small selection of relevant research findings. The reader also should bear in mind that the applicability to developing countries of lessons learned in advanced economies is not always clear. For instance, numerous deposit insurance schemes have been transplanted from advanced economy models and proved poorly adapted to the circumstances of their developing country hosts, resulting in excessive risk taking by banks and subsequent widespread fragility and crisis (Demirgüç-Kunt and Kane 2002). Regulatory institutions that have evolved in advanced country settings should not be unthinkingly transplanted to the very different political and institutional settings that prevail in most developing countries.[22]

The role of competition in enhancing access has already been discussed in chapter 2. Policy makers who seek to stimulate greater competition often have only a limited range of effective tools they can use, especially in small, low-income markets. A liberal entry policy vis-à-vis reputable financial service providers can help, but it may not be enough. Transparency of product pricing and the compulsory sharing of credit information can also help, as can rules about network access and interoperability of networks in the retail payments system, but these may not be fully effective either.

Because of their traditionally high unit costs, the main banks in most countries have been slow to provide products adapted to the needs of low-income households, even though they could be in a better position to do so than others because of the advantages of incumbency. More and more advanced economies have been adopting affirmative regulatory policies that require financial intermediaries to make appropriate products available to disadvantaged groups.[23] The features needed in such products can be deduced from the reasons given in surveys of those who do not use banking services, including the cost of banking and the risk of a costly loss of control of their finances. Among the products that could help are basic bank accounts that allow low-cost, simple transactions of modest size and that have mechanisms to protect low-income users from inadvertently triggering unauthorized overdrafts.[24] Where low-income customers represent only a fraction of a profitable banking market, the authorities can insist on such facilities being introduced without fear that the banks will exit. This might not be the case in many developing countries. But recently in South Africa, financial service providers introduced voluntarily (albeit under an implicit threat of legislation) a financial sector charter that included a basic bank account scheme.

—such as affirmative regulatory policies

More generally, as discussed in chapter 2, policies to promote competition in the banking system can also help restrain the exercise of market power that could be damaging to access. With their traditional lines of business coming under competitive pressures, incumbent institutions have an incentive to reach the underserved segments and increase the speed with which access-improving technologies are adopted.[25]

The same competition that can help foster access to financial services can also result in imprudent lending binges if it is not accompanied by a proper regulatory and supervisory framework. The financial market rules with the highest profile are the increasingly complex battery of prudential regulations imposed on banks to help minimize the risk of disruptive and costly bank failures. The contraction of credit often associated with systemic banking crises hits the poor as well as the rich—sometimes more so—and the poor are less able to bear losses (Honohan 2005a; Halac

Prudential regulation and supervision can reduce the risks of banking crises—

157

and Schmukler 2004). The goal of financial stability is thus generally aligned with that of access, although some stability-oriented measures have the potential to restrict access (box 4.1).[26]

Indeed, an important current debate among scholars centers on what style of prudential regulation works best, both in ensuring stability and avoiding potential side effects such as hindering financial sector development and facilitating corruption.

—but too much discretionary powers for bank regulators can be harmful

Barth, Caprio, and Levine (2006) have addressed this issue with regard to banking. They collected detailed information about the powers and conduct of bank supervisors in over 150 countries in 1997 and in 2001, searching for causal links between regulatory style and the performance of banking systems across the world. Based on regression analysis linking measures of national regulatory style to financial access and other economic outcomes at the individual firm level, the authors concluded that

---

Box 4.1 Basel II and access

FOLLOWING AGREEMENT AMONG THE REGULATORS of the largest industrial countries on a revised framework establishing minimum capital requirements for international trading banks and new supervisory practices, bank regulators all over the world have been taking steps to make comparable revisions in their bank regulation. The new framework, known as Basel II, is intended to avoid regulatory arbitrage by sophisticated banks by making required capital more sensitive to measurable differences in credit and other risks faced by banks. Although it is recognized as embodying technical compromises and could in certain circumstances amplify risk, Basel II's more elaborate approach to capital requirements has triggered technological advances in risk measurement by banks. There is much to be said for the drive to a more scientific approach to risk management, which has been encouraged by the Basel II process and which has the potential to improve access for creditworthy borrowers.

But Basel II also has the potential to limit firm access to finance in developing countries. For one

thing, the risk weight attached to international bank lending to some developing countries is likely to increase, especially at times of economic difficulty, and this could contribute to an onshore credit crunch affecting firm borrowers (Ferri, Liu, and Majnoni 2001).

Concerns have also been raised that foreign-owned banks, reluctant to incur the costs of multiple regulatory reporting, might pressure regulatory authorities to adopt the new system even in developing countries where the advanced risk measurement techniques of Basel II are impractical or premature (Honohan 2001). If that occurs and results in higher compliance costs for local banks and inappropriate risk rating of borrowers, access could be damaged. In addition, by failing to make full allowance for the potential for a portfolio of SME loans to achieve risk pooling, the Basel II rules miss an opportunity for banks to use improved information on the distribution of risks to make SME loans at more competitive rates (Adasme, Majnoni, and Uribe 2006).

Figure 4.1   Supervisory approaches and corruption in lending

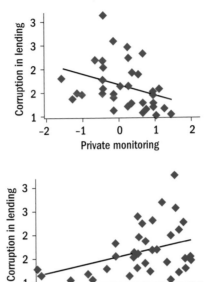

Source: Beck, Demirgüç-Kunt, and Levine (2006).
Note: This figure shows the correlation between the average financing obstacles due to corruption reported by firms and (a) the degree of private monitoring across countries and (b) the degree of supervisory power.

relying too much on discretionary powers given to government officials to keep the banking system safe, sound, and efficient may be misguided. Using the same data, Beck, Demirgüç-Kunt, and Levine (2006, figure 4.1) found that firms in countries that grant the largest discretionary powers to their bank supervisors tend to complain more that the corruption of bank officials is an obstacle to their firm's growth.[27]

Barth, Caprio, and Levine argue that for banks to promote social welfare, a country needs political and other institutions that induce its officials to develop policies that maximize social welfare, not the private welfare of officials or bankers. From this analysis, it seems that empowering and inducing large private market participants to conduct their own due diligence or monitoring of banks (for example, ensuring good disclosure of information) can be a powerful and often-neglected way of strengthening the stability of banking while at the same time improving the reach of the system. And this is not just a message for advanced economies. On the contrary, the potential for market discipline to be relatively effective even in low-income countries is often underestimated (Caprio and Honohan 2004). Similarly, ensuring that bank supervisors are independent of the political sphere and of the supervised entities themselves, while at the same time accountable to the general public is important, though often difficult to achieve given political and institutional traditions. In many countries, especially those whose law is based on civil code, supervisors are still liable for their actions, even if undertaken in good faith, making them subject to frivolous law suits. Similarly, many countries seem reluctant to give the same degree of political independence cum accountability to bank regulatory entities as they have given to central banks (Quintyn, Ramirez, and Taylor 2007).

Policies restraining abusive lending to the poor

Prudential policies, however, are important not only at the bank or system level but also at the borrower level. As discussed in chapter 3, when it comes to borrowing by the poor, more is not always better. Very poor people, especially those hit by adverse shocks, such as ill health or natural disaster, and those with chaotic lifestyles, can easily find themselves in an overborrowed situation where their inability to service accumulated debt has severe effects on their wellbeing. Most often this occurs by accident, but in some cases it can be attributable to predatory behavior by lenders deliberately exploiting the gullibility and ignorance of the borrowers to trap them in spiraling charges.

The approach of caveat emptor, which assumes that borrowers have a clear picture of the costs and benefits of entering a borrowing relationship and the capacity to make rational choices, is certainly not true for marginal groups—and the margin can be quite large in developing countries.[28] These borrowers need to be protected against abusive, deceptive, extortionate, or predatory behavior, but doing so is not easy. Although protecting the vulnerable from unwise borrowing and dealing with the overborrowed poor has long been considered an appropriate matter for public policy, as yet no generally agreed policy approach has emerged, even in the advanced economies. Policy measures to deal well with these kinds of situation may be beyond the technical capacity of many developing country governments.[29]

Interest rate ceilings are rarely effective—

One traditional approach, a ceiling on interest rates (usury laws), is still widely used, although it is increasingly considered rather ineffective as a measure, not least because opaque cost structures can result in total costs of credit greatly exceeding stated interest rates. Using what is known as "behavioral pricing," unscrupulous lenders advertise low interest rates knowing that they will attract naïve and disorganized borrowers who do not realize that their predictable behavior is sure to result in a very high overall cost of credit when penalties for late payments and other charges are factored in. At the same time, to the extent that regulators can detect and limit these extra charges, low ceilings on interest rates are clearly counterproductive if they exclude many low-income households that could be creditworthy even at the high rates needed by lenders to cover the costs of processing the borrowings. As a result, although most advanced countries still have usury ceilings, these have been relaxed or qualified by exemptions (Policis 2004; Helms and Reille 2004; Goodwin-Groen 2007). Constraints on interest ceilings do exist in numerous developing countries, and it is widely accepted that they inhibit the expansion of credit by formal and semiformal intermediaries. For some Muslims, prohibition of *riba* entails avoidance of all interest-based finance, although there are practical alternatives (box 4.2).

Allowing a category of licensed or supervised lenders to exceed the basic usury level is one device that many advanced jurisdictions have used to bring high-interest lending into the light of day, rather than consigning it to the shadows in illegality.[30] This licensing needs to be accompanied by enforceable consumer protection rules to ensure that charges are

---

Box 4.2 *Sharia*-compliant instruments for firm finance

RELIGIOUS SCRUPLES CAN RESULT IN SOME self-exclusion. To meet the financing and investment needs of Muslims whose beliefs and ethical frameworks may preclude them from using some conventional financial instruments, a large industry of *sharia*-compliant financial instruments has emerged in recent years and is being constantly refined. These instruments are scrutinized and authorized by legal scholars for their compliance with Islamic precepts. Financial instruments are prohibited if they allow forbidden forms of exploitation by charging riskless interest (*riba*); entail radically uncertain financial transactions (*gharar*) or zero-sum games of pure chance (*maysir*), especially those that involve actual or potential deception; or finance

forbidden (*haram*) activities. Experts have found ways of meeting the core financing requirements of modern economies (including insurance through *takaful*) without violating these precepts. Indeed, innovation in *sharia*-compliant financial engineering continues with the goal—shared with conventional finance—of providing for the needs of enterprise while pooling risk and assigning risk to where it can best be borne (Jaumdally 1999; Obaidullah 2005). For example, the global demand for *sukuk*, a type of Islamic bond that Malaysia helped popularize, has been growing very rapidly. In addition, many Muslims advance charitable funds (*qard al-hasan*) at a zero rate of return to help meet the financing needs of poor people.

transparent and that lenders do not make loans to those who cannot bear the service charges.[31] This approach is also used in South Africa, and it could be applied more widely in developing countries, though its effectiveness depends on the capacity of the licensing authority to enforce the accompanying rules of good lender practice. But even advanced countries have had difficulty enforcing the transparency requirements, and in an environment of widespread illiteracy, establishing what information has been provided to the borrower is not obvious. As a result, this approach is not practicable in many low-income countries.

—and may even be counterproductive

A recent comparison of consumer credit in the three largest EU economies displays the wide variation in regulatory philosophy and suggests the very considerable consequences that this variation may have for the scale and nature of the consumer credit market for middle- and low-income people. Although thorough econometric analysis is still lacking, the tighter interest ceilings (and other rules for lenders) in France and Germany may have had quite significant effects on restricting the range and availability of legally provided credit, compared with credit in the United Kingdom, and seem to have been associated with a *higher* incidence of overborrowing (Policis 2006). The fraction of borrowers who have defaulted on high-cost, subprime credit cards is much higher in U.S. states with binding usury laws than in states without such laws, pointing to the lack of other more suitable sources of credit for low-income borrowers (Policis 2004).

Even in the United Kingdom, which no longer has usury laws, a small minority of individuals in difficult circumstances has no access to legally provided credit. But when these individuals have recourse to illegal lenders, they pay on average about three times the prevailing cost of legal credit and are typically subjected to aggressive debt collection and predatory lending abuses. Usury laws in France and Germany are likely at the root of the finding that more of the destitute in those countries borrow in the illegal market than do the poor in the United Kingdom; if so, the usury ceilings effectively remove protection from them rather than giving it (Policis 2006).

Bankruptcy laws should take moral hazard into account

Overborrowing can result from misfortune as much as from abusive behavior of lenders. In that case, the primary need may be for assistance to the overborrower in finding a viable workout plan with the creditors. Some countries have formalized personal bankruptcy or administration schemes. The likely impact on credit market functioning should be borne in mind in designing public policy regarding overborrowing, respecting the danger of moral hazard behavior, the limited capacity of courts or bankruptcy tribunals, and the impracticality of having costly procedures to deal with debts of poor people that are small in absolute terms.

Public policy around the supply of credit for low-income households thus needs to ensure contract and pricing transparency, lender responsibility, and measures to facilitate workouts for the overborrowed. Many administrative resources must be used to implement and enforce these policies, and those costs must be factored into the policy design.

Government Interventions in the Market

If access to financial services is a powerful tool for reducing poverty, as many economists and policy makers argue, an a priori case might be made for subsidization. Subsidization of these fixed costs, however, would have to be justified in relation to competing demands for public funds. As chapter 3 discussed, the case for subsidization of financial services in this context is hotly contested in discussions of microfinance. The deadweight cost of diverting subsidies to intramarginal clients, especially when the target group cannot be well defined, and the risk of undercutting market innovation that could enhance access on a sustainable basis are but two of the problems cited. The fiscal costs of de facto credit subsidies can be high—often much higher than predicted ex ante (see, for example, Adams, Graham, and von Pischke 1984; and Micco, Panizza, and Yañez 2007[32]).

Interventions through taxes and subsidies—

The effectiveness of numerous official attempts to improve the reach of SME lending and the maturity structure of SME loans is doubtful (Caprio and Demirgüç-Kunt 1997; Beck and Demirgüç-Kunt 2006). Political subversion of directed credit programs has been a significant problem. Sometimes such schemes have ended up channeling sizable loans to political cronies, but politicization of small-scale lending has also been observed. It is easy to see why: extending small loans is an ideal political lever, with evident benefits and opaque costs. That is especially evident when the lenders are state-owned banks, as discussed below. Even where politicization is not a problem, attempts to redirect credit toward disadvantaged groups often seem to be ineffective.[33]

—can be politicized

Perhaps the most widely discussed policy intervention of this type was the restrictive branching law adopted in India in 1977; under this law banks wishing to open additional urban branches were first obliged to open additional rural branches. The rural locations benefited from additional banking services, although the process was not costless (box 4.3). This intriguing scheme can be considered an implicit self-financing combination of tax and subsidy, but it would be hard to judge whether the tax fell more heavily on the banks or the urban dwellers.

Ease of raising revenue from the sector has resulted in numerous other forms of tax or quasi-tax being imposed on the financial sector in most countries; not least are large and underremunerated reserve requirements and—a recent fashion—financial transactions taxes. The distortions created by these taxes have sometimes been very severe, especially when inflation is high. The potential negative impact on the outreach of the financial system from the introduction of such taxes needs to be borne carefully in mind (Honohan 2003).

Interventions through government-owned intermediaries have a poor record—

Despite a few success stories, substituting government provision of financial services for that of the market is generally considered problematic. The poor record of government development banks in delivering broad access or lowering poverty weakens the case for using this tool

---

Box 4.3 Rural branching in India

Between 1977 and 1990, the Reserve Bank of India mandated that a commercial bank could open a new branch in a location that already had bank branches only if it opened four in locations with no branches. This regulation was part of a social banking program that tried to expand access to financial services in rural areas. An ex post evaluation of this policy (Burgess and Pande 2005) shows that it had sizable effects. The 1:4 rule was a binding constraint on banks and together with a regulated branch-level loan-deposit ratio of 60 percent led to an increase in bank branches and in rural credit in less densely banked states, even after controlling for other state characteristics that might have driven branch and credit expansion. One interesting finding: whereas the presence of more bank branches in a state was associated with more rapid poverty reduction in that state in the period before and after the policy was in effect, this correlation was absent between 1977 and 1990. This finding, which is robust to

other policies introduced over the period and to controlling for endogeneity, suggests that availability of a bank branch is poverty reducing, even where the branch has been opened only as a result of the policy. The regression results imply that rural branch expansion during the policy period may have accounted for 60 percent of all rural poverty reduction during the period, largely through an increase in nonagricultural activities, which experienced higher returns than in agriculture, and especially through an increase in unregistered or informal manufacturing activities. But there was a significant downside: commercial banks incurred large losses attributable to subsidized interest rates and high loan losses—suggesting potential longer-term damage to the credit culture. Furthermore, many governments do not have the carrot of licensing branches in markets as dynamic as those of some of the largest Indian cities to compensate for the stick of compulsory rural branches.

on the credit side. Instead the evidence is that state-owned banks tend to lend to cronies, especially around the time of elections, as vividly displayed by recent detailed analysis of statistics on bank credit by Cole (2004), Dinç (2005), and Khwaja and Mian (2005), whose findings confirm numerous anecdotes.

For example, Cole has shown that government-owned banks in Indian states ramped up agricultural lending in tightly contested districts in election years. Given a history in which state governments cancelled banking debts in the past, borrowers might not only have been glad of the loan, but likely assumed that it might not have to be repaid if times became hard.[34] Dinç showed that increased lending by government-owned banks right before elections is not specific to India but can be observed in data from 22 developing countries.[35]

Drilling down to the individual loan level, Khwaja and Mian found evidence from Pakistan that politically active borrowers were able to secure larger and cheaper loans from state-owned banks and defaulted on these loans much more than other business borrowers (figure 4.2).[36] Even though not all state-owned banks performed poorly (Levy Yeyati, Micco, and Panizza 2006), this and a large body of other evidence make

—including the use of political criteria to grant loans

Figure 4.2 Size of loans by Pakistani banks

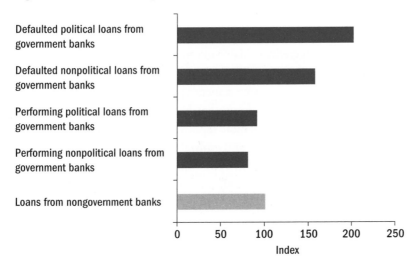

Source: Based on Khwaja and Mian (2005).

Note: Larger, politically connected loans default more than nonpolitical loans and are more likely to be from government-owned banks. There was no significant correlation between political connections and size of loan from nongovernment banks.

it easy to see why many countries have preferred to sell large state-owned banks, even to foreign-owned entities.[37]

The record is better for state-supported savings and payment services

In the case of depository services, experience has been more mixed. The postal banking service and state-supported savings banks have traditionally been seen as the providers of depository services to low-income groups. The wide geographic network of post offices and agencies makes it the tool of choice for offering basic payment and savings products in more remote areas. Japan Post Bank and the Russian Sberbank (formerly a savings bank) are among the largest retail financial institutions in the world. Indeed, in France, the right to a banking account is essentially ensured through the postal savings system. Given the sunk cost nature of the post office infrastructure, banking services can be offered at marginal costs, a fact that implies significantly lower costs in the case of low-income clients with the need for small transactions (World Bank 2006b). At the same time, examples abound of postal banks with weak financial structures because they lack a clear legal and accounting separation from the post office. Preliminary cross-country evidence on access barriers suggests that, despite explicit mandates for government banks to expand outreach, in banking systems dominated by state banks, there are fewer bank branches and automated teller machines. Customers in such systems do face lower fees, but they also experience poorer service quality (Beck, Demirgüç-Kunt, and Martinez Peria, 2007a, b).

DFIs could become more effective as providers of know-how than of credit

Some state-owned banks, designated as development finance institutions (DFIs) or development banks, have a specific public policy mandate to make long-term credit available to promote economic development in particular regions or sectors. While these banks have typically been urged to operate in as commercial a manner as is consistent with fulfilling their mandate, the difficulty of doing that has led many to reconsider their business model. A handful of more sophisticated government-owned DFIs have moved away from credit and evolved into providers of more complex financial services. Their know-how, willingness, and capacity to take initiatives that are consistent with their social remit—even at the cost of a lengthy initial period of loss-making—has allowed them to introduce into developing countries financial products and markets that have been proven elsewhere but that entail heavy setup costs without certainty of high financial return. Involving few if any credit risks, these services are less subject to political subversion. Moreover, employing public-private partnerships, the DFIs can help overcome coordination failures, first-mover disincentives, and obstacles to risk sharing and distribution.

Three examples from Mexico illustrate. One is the electronic brokerage of reverse factoring, developed by Nafin, a government development bank, which allows many small suppliers to use their receivables from large creditworthy buyers to obtain working capital financing (Klapper 2006). Another example is the electronic platform implemented by BANSEFI, another government-owned institution, to help semiformal and informal financial intermediaries reduce their operating costs by centralizing back-office operations. Finally, a government-owned DFI, turned investment bank, FIRA, has brokered quite complicated structured financial products to realign credit risks with the pattern of information between financial intermediaries and the different participants in the supply chains for several industries, including shrimp and other agrifish products (De la Torre, Gozzi, and Schmukler 2007). Given patient capital, the private sector could have undertaken each of these successful initiatives. Indeed, the Mexican government explicitly envisages privatization of at least some of these initiatives. But they have had a useful catalytic function in "kick-starting" certain financial services in Mexico.

Evaluation of interventions

It is increasingly recognized that direct interventions to support access need careful evaluation. There are at least three potentially important dimensions to the needed evaluations.

- First, a management audit is necessary to try to ensure that delivery is cost effective and that decision and control structures are optimized against best practice, with, for example, clear and effective procedures for measuring intended outputs and desired outcomes.[38]
- Second, the impact of the scheme on the intended beneficiaries must be assessed. Comparing beneficiaries before and after the intervention is not sufficient, as a recent example of a government-sponsored scheme of poverty reduction loans in China shows (Chen, Mu, and Ravallion 2006). Once the researchers controlled for the selection bias of the program targeted to poor households and for potential spillover effects to villages that were not in the program, they did not find any long-term effect on incomes, except for the poor who were relatively well educated.

The best methodology is often randomized evaluation, as discussed in chapter 3.[39] This methodology requires recording the experience both of program beneficiaries and of a control group; the latter must be selected with care to ensure that they were not excluded from the program as a result of the program's design. Unfortunately, most control groups are not selected until after the program has been started, complicating the subsequent evaluation.

- Third, general equilibrium, or "system," effects, especially of large-scale programs, must be taken into account. These are especially difficult to assess, given that they affect nonparticipants as well as participants and may be subtle. Thus, for example, it is often argued that direct provision of services below cost can undermine the capacity or motivation of private service providers to incur setup costs for competing services. This is especially important in cases where there is no clear provision that the government intervention or subsidy will end after a certain time period. Not only can governance problems undermine the effectiveness of the program but they also can have negative spillover effects on the economy at large. This is where it is important to have a good conceptual understanding of the potential processes at work and the honest and skilled use of econometric techniques to deal with endogeneity, selection bias, and errors in variables.

Overall, whereas better nutrition or education for the poor may be uncontroversial as overarching goals, the immediate goals of policy interventions to improve financial access need careful definition. Direct policy intervention has a chance of working only if attention is paid to getting four things right:

- Clarity and logical coherence of the objectives of intervention
- Governance structures that inhibit subversion of these objectives
- Control over agency costs, especially credit risk related to adverse selection and moral hazard
- Adequate technical and administrative arrangements.

A canonical example of direct intervention: the credit guarantee scheme

In the following pages we take a close look at one type of direct intervention—government-backed credit guarantees. Most of the issues that arise in designing credit guarantee schemes have their counterparts in other types of direct intervention. The details described here for credit guarantees thus carry lessons for a wide range of policy initiatives.[40]

With direct and directed lending programs somewhat in eclipse in recent years, the direct intervention mechanism of choice for SME credit activists in recent years has been the government-backed partial credit guarantee. According to Green (2003), well over 2,000 such schemes exist in almost 100 countries.[41] Thus more than half of all countries—and all but a handful of the developed countries—have some form of credit guarantee scheme, usually targeted at some sector or category of firm that is thought to be underserved by the private financial sector. Typically, these guarantee programs seek to expand availability of credit to SMEs and are sometimes focused on specific sectors, regions, or ownership groups, or on young or new technology firms (or even on firms that have been hit by an adverse shock and risk failure). Often there is a subsidiary employment, innovation, or productivity growth objective.

But these trends reflect more the disappointing experience of other forms of intervention than any substantial body of evidence that publicly funded credit guarantee schemes work well. Indeed, while new guarantee schemes are contemplated in several countries, some of the countries with the largest and longest-established guarantee schemes have been downsizing or drastically redesigning their programs.

Of course, credit guarantees are observed in private financial markets without explicit government support. They emerge typically for one of three main reasons: first, because of differential information, as where the borrower's creditworthiness is better known by a well-capitalized guarantor than by the lender; second, as a means of spreading and diversifying risk; and third, as a regulatory arbitrage, as when an unregulated firm provides a guarantee allowing the lender to bring an otherwise insufficiently secured loan into compliance with regulatory requirements or other government programs or financial industry risk-rating practices and conventions.

Government involvement in creating a credit guarantee company is often rationalized by the observation that SMEs commonly do not have the kinds of collateral that bankers require. Given that financial markets are not perfectly efficient, a decision by the government to step in where private financiers have not found it profitable to do so need not necessarily involve subsidy and fiscal outlay—although typically it does.[42] With many competing pressures for public funds, an economically coherent argument in favor of a subsidized credit guarantee system needs to go

Weighing the welfare benefits against the costs of subsidies

a lot further than the observation that such a scheme would increase the availability of credit. The government needs to be sure that such a scheme will increase overall welfare by enough to justify the subsidy cost, and not simply result in a costly distortion. A welfare economics perspective suggests three possible sources from which a net welfare improvement could come:

- *Market failure related to adverse selection.* Lending may be rationed and undersupplied relative to the social optimum (see box 1.2); in such circumstances a credit subsidy might improve overall welfare.[43]
- *Correcting for unequally distributed endowments.* Lack of collateral is most acute for low-wealth individuals and groups of people and for poorer geographical areas. However, it is far from clear that credit allocation is the best or even a good instrument to correct for unequal initial endowments.
- *Kick-starting SME lending.* SME lending is not well developed in part because lenders have not accumulated the needed practical experience and the stock of credit information, and therefore face a lengthy loss-making startup period. Credit appraisal and management can build on experience, including systemwide credit history data and credit scoring.

Reading between the lines of the diverse and often rather vaguely stated goals of publicly sponsored credit guarantee schemes, one can usually detect hints of one or more of these economists' arguments, perhaps most often the last one mentioned.[44] Whether these goals are fully achieved and at what cost is something that has never been evaluated in a fully satisfactory way even after the event, much less in advance. The evaluations that have been carried out focus on operational aspects such as ensuring that sufficient take-up or keeping the cost of the scheme within bounds.

The cost issue sometimes attracts less attention in the early days of the scheme. After all, one obvious but superficial attraction for promoters of credit guarantee schemes is that the upfront cash commitment by the government is small in relation to the total volume of credit supported by such schemes. The liabilities are contingent and in the future, while operating costs can be covered by fees and premiums paid by beneficiaries. The endowment of capital may be a small fraction—often 5 percent—of the allowed total sum guaranteed and need not be paid in cash. In due course, loan losses do emerge, and the adequacy of the

It can be difficult to evaluate the total costs of a scheme at its inception—

fees and premiums becomes evident only over time as the contingent liabilities inherent in this soft budget constraint crystallize.

Estimating likely future underwriting losses is not as easy as it might seem, especially at start-up.[45] If the target group has not been borrowing, there is little experience on which to project defaults and the consequent losses. Furthermore, default experience is highly dependent on the state of the business cycle, so that it is unwise to extrapolate from the experience of a few years. If there is a major economic downturn, then default rates and resulting losses can soar, as was seen in several East Asian countries in recent years.

In practice the range of experience regarding cost has been enormous (figure 4.3).[46] While numerous schemes have experienced much higher-than-expected losses, heavy and unanticipated underwriting costs are by no means a universal experience of credit guarantee schemes (Doran and Levitsky 1997; Bennett, Doran, and Billington 2005). This finding is consistent with the belief of many bankers that loan losses can be held to acceptable levels through good credit appraisal and monitoring practices, but that it is the cost per loan of appraisal and monitoring that under-

Figure 4.3 Estimated annual subsidy cost of selected credit guarantee schemes

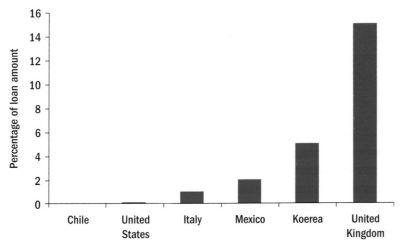

Source: Approximate figures based on data in Benavente, Galetovic, and Sanhueza 2006; Bennett, Doran, and Billington 2005; Benavides and Huidobro 2005; Zechinni and Ventura 2006; Shim 2006; and Graham 2004. The U.S. figure assumes average maturity of 13 years (U.S. General Accounting Office 1996). The U.K. figure is the 2003–4 outlay divided by that year's flow of new guarantees (Graham 2004, para 1.12); using the average of the previous 10 years' new guarantees would give a much higher figure.

mines the profitability of SME lending. If so, a well-run credit guarantee scheme may not need to be very expensive, but it may also not be enough to attract bankers into the market for loans to the target group.

—and even harder to calculate the benefits

If it is difficult to estimate the likely future cost of a credit guarantee scheme, it is even more difficult to evaluate the social benefit that results. Evidently the volume of loans guaranteed is a wholly inadequate measure of social benefit. On one hand, there might be no additionality involved—the loans might have been forthcoming anyway even in the absence of the guarantee. On the other hand, additionality might be greater than the loan amount guaranteed, as receipt of the guarantee might leverage a much more substantial, unguaranteed financing package. Most evaluations of guarantee schemes rely on the qualitative assessment of bankers and SME insiders to determine whether availability of credit to SMEs has eased. Depending on the design of the scheme and in particular on the nature of eligibility rules, formal econometric methods can sometimes be used to throw light on this question, but only a few systematic attempts to do so have been made.[47] A specific policy change in Pakistan allowed Zia (2007) to uncover credible evidence of very substantial deadweight (lack of additionality) in the subsidized export credit scheme in Pakistan.[48] By distinguishing between the experience of Chilean firms whose main bank began using the FOGAPE scheme at different times, Larraín and Quiroz (2006) estimated that microfirms whose bank used the FOGAPE scheme had a 14 percent higher probability of getting a loan. At the same time, Benavente, Galetovic and Sanhueza (2006) note evidence of sizable displacement in the scheme—for example, a large and growing share of successive guarantees being granted to the same firms.

Second, even if there is additionality, it might involve such heavy loan losses or transaction costs as to result in net welfare losses for the economy as a whole. And even if fiscal costs are low, the economic costs of misallocated resources can be high. In the Pakistan case, Zia calculated that diversion of unneeded credit to beneficiary firms could have held GDP below its potential by 0.75 percent.

Operational design is important

The operating expenses and underwriting experience of a credit guarantee scheme depend on the design of the scheme (as well as on the effectiveness of its administration). These will also clearly affect the success of the scheme in improving the availability of credit and achieving any other goals of the scheme. The first issue is pricing: systematic underpricing clearly adds to the fiscal cost of any such scheme. Three other design dimensions are worth noting.

- First is the question of whether the guarantee scheme should carry out its own credit appraisal of each final borrower who is being guaranteed. Some of the best-regarded schemes do not conduct such retail assessments but instead rely on an assessment of the intermediary whose portfolio of loans is being guaranteed.[49]

- Second is the rate of guarantee, that is, the proportion of the total loan that is guaranteed (along with related aspects, such as whether the losses are shared proportionately between lender and guarantor, or if the guarantor covers the first or last portions). Many practitioners argue that the lender should retain a significant part of the risk (at least 20 percent and preferably 30–40 percent, according to Levitzky 1997 and Green 2003), so that there will be an incentive to conduct credit appraisal. In practice, most schemes offer slightly higher rates of guarantee—70 to 80 percent being about the norm—and up to 85 percent in the case of the U.S. Small Business Administration and 100 percent in some other cases (for example, Japan). Guarantee rates significantly under 50 percent fail to attract lenders. Scaling guarantee rates according to the claims experience from each lender can improve lender incentives without the adverse distributional impact that would result from requiring final borrower guarantees. Chile's FOGAPE has started to auction available guarantee amounts, with the lenders bidding on the rate of guarantee.[50] Bankers who bid for lower guarantee rates than the maximum allowable have their requests filled; others are rationed. In practice, the auctions have resulted in the primary lender retaining between 20 and 30 percent of the risk (Benavente, Galetovic, and Sanhueza 2006; Bennett, Doran, and Billington 2005).

- Third is the nature of the lending criteria, such as the categories of eligible borrowers and the terms of the lending. Some schemes have relatively broad eligibility rules (for example, a ceiling on borrower size as measured by turnover, and a ceiling on the guarantee fund's overall exposure to the borrower). The more complex the criteria, the more likely opaque political interference with the granting of guarantees. At the same time, a broad set of criteria leaves the door open to deadweight in the allocation of subsidy to borrowers that have no need of it. Restrictions on the lending terms, such as interest ceilings, seek to limit the degree to which the lenders in an uncompetitive market capture rent from the scheme, but if these restrictions are set at unrealistic levels, they can open the door to corrupt side-payments. In practice the trend has been to move toward less complicated eligibility criteria over time.

Although Japan and Korea have had very extensive credit guarantee schemes, with the stock of guarantees exceeding 7 percent of GDP in 2001, and still in excess of 5 percent of GDP at the time of writing,[51] guarantee schemes in most countries have typically covered only a small fraction of total SME lending, and guarantees amount to a fraction of 1 percent of GDP. Sometimes this is due to capacity constraints (as in the well-regarded Chilean scheme, which covers only about one-sixth of micro-, small-, and medium-enterprise lending). In other cases it is attributable to lack of demand, which in turn can be traced to such features as excessive procedural costs, lack of lender confidence, delays in claims payments, or narrow eligibility criteria.

Subsidies are not an ingredient for success

Systematic economic evaluations do not yet offer enough evidence to form an impression of which schemes, if any, truly represent value for money. But as this brief review suggests, the lessons of operational experience are that government-sponsored credit guarantee schemes have the most to show for their efforts where they have effectively and credibly delivered an attractive package of services to lenders, with a view to enhancing their capacity to lend to the underserved sector, thereby propelling them to a sustainably higher level of lending. Innovative pricing can induce improved results (for example, better loan appraisal by lenders); even without subsidy, demand from lenders may be high where the scheme operator can add value, for example, by disseminating industry information on SME loan performance. More and more guarantee schemes are likely to move to broad eligibility and other criteria, reduced subsidies, and more use of the portfolio and wholesaling approach in preference to case-by-case evaluation by the guarantor of retail loans.

Government-sponsored credit guarantee schemes will never substitute for reform of the underlying institutional requirements of an effective credit system. The best of them can probably survive and add value even without ongoing government subsidies.

Given the checkered record of such schemes in the advanced economies, and this is true of many other types of direct government intervention in the financial market, the question is not just one of avoiding unthinking transplantation of success stories; it is more a matter of pausing to consider whether, if success is unlikely in a favorable governance and general institutional environment, an adaptation can work in the more difficult environment of the developing world?

Box 4.4   Subsidy and access

THE NET FISCAL COST INCURRED BY PUBLICLY funded credit guarantee schemes is just one example of a variety of access-related subsidies. As in other areas of development, the use of public funds is easy to justify in the interest of improving access and thereby promoting pro-poor growth. Such subsidies of course need to be evaluated against the many alternative uses of the donor or scarce public funds involved, not least of which are alternative subsidies to meet education, health, and other priority needs for the poor themselves. In practice, such a cost-benefit calculation is rarely made. Indeed, the scale of subsidy is often unmeasured.

Furthermore, as with financial sector taxation, subsidies in finance can be more liable to deadweight costs than is the case for many other sectors (Honohan 2003). It is often especially hard to ensure that finance-related subsidies reach the target group or that they have the hoped-for effect.

But an even more serious problem is the possible chilling effect of subsidies on the commercial provision of competing and potentially better services to the poor. Subsidizing finance is likely to undermine the motivation and incentive for market-driven financial firms to innovate and deliver. It is this danger—that subsidies will inhibit the viability of sustainable financial innovation—that can be the decisive argument against some forms of subsidy.

Note that it is not subsidization of the poor that should be questioned: the poor need help and subsidies in many dimensions. Subsidies to cover fixed costs (for example, in payments systems, especially when these generate network externalities) may be less subject to this chilling effect than those that operate to subsidize marginal costs. But every case must be assessed on its own merits.

Microfinance is the area of financial access where subsidies have been most debated. Many well-intentioned people have sought by means of subsidy to make credit affordable for the poor. As a result, a majority of microfinance institutions (MFIs) today—though fewer of the largest ones—operate on a subsidized basis (Cull, Demirgüç-Kunt, and Morduch 2007). Some of these subsidies are for overhead, and the MFIs do not think of them as subsidizing the interest rates. Many currently subsidized MFIs aspire to reach a break-even point and ultimately become fully profitable. Others, including the famous Grameen Bank, consciously apply subsidies to keep interest rates down. MFIs that operate group-lending schemes and that in practice are more focused on the poor rely on the highest subsidies.

While many borrowers are able and willing to service interest rates at levels that allow efficient MFIs to be fully profitable, there is no doubt that demand and borrower surplus would be even higher if interest rates were lower. Many would agree with Morduch (1999) that the prospects of reaching many of the very poor with unsubsidized credit are low. But even with a subsidy, credit will rarely be the first financial service need of the very poor. Also, apart from ensuring that the subsidy does reach its target group, the question, as always, is whether introduction of subsidy undermines the emergence of a sustainable industry with extensive—albeit incomplete—outreach.

Political Economy of Access

Politics and finance are the keys to economic access. If North, Wallis, and Weingast (2006) are correct in their view that the decisive transition in economic history is that between limited and open-access societies, to understand this transition is, as they point out, to understand modern development.

It is one thing to identify a policy measure that will achieve a net improvement in financial access at reasonable cost and limited overall side-effects. It is quite another to suppose that such a policy will automatically be implemented by an enthusiastic government.[52] Governments are, after all, operating in a political environment, and the package of policies that is implemented often owes more to the balance of political influence than to the state of knowledge about policy effectiveness.[53] Why should governments introduce reforms that might be at the expense of incumbent elites?

Existing elites may benefit from restricted access—

When the political and social structure of the state is predicated on limited access and the resulting rents, existing elites have limited enthusiasm for policies that would increase access to financial services (Rajan and Zingales 2003). It may well be, as Rajan (2006a) argues, that in unequal societies the desire of each subgroup to preserve its economic rents against all others tends to reinforce the status quo. The policy reform agenda is therefore not a simple matter of adjusting a flawed policy stance or adapting existing laws to changing market and technological realities. Instead the reforms must be far-reaching if the gain in economic performance is to be large enough to be attractive to existing elites, who will have a smaller share of the larger postreform cake. Vested interests must be convinced of the merits of transition. Making that argument is a more effective way of inducing change than direct attacks on privileges. And prioritizing financial access generates a detailed policy agenda for converting the aspiration for transition into concrete measures. For, despite the far-reaching nature of the institutional changes involved in the transition to an open-access society, it seems clear that reforms that really do improve financial access should also help drive the societal transformation. The financial access agenda thus points back to the nature of the institutional changes that are needed in society and as such provides a touchstone for reform.

The reforms needed to improve financial access as the decisive change mechanism in the economy are not only necessary but almost sufficient to define that wider policy agenda. This agenda ranges from matters of great generality down to questions of operational implementation and design. Delivering on this agenda calls on many different agencies of government and also typically needs support from external development partners. Engagement of civil society is essential to create the political environment within which governments will be induced to act.

Numerous examples can be cited from research on policy adoption to illustrate the pressures that are involved. When and how do financial sector reforms occur? What is the relative importance of private and public interest and ideology? In a classic paper, Kroszner and Strahan (1999) argued that the sequence in which U.S. states liberalized banking was consistent with the view that resistance to such policy changes was driven by the well-organized private special interest of the bankers and not by an objective or ideologically driven view of the public interest.[54] Eventually, technological progress and a competitive political system overcame the special interests of small bankers who benefited from the constraints. In contrast, Haber (2005) argues that a less competitive political system in Mexico meant that the government limited entry into the banking sector in return for favors and for financing for much longer than did the United States; as a result, by the early 20th century, Mexico was left with a much smaller, more concentrated, and more inefficient banking system.

—but vested interests can be overcome in a competitive political system—

The example of branch deregulation in the United States also shows the potential for exogenous events, such as technological innovation, to overcome political resistance to competition-enhancing reforms. As the introduction of ATMs, money market checking accounts, and improvements in communication technology have reduced the banks' need to be physically close to their clients, the monopoly power of small local banks declined and with it political resistance to change. The prospect of accession to the European Union helped many governments in transition economies to overcome political resistance against institutional reform (Beck and Laeven 2006). It is worth looking for such windows of opportunity when political resistance to reform may be weaker.

—and through technological innovation

Once started, there seems to be an internal dynamic to the process of financial sector reforms, though timing can be also be influenced by macroeconomic conditions. Based on the timing of financial liberalization in 35 countries over the period 1973–96, Abiad and Mody (2005) found that countries with highly repressed financial sectors are unlikely to reform.[55] Once reforms, even small ones, take place, however, the process builds momentum and further reforms become more likely. A balance-of-payments crisis typically triggers financial sector reforms, but a banking crisis is often associated with an interruption or reversal of liberalization.

Many other examples of political influence on financial sector policy are reported in the literature. For example, seeking to explain the frequency with which underpriced privatizations are observed, Biais and Perotti (2002) discuss how a strategic privatization program allocating left-leaning voters enough underpriced shares can induce a voting shift away from left-wing parties whose policy would reduce the values of shareholdings. Perotti and Volpin (2004) argue, with some supporting evidence, that in countries with low political accountability, incumbent firms succeed in persuading politicians not to strengthen effective investor protection in order to prevent potential entrants from raising capital.[56] Along similar lines, Feijen and Perotti (2005) suggest that, following financial liberalization (which typically results in improved access to finance by new entrants), elites successfully lobby politicians to ensure weak contract enforcement with the result that their highly leveraged recent entrant competitors are unable to refinance in downturns, and have to exit the market. And lobbying can be effective even at the micro level. Claessens, Feijen, and Laeven (2007) discovered, using data on every political donation made by Brazilian firms in the runup to the 1998 elections, that political contributions are somehow rewarded by subsequent excess returns in the stock market.

The middle classes can be powerful allies for the poor

How to help align reform-making process with public interest? This is another area where much more research is needed. Greater public awareness of the potential benefits of policies to broaden access will also be important to shift the political equilibrium in the direction of reforms that promote the public good. In this context, the challenges of financial access and financial inclusion clearly go well beyond ensuring financial services for the poor. The middle classes too have insufficient access to finance. Advertising the access agenda as a broad one that includes the middle class helps mobilize a powerful supporter in the struggle to broaden access (Rajan 2006b). The same mechanisms that expand access for middle-class households and SME entrepreneurs will often help expand the access for the very poor as well. This process will also help strengthen the links between formal and informal financial systems and allow the poor to migrate upward.

Conclusions

This chapter has highlighted the complexity of the policy challenge in improving access. The discussion has been necessarily selective, setting out principles for effective government policy by drawing on and generalizing lessons from specific examples.

Deep institutional reform that above all ensures security of property rights against expropriation by the state is an underlying, albeit often long-term, goal. Meanwhile legal and especially informational infrastructures can be strengthened to help financial institutions work around a difficult environment, thereby making the provision of wider access privately profitable.

Institutional reform and building infrastructure are key long-term priorities

Ensuring competition is an essential part of broadening access as competition encourages incumbent institutions to seek out profitable ways of providing services to previously excluded segments of the population and increases the speed with which new, access-improving technologies are adopted. In this process, providing the private sector with the right incentives is key, hence the importance of good prudential regulations. A variety of regulatory measures is needed to support wider access. Taking consumer protection against abusive lending as an example, we have shown that interest ceilings fail to address the problem adequately and can even be counterproductive; increased transparency and formalization and enforcement of lender responsibility are a more coherent approach, along with support for the overborrowed. However, delivering all of this is administratively demanding.

Ensure competition and provide the private sector with the right incentives

The scope for direct government interventions in improving access is more limited than often believed. Here, we have used credit guarantee schemes as an example of direct government intervention aimed at increasing access for SMEs. These programs can be more costly in budgetary terms than anticipated, and their performance can be improved by careful scheme design. In the absence of thorough economic evaluations of most schemes, their net effect in cost-benefit terms remains unclear.

A limited role for direct government interventions

If the interest of powerful incumbents is threatened by the potential emergence of new entrants financed by a system that has improved access and outreach, lobbying by those incumbents can block the needed reforms. A comprehensive approach to financial sector reform aiming at better access must take these political realities into account. Given that the challenges of financial inclusion and benefits from broader access go

The middle class may have the power to overcome the vested interests of the elites

179

well beyond ensuring financial services for the poor, defining the access agenda more broadly to include the middle class will help mobilize greater political support for advancing the access agenda around the world.

Notes

1. For a theoretical analysis, see Huybens and Smith (1998, 1999), among others, and for empirical analysis of the cross-country relationship between finance and inflation, see Boyd, Levine, and Smith (2001); Honohan (2003).

2. This infrastructure can also be seen as a public good that private providers are not willing to provide.

3. Recently more country-specific evidence has been accumulated through two programs conducted by the World Bank, in the latter case jointly with the International Monetary Fund. The Reports on Observance of Standards and Codes on insolvency and creditor rights, corporate governance, auditing and accounting standards, and other areas are detailed assessments of the contractual, information, and regulatory frameworks of countries and provide detailed reform suggestions. The Financial Sector Assessment Program provides a detailed assessment of the stability and development of countries' financial systems as well as road maps to short-, medium- and long-term deepening and broadening.

4. LaPorta and others (1997, 1998) (and the literature that ensued) showed that, compared with French legal origin countries, the English common law countries have deeper banking systems and securities markets, more initial public offerings, more diffuse ownership of public equity, a higher ratio of market to book value of shares (Tobin's Q), and higher dividend payouts that are more closely tied to profits. The interpretation of these findings remains quite controversial. LaPorta and others relate these outcomes to cross-legal system variation in the protection of minority shareholders and creditors and enforcement of law. Thus, to oversimplify, the common law system tends to offer stronger legal protection of shareholders and creditors, together with more efficient courts and judicial systems.

5. While most scholars believe that efficient protection of creditor and investor rights is an important determinant of financial development, there has been considerable debate as to whether the legal origin variable proposed by La Porta and others (1997, 1998) is at the root of international differences in these rights, let alone their enforcement. This variable is correlated across countries with other predetermined variables such as geographical endowments, political structures, and ethnic diversity (Beck and Levine 2005; Ayyagari, Demirgüç-Kunt, and Maksimovic 2006b, 2007c).

6. However, related work shows that the distinction between legal systems according to adaptability is not completely aligned with the difference between civil and common law (Beck, Demirgüç-Kunt, and Levine 2003). German civil code legal systems are found to be as adaptable as common law systems, suggesting reform possibilities to policy makers within the civil code legal tradition.

7. A proxy indicator for the quality of institutions that colonizers established during the 18th and 19th centuries, introduced by Acemoglu, Johnson, and Robinson (2001, 2002).

8. That is not to say that contracting institutions are of no importance. Far from it, as is shown, for example, in Cull and Xu's (2005) analysis of the contrasting experience on both of these dimensions in Chinese provinces. They find that both property rights protection and contract enforcement matter for firms' reinvestment decisions.

9. This conjecture is not inconsistent with Acemoglu and Johnson's (2005) finding that it is the private contracting institutions that remain significant in explaining stock market capitalization.

10. Given their heavier reliance on secured lending, it is not surprising that foreign bank lending increases by even more.

11. This is not to say that reform of bankruptcy code cannot have an important impact, as Gine and Love (2006) show for the case of Colombia. Once it was reformed, the country's insolvency system managed to separate viable from nonviable enterprises, allowing the former to restructure and liquidating the latter. Further, systems with effective collateral systems and ineffective insolvency systems can result in severe imbalances in the long term. In practice, designing the needed reforms requires great attention to detail if they are to work effectively. For example, practitioners may have to scrutinize such aspects as the relative priority of secured and unsecured creditors in an insolvency, the availability of corporate workout solutions, the remuneration of insolvency professionals, personal liability for officers and directors, discrimination between local and foreign creditors, stays on the premature dismemberment of a debtor's assets, and so on.

12. It is not only intermediaries that can perform the work-around. Fisman and Love (2003) found evidence that trade credit partly offsets national weaknesses in financial sector deficiencies; industries with higher dependence on trade credit financing (measured by the ratio of accounts payable to total assets) exhibit higher rates of growth in countries with relatively weak financial institutions.

13. Field and Torero (2006) and Galiani and Schargrodsky (2005) find similar results for land titling in the cases of Peru and Argentina, respectively.

In both cases the effect of land titling programs on access to finance was low or zero. In Peru, Field and Torero explain their finding with the political economy observation that freshly titled landowners feared less expropriation from lenders than before.

14. The Brazilian authorities have introduced several shortcuts to allow contracting parties to work around the painfully slow process of enforcing contracts through the court system, which can take several years. Apart from allowing payroll deduction of consumer loans, certain contract forms allow for expedited court procedures or even out-of-court enforcement (Kumar 2005).

15. Tax concessions to boost specific financial markets risk misfiring, because of the considerable potential for arbitrage. For a discussion and some overall principles, see Honohan (2003).

16. In this market, licensed lenders visit the borrowers in their homes on a weekly basis to collect the repayments, typically 3 percent of the initial amount borrowed over 55 weeks. (Ellison, Collard, and Forster 2006).

17. Pensions represent another area where details of legislative and regulatory design can be crucial. Practitioners have been studying the performance of innovative regimes such as the one in Chile, and much research still needs to be done on ensuring that pensioners get value for money and a reasonable risk-return balance (both in the accumulation and the payout phases) and that pension funds contribute to the availability of long-term and risk finance to the private sector (Rocha and Impavido 2006; Rocha and Thorburn 2007).

18. Regulatory design should ensure sufficient certainty around electronic contracting, protecting customers adequately against fraud and abuse and aiming for interoperability between the technical platforms of different suppliers. In addition, Porteous (2006) proposes three principles of good regulatory design if m-finance is to transform the payments environment for low-income customers in developing countries. First, customer due diligence procedures for account opening should be risk based and should not unduly prejudice remote account openings by small customers. Second, customers should be able at least to make deposits and withdraw cash through agents and remote points outside of bank branches. Third, adequate provision must be made for the issuance of e-money by appropriately capitalized and supervised entities, which are not necessarily banks.

19. A regulatory decision in Brazil to allow limited banking services to be operated on an agency basis by lottery offices and other bank correspondents raised similar issues, but in practice this initiative has worked effectively and has greatly improved access. By 2004 all municipalities in Brazil had some form of banking service, whereas only 29 percent had access to these services in 2000; half of the increase was exclusively attributable to correspondents (Kumar 2005).

20. More generally, the need to make AML-CFT regulations as access-friendly as possible is recognized by specialists in the field (Hernández-Coss and others 2005). To do so requires ensuring that these requirements are risk based and that they therefore do not impose documentation and verification requirements for low-income customers accessing services that have limited scope for abuse. Regulatory authorities need to engage with financial service providers to design services needed by the poor, such as basic bank accounts, in such a way that they can be safely offered without triggering AML-CFT concerns.

21. Early evidence with these separate boards suggests a higher entry and exit rate of listed companies (potentially reflecting the dynamism of the SME sector), but also lower liquidity, as most of the trading is done by institutional investors (Yoo 2007).

22. This is the case not least where regulation is in flux in the advanced economies, as with recent rules on corporate financial information. Low-income countries in particular should not be made guinea pigs for novel and untested regulatory ideas that could impose costs. Assessments being carried out by the World Bank—often in the context of the already mentioned joint World Bank-IMF Financial Sector Assessment Program, and the wider Reports on the Observance of Standards and Codes—of the compliance of individual financial systems with international financial regulations have sought to bear this potential problem in mind.

23. In the United States, there are no such requirements, but the U.S. Treasury has negotiated with a wide range of deposit-taking institutions for the establishment of limited service, low-cost accounts known as electronic transfer accounts (ETAs), into which federal payments such as Social Security can be electronically deposited, even for beneficiaries with poor credit histories (Caskey, Ruiz Duran, and Solo 2006; Claessens 2006). So far, however, only a tiny fraction of the unbanked beneficiaries of federal payments have opened such accounts.

24. For example, arranging for money entering the account to trigger automated, direct debit, bill-payment instructions so that payments cannot be made without money to cover them, a feature still lacking in the basic bank accounts recently introduced in several countries (Collard and Kempson 2005).

25. Competition policy for payments systems is an especially complex issue: new technology for retail payments requires novel theoretical analysis of the resulting two-sided markets involving both merchants and consumers (for an accessible survey, see Evans and Schmalensee 2005). There can be a tension between the desirability of achieving scale and network economies (through cooperation) and keen pricing (through competition). Specialists are still debating optimal competition policy for advanced economies, with practitioners only beginning to look at the issues for developing countries (Guadamillas 2007).

26. While protection of small depositors is important, the design of the financial safety net should minimize moral hazard, thereby reducing risk-shifting behavior from bankers to society at large.

27. Once again these are the responses to the WBES survey. Numerous firm- and country-level controls were included in the regressions, which used a sample of about 2,500 firms in 37 countries, and the likely correlation of errors across firms within countries was carefully taken into account using a clustering technique. The authors also control for each firm's response to financing obstacles generally to ensure that what is being measured as corruption is not just a generalized complaint about lack of access.

28. Indeed, the notion that consumer borrowing decisions are rationally made is undermined by clear evidence from an interesting experiment conducted recently in South Africa by a large consumer lender. Loan offers with randomized interest rates were mailed to some 50,000 customers, along with numerous variants of advertising material. The researchers (Bertrand and others 2005) found that loan demand was sensitive not only to the quoted interest rates but to several of the advertising devices. For example, including a photograph of a woman in the accompanying literature (as opposed to a man) was, in terms of its influence on loan take-up, equivalent to lowering the rate of interest by over 4 percentage points a *month*.

29. Extortionate or predatory behavior is particularly hard to define. In more than 30 years of operation, the U.K. legislation against "extortionate lending" led to only 10 successful claims by borrowers. New legislation enacted in 2006 broadens the criteria by which lending may be found "unfair" and thus illegal (U.K. Department of Trade and Industry 2003).

30. This could happen either by removing the ceiling altogether or by retaining it at a fairly high rate for licensed lenders. In Ireland the annual percentage rate of 200 percent still applies to licensed money lenders (compared with the traditional ceiling of 23 percent for unlicensed lenders). The 200 percent ceiling appears to be constraining at very short maturities for the main lenders in the high-risk market but not for maturities of several months or more (U.K. Competition Commission 2006). Of course much higher interest rates (in the millions of percent per year) have been documented all over the world in illegal or unregulated lending to unfortunate individuals.

31. Such requirements should not be too draconian, as where unfavorable registration on the national credit registry is enough to exclude a borrower from future loans.

32. Using an eight-year bank-level dataset for over 100 countries Micco, Panizza, and Yañez (2007) confirm that state-owned banks in developing countries are less profitable than privately owned banks because of lower margins and higher overhead costs, even after controlling for the dynamics of ownership over time, most notably regarding privatization. The relationship is much weaker in

developed countries. Of special interest is the finding that state-owned banks report higher profits in years of economic expansion compared to privately-owned banks, but they are much less profitable in election years, a result which, because it is driven by differences in net interest margins rather than overhead costs, points to loan losses (or debt forgiveness) in those years.

33. Even the U.S. Community Reinvestment Act may have had little effect, at least in its early years. Introduced in 1977, this law is sometimes pointed to as an example of a well-functioning directed credit program. Banks are rated on their "efforts in determining community credit needs, marketing credit, participating in community development, maintaining branch offices and avoiding discriminatory credit policies" in low-income neighborhoods. But, at least before 1997–98, they were not assessed on whether they actually lent more to target groups. Indeed, Dahl, Evanoff, and Spivey (2000) found that banks whose performance under the law was downgraded did not respond by increasing the share of their lending to target groups.

34. Cole analyzed the allocation of agricultural credit from government-owned banks in India and found a strong suggestion of political influence. Across a sample of 412 districts in 19 Indian states in each year 1992–99, and including 32 elections, he finds that not only did credit increase in election years but the election-year credit surge was greatest in the districts most closely contested. Given that it is state-level governments that appoint members of the coordinating committee for lending practices and policies, political pressure can be coming from different parties in different states even in the same year, a feature of the data that helped pinpoint likely political effects.

35. Using a sample of 22 developing countries with 10 banks from each country over the period 1993–2000, Dinç found that in the months before elections, government-owned banks increase their lending—and the amount of loans restructured or overdue—relative to privately owned banks. This suggests not only politically motivated lending at government-owned banks but also loan forgiveness before elections.

36. Khwaja and Mian analyzed all 112,685 business loan accounts at banks in Pakistan during 1996–2002 and uncovered strong circumstantial evidence of corruption at state-owned banks. The loan files contained the names of the borrowing companies' directors, which allowed the authors to link them with the names of all of the candidates in the 1993 and 1997 general elections. Fully one-quarter of the candidates were directors of borrowing firms. More important, their firms borrowed more, paid lower interest rates, and defaulted more often (a 24 percent default rate, compared with a 6 percent for others, even after inclusion of firm-level control variables). These effects proved to be entirely attributable to borrowing from state-owned banks—implying sizable fiscal costs as well as the costs from misallocation of investable funds—and they were larger, the more electorally successful the politician. The effects are smaller in districts with a healthier democratic process, as measured by voter turnout.

37. See World Bank (2001) and Hanson (2004) for other reviews of the experience with state-owned banks.

38. For some examples related to financial access, see http://www.ifc.org/ifcext/sme.nsf/Content/Publications.

39. Also see Duflo and Kremer (2005) for a discussion of the relative merits of randomized evaluation and competitors such as propensity score testing and the difference-in-difference methods for estimating the partial equilibrium effects on beneficiaries of direct policy interventions.

40. The analysis of credit guarantee schemes displays some similarities and some contrasts with that of deposit insurance schemes (Demirgüç-Kunt and Kane 2002). In both types of schemes, the benefits of expanding access have to be balanced with the moral hazard risk. Perhaps the main difference is that coverage of a credit guarantee scheme can be credibly limited, whereas deposit insurance guarantees tend to be extended to all depositors, especially in a crisis. In addition, pricing and other features of credit guarantees can more easily be made realistically risk-related. For example a sizable degree of coinsurance is the norm with credit guarantees, and coverage can vary. But, as is argued in the text, just as with deposit insurance, success is less likely in poor institutional environments.

41. Curiously, the large, publicly funded SHG-bank linkage program in India, which provides subsidized refinancing (by NABARD) of bank loans to self-help groups, directly benefiting about 14 million households, offers no loan-loss guarantee to the bank.

42. For example, government interventions in every one of the 25 EU member states involve subsidies or fiscal outlays, according to Dorn (2005); 47 EU schemes are reviewed by Gracey (2001).

43. Note, however, that this line of reasoning is more specific than is often portrayed. Depending on the exact nature of project risks and of the information asymmetries between lenders and borrowers, there might even be *more* lending than is socially optimal (DeMeza and Webb 1987; Besley 1994). The successful operation of MFIs that charge high interest rates shows that this problem is not decisive in all markets.

44. Even in the United Kingdom, the stated purpose of the government's Small Firms' Loan Guarantee (SFLG) scheme has been simply the limited, instrumental one of assisting "SMEs who have a viable business plan but lack the collateral necessary to secure the loan that they seek."

45. Even the U.S. Small Business Administration's (SBA) long-established SME guarantee scheme (the so-called section 7a scheme) has been criticized for poor underwriting loss estimates (U.S. General Accounting Office 2001). Curiously,

though, the SBA erred on the conservative side in this matter; its actual underwriting losses turned out to be considerably lower than had been budgeted.

46. The highly regarded Chilean FOGAPE scheme has increased its annual charge to between 1 and 2 percent of the loan amount depending on the claims performance of participating banks; to date, the charges have been sufficient to cover the administrative expenses of the scheme as well as claims (Benavente, Galetovic, and Sanhueza 2006; De la Torre, Gozzi, and Schmukler 2007). Schemes in Malaysia and Thailand have also required very little subsidy over the years. The long-running SBA section 7a program in the United States entails a one-time subsidy of only about 1.3 percent of the value of the guaranteed loans, including provision for calls on the guarantee and operating expenses. The annual subsidy for the Italian SGS system grew to about 1 percent by 2004. Other programs have had higher costs. The charges of between 0.5 and 4 percent of the sum guaranteed by Mexican schemes cover only about half of the operating costs and underwriting losses (Benavides and Huidobro 2005). The very large Korean KCGF charges between 0.5 percent and 2 percent depending on the borrower's credit rating, with an average of just over 1 percent, but this revenue covers only a fifth of the scheme's outlays. Indeed the two major Korean schemes operated at a loss of almost 4 percent a year of the stock of outstanding guarantees in 2001–5 (Shim 2006). Over the years, the (much smaller) U.K. SFLG scheme—which charges an annual 2 percent fee—had experienced defaults on more than one in three of its guaranteed loans, requiring a subsidy amounting in a recent year to 15 percent of gross new guarantees in that year (Graham 2004).

47. One recent attempt to use quantitative information to estimate additionality is Zecchini and Ventura (2006), who compare data on some 4,000 Italian firms eligible for the SGS guarantee scheme and 6,000 controls—firms that were not eligible because of their sector. Estimating a regression equation explaining the level of bank borrowing by firm in terms of the firm's number of employees, sales, tangible and intangible assets, nonbank debt, net worth, and net earnings, they find that, even after taking account of eligibility (using an instrumental variables technique), a firm's use of SGS guarantees is associated with a modestly higher level of bank borrowing (about 10–13 percent). Another econometric effort was made by KPMG Management Consulting (1999), but it looked only at assisted borrowers and did not include a control group.

48. The key natural experiment allowing identification of the effect of subsidized export credit was the removal of one important sector, cotton yarn, from eligibility for subsidy. Apparently the authorities wanted to concentrate available funds on export sectors with higher value added. The cotton yarn sector, which had accounted for over half of the 100,000 individual loans made in the scheme between 1998 and 2003, survived this removal with output and exports almost unaffected. While some smaller, unlisted firms without multiple banking relationships were hit by the change, the larger firms just saw a reduction in their profits. An estimated one-half of the subsidized funds had gone to financially

unconstrained firms that did not need it. Interestingly, it was not systematically the less-productive firms that were hit by the removal of the subsidy.

49. A third form is the wholesale guarantee of, for example, a bond issue by a specialized SME lender, a securitization of the underlying loans, or a block loan to a specialized lender by another intermediary. The Italian SGS provides counterguarantees on a wholesale basis to mutual guarantee associations for bank loans of their members. Accion International has had many years of experience on a cross-country basis in wholesale guarantees of facilities provided to its local affiliates.

50. This can be seen as an application of the increasingly fashionable idea of auctioning a block of subsidy funds to the highest bidder. In finance, the risk that the beneficiary will ultimately default, thereby eventually paying much less than she promised, makes auctioning of rather limited application. It can work in the case at hand, where the block of funds and the subsidy involved is only a small part of the bidder's business.

51. Chinese guarantee funds, some of which are publicly backed but result from regulatory arbitrage, were estimated to cover loans amounting to 2.6 percent of GDP in 2005 (Shim 2006).

52. Sometimes such measures can also be undermined by judicial decisions, as is illustrated by the case of payroll loans in Brazil, which were declared unconstitutional by a court, leading to higher borrowing costs (Costa and de Mello 2006).

53. The study of Braun and Raddatz (2007) provides an excellent example of this. Distinguishing between economic sectors that are more or less likely to favor financial liberalization, the authors were able to show that in countries in which the economic power of the former grew (as a result of trade liberalization), subsequent financial deepening was faster.

54. Specifically, Kroszner and Strahan (1999) examined the removal of restrictions on branch banking. They trace the origin of these restrictions to the interest that 19th century state governments had in creating local banking monopolies that could be taxed. Resistance in the 20th century to deregulation came from the incumbent small banks, and indeed it was the states with many small banks that deregulated last.

55. They constructed an indicator of financial liberalization encompassing credit and interest rate controls, entry barriers, restrictive regulations, government ownership, and restrictions on international financial transactions.

56. From cross-country evidence from 38 countries they find that greater political accountability is associated with higher entry in sectors that are more dependent on external capital and have greater growth opportunities.

Data Appendix

TABLES A.1 TO A.7 PRESENT DATA COLLECTED FOR AND USED IN THIS book and its background papers on indicators of use of, access to, and bariers to financial services. The data are also available at http://econ .worldbank.org/programs/finance.

Table A.1 Composite measure of access to financial services

		Percent with access			Percent with access			Percent with access
Albania		34	Gambia, The		21	Panama		46
Algeria		31	Georgia		15	Papua New Guinea		8
Angola		25	Germany	s	97	Paraguay		30
Antigua and Barbuda		48	Ghana		16	Peru		26
Argentina		28	Greece	s	83	Philippines		26
Armenia	s	9	Grenada		37	Poland	s	66
Austria	s	96	Guatemala		32	Portugal	s	84
Azerbaijan		17	Guinea		20	Romania	s	23
Bahamas, The		53	Guyana		20	Russian Federation		69
Bangladesh		32	Haiti		15	Rwanda		23
Barbados		56	Honduras		25	Samoa		19
Belarus		16	Hungary	s	66	Saudi Arabia		62
Belgium	s	97	India	s	48	São Tomé and Principe		15
Belize		46	Indonesia		40	Senegal		27
Benin		32	Iran, Islamic Rep. of		31	Seychelles		41
Bermuda		48	Iraq		17	Sierra Leone		13
Bhutan		16	Ireland	s	88	Singapore		98
Bolivia		30	Italy	s	75	Slovak Republic	s	83
Bosnia and Herzegovina		17	Jamaica	s	59	Slovenia	s	97
Botswana	s	47	Jordan		37	Solomon Islands		15
Brazil	s	43	Kazakhstan		48	South Africa	s	46
Bulgaria	s	56	Kenya	s	10	Spain	s	95
Burkina Faso		26	Korea, Rep. of		63	Sri Lanka		59
Burundi		17	Kyrgyz Republic		14	St. Kitts and Nevis		49
Cambodia		20	Latvia	s	64	St. Lucia		40
Cameroon		24	Lesotho	s	17	St. Vincent		45
Canada	s	96	Liberia		11	Sudan		15
Cape Verde		40	Libya		27	Suriname		32

Table A.1 Composite measure of access to financial services *(continued)*

Central African Republic		19	Lithuania	s	70	Swaziland	s	35
Chile		60	Luxembourg	s	99	Sweden	s	99
China	s	42	Macedonia, FYR		20	Switzerland		88
Colombia	s	41	Madagascar		21	Syrian Arab Rep.		17
Comoros		20	Malawi		21	Tajikistan		16
Congo, Rep. Of		27	Malaysia		60	Tanzania	s	5
Costa Rica		29	Mali		22	Thailand		59
Cote d'Ivoire	s	25	Malta	s	90	Togo		28
Croatia		42	Mauritius		54	Trinidad andTobago		53
Cuba		45	Mexico	s	25	Tunisia		42
Cyprus	s	85	Moldova		13	Turkey		49
Czech Republic	s	85	Mongolia		25	Uganda		20
Denmark	s	99	Morocco		28	Ukraine		24
Dominica		66	Mozambique		12	United Kingdom	s	91
Dominican Republic		29	Myanmar		19	United States	s	91
Ecuador	s	35	Namibia	s	28	Uruguay		42
Egypt, Arab. Rep. of		41	Nepal		20	Uzbekistan		16
El Salvador		26	Netherlands		100	Venezuela, R. B. de		28
Eritrea		12	Nicaragua	s	5	Vietnam		29
Estonia	s	86	Niger		31	West Bank and Gaza		14
Ethiopia		14	Nigeria		15	Yemen, Republic of		14
Fiji		39	Norway		84	Yugoslavia, former		21
Finland	s	99	Oman		33	Zambia		15
France	s	96	Pakistan	s	12	Zimbabwe		34
Gabon		39						

Note: The composite indicator measures the percentage of the adult population with access to an account with a financial intermediary. The indicator is constructed as follows: for any country with data on access from a household survey, the surveyed percentage is given and designated by an *s*. For other countries, the percentage is constructed as a function of the estimated number and average size of bank accounts, as discussed in box 1.4 and Honohan (2007). These numbers are subject to estimation error. This is a "live" data set, and figures will be replaced as survey data become available for each country. See http://econ.worldbank.org/programs/finance for updates.

Table A.2 Use of loan and deposit services across economies

	Loan accounts per capita (number)	Loan-income ratio	Deposit accounts per capita (number)	Deposit-income ratio	Ratio of private credit to GDP (average 1999 to 2003)	GDP per capita, 2003 ($)
Albania	4.42	15.41	161.25	2.75	—	1,933
Argentina	154.19	1.77	368.73	0.58	0.205	3,381
Armenia	41.23	1.93	111.38	1.00	0.076	915
Austria	647.64	1.84	3,119.95	0.26	1.025	31,202
Bangladesh	54.73	5.22	228.75	1.60	0.245	376
Belgium	59.47	21.09	3,080.31	0.38	0.773	29,205
Bolivia	9.53	27.89	40.63	5.81	0.558	894
Bosnia and Herzegovina	114.09	3.19	429.40	1.87	—	1,682
Brazil	49.59	6.18	630.86	0.40	0.346	2,788
Bulgaria	73.85	4.24	1,351.37	0.26	0.149	2,538
Chile	417.74	1.6	1,044.82	0.46	0.694	4,591
Colombia	—	—	612.21	0.42	0.262	1,747
Czech Republic	—	—	1,922.83	0.42	0.424	8,375
Denmark	450.99	2.09	2,706.07	0.22	1.100	39,429
Dominican Republic	50.10	6.71	719.52	0.10	0.335	1,821
Ecuador	77.09	2.63	419.54	0.63	0.353	2,066
El Salvador	126.89	0.39	456.69	0.12	0.047	2,204
Fiji	67.09	4.75	444.42	1.13	0.322	2,696
France	—	—	1,800.84	0.40	0.857	29,267
Greece	776.48	0.83	2,417.64	0.29	0.546	16,203
Guatemala	45.79	3.19	403.54	0.55	0.189	2,009
Guyana	—	—	571.03	1.37	—	965
Honduras	67.27	6.13	287.27	0.74	0.388	1,001
Iran, Islamic Rep. of	48.19	2.91	2,249.28	0.04	0.281	2,061
Israel	709.90	1.58	—	—	0.859	16,686
Italy	328.15	2.35	975.64	0.47	0.750	25,429
Jordan	80.39	8.2	465.48	1.41	0.721	1,858
Kenya	—	—	69.98	6.26	0.258	434
Lebanon	93.42	9.13	382.53	6.65	—	4,224
Lithuania	58.86	3.65	1,166.45	0.21	0.128	5,273
Madagascar	4.38	18.35	14.46	9.31	0.081	323
Malaysia	328.97	2.95	1,250.10	0.92	1.352	4,164
Malta	407.21	6.24	2,495.81	1.22	1.083	9,699

Table A.2 Use of loan and deposit services across economies *(continued)*

	Loan accounts per capita (number)	Loan-income ratio	Deposit accounts per capita (number)	Deposit-income ratio	Ratio of private credit to GDP (average 1999 to 2003)	GDP per capita, 2003 ($)
Mauritius	207.13	2.75	1,585.99	0.53	0.559	4,265
Mexico	—	—	309.57	0.46	0.181	6,121
Namibia	80.74	5.16	422.96	1.27	0.438	2,312
Nicaragua	95.61	2.49	96.12	4.70	0.424	748
Norway	—	—	1,610.78	0.23	0.870	48,592
Pakistan	21.93	14.26	191.84	2.63	0.260	464
Panama	297.84	5.32	—	—	0.922	4,328
Papua New Guinea	—	—	119.77	2.48	0.147	617
Peru	77.92	2.45	316.19	0.74	0.248	2,247
Philippines	—	—	302.05	1.77	0.405	989
Poland	773.87	0.33	—	—	0.265	5,487
Romania	—	—	1,207.88	0.25	0.073	2,719
Russian Federation	54.11	4.23	1,892.28	0.07	—	3,022
Saudi Arabia	47.45	7.73	214.13	2.28	0.554	8,366
Singapore	513.23	3.84	1,670.88	1.62	1.159	21,492
Spain	556.48	1.91	2,075.96	0.44	0.992	20,343
Switzerland	—	—	1,985.84	0.29	1.589	42,138
Thailand	247.87	4.56	1,423.12	0.83	1.044	2,309
Trinidad and Tobago	—	—	1,073.48	0.35	0.404	7,769
Turkey	264.51	0.65	1,114.23	0.68	0.171	3,365
Uganda	5.79	10.74	46.64	3.93	0.051	245
Venezuela, R. B. de	93.04	1.02	486.74	0.48	0.110	3,319
West Bank and Gaza	50.15	8.25	253.99	4.91	—	1,026
Zimbabwe	—	—	173.56	7.98	0.235	634

Note: Reported indicators are based on data collected through a survey of bank regulators, as discussed in box 1.4 and Beck, Demirgüç-Kunt, and Martinez Peria (2007b). Loan (deposit) accounts per capita refer to the number of loans (deposits) per 1,000 people. Loan (deposit)-income ratio refers to the average size of loans (deposits) per GDP per capita. The survey questions asked are: "How many loans are there in your country right now that have been issued by deposit money banks? (Please include loans from deposit money banks to individuals, businesses and others, including home mortgages, consumer loans, business loans, trade loans, student loans, emergency loans, agricultural loans, etc.)," "What is the total value of these loans? (Please specify currency and units.)," "How many deposit accounts are there at deposit money banks in your country right now? (Please include all current (checking) accounts, savings accounts, and time deposits for businesses, individuals, and others.)," and "What is the total value of these deposits? (Please specify currency and units.)." Private credit to GDP is the ratio of claims of financial institutions on the private sector to GDP and is obtained from the World Bank Financial Structure and Economic Development Database. GDP per capita is in US$ and is taken from World Development Indicators. Data are available at http://econ.worldbank.org/programs/finance. — = data not available.

Table A.3 Branch and ATM penetration across economies

	Geographic branch penetration (number)	Demographic branch penetration (number)	Geographic ATM penetration (number)	Demographic ATM penetration (number)	Ratio of private credit to GDP (average 1999 to 2003)	GDP per capita, 2003 ($)
Albania	2.45	2.11	2.74	2.37	—	1,933
Argentina	1.40	10.01	2.09	14.91	0.205	3,381
Armenia	8.23	7.59	1.49	1.37	0.076	915
Australia	0.77	29.86	1.66	64.18	0.879	26,062
Austria	52.47	53.87	84.95	87.21	1.025	31,202
Azerbaijan	3.90	4.11	—	—	—	865
Bahrain	135.21	13.48	269.01	26.83	0.576	10,791
Bangladesh	47.46	4.47	0.61	0.06	0.245	376
Belarus	2.28	4.79	2.41	5.06	0.070	1,770
Belgium	181.65	53.15	229.28	67.09	0.773	29,205
Belize	1.67	14.67	—	—	0.543	3,583
Bolivia	0.13	1.53	0.40	4.80	0.558	894
Bosnia and Herzegovina	3.15	3.86	4.38	5.36	—	1,682
Botswana	0.11	3.77	0.27	9.00	0.163	4,290
Brazil	3.05	14.59	3.72	17.82	0.346	2,788
Bulgaria	9.81	13.87	21.09	29.79	0.149	2,538
Canada	1.56	45.60	4.64	135.23	0.967	26,380
Chile	1.98	9.39	5.06	24.03	0.694	4,591
China	1.83	1.33	5.25	3.80	1.236	1,094
Colombia	3.74	8.74	4.10	9.60	0.262	1,747
Costa Rica	7.52	9.59	10.07	12.83	0.240	4,365
Croatia	18.62	23.36	31.96	40.10	0.416	6,356
Czech Republic	14.73	11.15	25.84	19.57	0.424	8,375
Denmark	47.77	37.63	66.51	52.39	1.100	39,429
Dominican Republic	10.83	6.00	27.24	15.08	0.335	1,821
Ecuador	4.38	9.30	2.97	6.32	0.353	2,066
Egypt, Arab Rep. of	2.45	3.62	1.21	1.78	0.579	1,220
El Salvador	14.58	4.62	34.89	11.07	0.047	2,204
Estonia	4.85	15.19	18.43	57.7	0.248	6,210
Ethiopia	0.28	0.41	—	—	0.294	97
Fiji	2.52	5.51	5.69	12.46	0.322	2,696
Finland	3.26	19.06	13.55	79.21	0.558	31,007
France	46.94	43.23	76.33	70.30	0.857	29,267
Georgia	2.32	3.14	0.86	1.17	—	768
Germany	116.90	49.41	144.68	61.16	1.178	29,081
Ghana	1.43	1.60	—	—	—	375
Greece	25.53	30.81	39.39	47.55	0.546	16,203
Guatemala	11.49	10.12	22.93	20.20	0.189	2,009
Guyana	0.12	3.12	0.25	6.50	—	965

Table A.3 Branch and ATM penetration across economies *(continued)*

	Geographic branch penetration (number)	Demographic branch penetration (number)	Geographic ATM penetration (number)	Demographic ATM penetration (number)	Ratio of private credit to GDP (average 1999 to 2003)	GDP per capita, 2003 ($)
Honduras	0.46	0.73	2.22	3.56	0.388	1,001
Hungary	31.04	28.25	32.30	29.40	0.309	8,182
India	22.57	6.30	—	—	0.277	563
Indonesia	10.00	8.44	5.73	4.84	0.236	971
Iran, Islamic Rep. of	3.40	8.39	0.51	1.25	0.281	2,061
Ireland	13.41	23.41	27.78	48.49	1.020	37,637
Israel	47.82	14.74	61.01	18.81	0.859	16,686
Italy	102.05	52.07	131.71	67.20	0.750	25,429
Japan	34.82	9.98	396.98	113.75	1.115	34,010
Jordan	5.98	10.02	5.60	9.38	0.721	1,858
Kazakhstan	0.14	2.47	0.39	7.01	0.125	1,995
Korea, Rep. of	65.02	13.40	436.88	90.03	1.197	12,634
Kuwait	11.05	8.27	26.32	19.69	0.644	14,848
Kyrgyz Republic	0.82	3.11	—	—	0.041	344
Lebanon	79.18	18.01	73.90	16.81	—	4,224
Lithuania	1.81	3.39	15.34	28.78	0.128	5,273
Madagascar	0.19	0.66	0.07	0.22	0.081	323
Malaysia	7.39	9.80	12.40	16.44	1.352	4,164
Malta	375.00	30.08	462.50	37.09	1.083	9,699
Mauritius	71.92	11.92	133.00	22.04	0.559	4,265
Mexico	4.09	7.63	8.91	16.63	0.181	6,121
Namibia	0.11	4.47	0.30	12.11	0.272	2,312
Nepal	2.96	1.72	0.15	0.09	0.272	237
Netherlands	163.81	34.23	223.02	46.60	1.407	31,548
New Zealand	4.19	28.04	7.53	50.36	1.101	19,021
Nicaragua	1.29	2.85	1.18	2.61	0.424	748
Nigeria	2.41	1.62	—	—	0.136	370
Norway	3.41	22.92	—	—	0.870	48,592
Pakistan	9.10	4.73	1.02	0.53	0.260	464
Panama	5.16	12.87	6.49	16.19	0.922	4,328
Papua New Guinea	0.20	1.64	—	—	0.147	617
Peru	0.89	4.17	1.24	5.85	0.248	2,247
Philippines	21.40	7.83	14.52	5.31	0.405	989
Poland	10.25	8.17	21.72	17.31	0.265	5,487
Portugal	57.45	51.58	121.50	109.09	1.318	14,665
Romania	13.26	13.76	12.02	12.47	0.073	2,719
Russian Federation	0.19	2.24	0.53	6.28	—	3,022
Saudi Arabia	0.56	5.36	1.54	14.70	0.554	8,366
Singapore	636.07	9.13	2,642.62	37.93	1.159	21,492
Slovak Republic	11.33	10.28	32.21	29.21	0.441	5,922

(continued)

Table A.3 Branch and ATM penetration across economies *(continued)*

	Geographic branch penetration (number)	Demographic branch penetration (number)	Geographic ATM penetration (number)	Demographic ATM penetration (number)	Ratio of private credit to GDP (average 1999 to 2003)	GDP per capita, 2003 ($)
Slovenia	2.14	2.19	64.56	66.14	0.352	13,383
South Africa	2.22	5.99	6.49	17.50	0.689	3,530
Spain	78.90	95.87	104.18	126.60	0.992	20,343
Sri Lanka	20.41	6.87	10.91	3.67	0.274	965
Sweden	4.74	21.80	6.43	29.56	0.830	33,586
Switzerland	70.54	37.99	131.10	70.60	1.589	42,138
Tanzania	0.23	0.57	0.07	0.17	—	275
Thailand	8.71	7.18	20.69	17.05	1.044	2,309
Trinidad and Tobago	23.59	9.22	52.44	20.49	0.404	7,769
Turkey	7.81	8.50	16.54	18.00	0.171	3,365
Uganda	0.67	0.53	0.90	0.70	0.051	245
Ukraine	—	—	0.78	0.93	—	1,024
United Kingdom	45.16	18.35	104.46	42.45	1.301	30,278
United States	9.81	30.86	38.43	120.94	1.628	37,388
Uruguay	1.23	6.39	—	—	0.517	3,308
Venezuela, R. B. de	1.28	4.41	4.81	16.60	0.110	3,319
West Bank and Gaza	18.33	3.27	18.17	3.24	—	1,026
Zambia	0.21	1.52	0.09	0.65	—	413
Zimbabwe	1.11	3.27	1.15	3.38	0.235	634

Note: Reported indicators are based on data collected through a survey of bank regulators, as discussed in box 1.4 and Beck, Demirgüç-Kunt, and Martinez Peria (2007b). Geographic branch (ATM) penetration refers to the number of branches (ATMs) per 1,000 square kilometers. Demographic branch (ATM) penetration refers to the number of branches (ATMs) per 100,000 people. The questions asked were: "How many bank branches do deposit money banks have (combined for all banks) in your country?" "How many ATMs (automated cash withdrawal machines) are there in your country?" Private credit to GDP is the ratio of claims of financial institutions on the private sector to GDP and is obtained from the World Bank Financial Structure and Economic Development Database. GDP per capita is in US$ and is taken from World Development Indicators. Data are available at http://econ.worldbank.org/programs/finance. — = data not available.

Table A.4 Barriers to deposit services

| | Physical access | | | Affordability | | | | | | Eligibility | |
	Number of banks responding	Deposit market share (respondents share out of total system) 2004	Locations to open deposit account (out of 3)	Minimum amount to open checking account (% of GDPPC)	Minimum amount to open savings account (% of GDPPC)	Minimum amount to be maintained in checking account (% of GDPPC)	Minimum amount to be maintained in savings account (% of GDPPC)	Annual fees checking account (% of GDPPC)	Annual fees savings account (% of GDPPC)	Number of documents to open checking account (out of 5)	Number of documents to open savings account (out of 5)
Albania	5	91.42	2.73	0.85	6.08	0.85	6.08	0.19	0.39	1.00	1.00
Argentina	2	17.90	1.59	4.85	2.85	0.00	0.00	2.06	1.13	3.41	2.00
Armenia	4	59.63	1.81	10.97	15.25	10.56	15.25	0.35	0.00	2.85	2.19
Australia	2	32.59	2.59	0.00	0.00	0.00	0.00	0.16	0.10	3.00	3.00
Bangladesh	5	56.98	2.00	2.28	0.89	2.28	0.79	0.00	0.00	4.57	4.57
Belarus	3	74.58	2.71	0.00	0.04	0.00	0.00	0.09	0.00	1.44	1.00
Belgium	3	72.56	2.00	0.00	0.00	0.00	0.00	0.09	0.00	1.80	1.80
Bolivia	4	58.04	2.00	17.40	0.81	25.44	3.93	0.83	1.78	2.53	2.33
Bosnia and Herzegovina	4	64.04	2.60	0.04	0.04	0.19	0.15	0.34	0.35	1.74	1.34
Brazil	4	64.35	2.44	0.00	0.10	0.00	0.00	0.81	0.03	2.67	2.16
Bulgaria	3	34.87	2.02	0.59	0.88	0.59	0.91	0.14	0.00	1.72	1.72
Cameroon	5	83.83	1.88	116.39	68.26	55.88	64.75	7.87	1.22	4.00	3.11
Chile	2	35.50	2.42	4.33	0.00	0.00	0.00	3.38	0.42	4.42	1.58
China	2	23.33	3.00	0.00	0.01	0.00	0.00	0.00	0.00	1.00	1.00
Colombia	5	50.48	1.93	8.78	1.22	0.00	0.18	0.78	0.56	3.08	2.25
Croatia	4	63.42	2.63	0.00	1.19	0.00	0.00	0.07	0.00	2.16	2.00
Czech Republic	2	43.00	2.00	0.23	1.41	0.00	1.24	0.26	0.00	1.00	1.00
Denmark	2	72.71	2.32	0.00	0.00	0.00	0.00	0.09	0.00	1.32	1.32
Dominican Republic	2	39.27	2.67	2.94	0.70	0.58	0.41	0.66	0.00	2.66	1.99
Egypt, Arab Rep. of	2	32.05	2.00	0.35	0.00	0.18	0.18	0.40	0.07	2.00	1.00
Ethiopia	4	93.73	1.92	55.41	5.50	6.04	5.11	0.00	0.00	3.77	2.14
France	2	26.23	1.46	0.00	0.03	0.00	0.03	0.00	0.00	2.00	2.00
Gabon	3	—	1.83	141.84	70.92	6.96	8.70	3.39	0.00	4.00	3.83

(continued)

Table A.4 Barriers to deposit services (continued)

		Physical access	Affordability						Eligibility	
	Number of banks responding	Deposit market share (respondents share out of total system) 2004	Locations to open deposit account (out of 3)	Minimum amount to open checking account (% of GDPPC)	Minimum amount to open savings account (% of GDPPC)	Minimum amount to be maintained in checking account (% of GDPPC)	Minimum amount to be maintained in savings account (% of GDPPC)	Annual fees checking account (% of GDPPC)	Annual fees savings account (% of GDPPC)	Number of documents to open checking account (out of 5)	Number of documents to open savings account (out of 5)
Georgia	5	85.71	2.56	0.00	33.18	0.00	8.09	0.33	0.33	1.66	1.78
Germany	3	31.91	2.65	0.00	0.01	0.00	0.00	0.26	0.00	1.74	1.74
Ghana	4	69.49	2.15	22.69	21.89	0.09	11.99	5.90	0.58	3.62	3.24
Greece	3	56.92	1.21	0.64	1.27	0.64	1.27	0.02	0.02	2.53	2.26
Hungary	3	53.09	2.53	0.14	2.04	0.00	0.82	0.17	0.00	1.55	1.00
India	4	36.87	2.00	8.85	5.02	5.83	5.02	0.00	0.17	2.69	2.55
Indonesia	4	44.73	2.53	9.54	3.03	6.14	0.65	2.80	0.66	3.18	2.66
Iran, Islamic Rep. of	2	29.86	2.06	0.03	0.59	0.03	0.30	0.00	0.00	3.53	3.53
Israel	2	36.17	2.00	0.00	0.00	0.00	0.00	0.04	0.00	1.22	1.00
Italy	4	22.79	2.14	0.00	0.00	0.17	0.17	0.40	0.21	1.67	1.67
Japan	4	29.63	1.75	0.00	0.00	0.66	0.00	0.02	0.00	2.03	1.24
Jordan	3	83.61	1.93	16.55	5.34	1.73	0.87	0.00	0.00	2.04	2.04
Kenya	3	43.82	2.78	11.71	44.30	0.00	41.82	12.82	2.07	3.78	2.86
Korea, Rep. of	6	68.95	2.11	3.32	0.01	0.00	0.01	0.06	0.00	1.94	1.20
Lebanon	3	38.00	1.58	4.22	23.98	4.22	23.98	1.96	1.90	2.54	2.36
Lithuania	5	88.87	2.71	0.00	1.45	0.00	1.55	0.01	0.00	1.59	1.00
Madagascar	5	72.44	1.95	38.86	19.35	0.00	17.59	5.15	0.00	2.94	2.71
Malawi	3	82.36	2.00	0.00	17.89	0.00	17.89	21.98	3.63	3.65	2.84
Malta	4	44.56	2.00	0.22	0.71	0.00	0.68	0.00	0.00	3.17	3.07
Mexico	3	48.95	2.18	1.11	0.62	0.90	0.67	0.43	0.18	2.80	2.18
Moldova	3	40.16	3.00	0.00	13.13	0.00	8.26	0.53	0.00	2.31	2.06
Mozambique	2	48.78	2.00	29.61	15.71	14.19	7.20	11.56	0.30	1.00	1.00
Nepal	5	37.86	2.34	90.66	63.39	123.77	73.83	8.28	4.97	4.11	3.92
Nigeria	3	32.22	2.44	106.42	22.07	0.00	1.96	0.05	0.00	3.66	1.99
Pakistan	3	47.50	2.00	1.59	1.59	0.33	0.71	0.00	0.00	2.64	2.43

DEPOSITS

Table A.4 Barriers to deposit services *(continued)*

		Physical access		Affordability						Eligibility	
				DEPOSITS							
	Number of banks responding	Deposit market share (respondents share out of total system) 2004	Locations to open deposit account (out of 3)	Minimum amount to open checking account (% of GDPPC)	Minimum amount to open savings account (% of GDPPC)	Minimum amount to be maintained in checking account (% of GDPPC)	Minimum amount to be maintained in savings account (% of GDPPC)	Annual fees checking account (% of GDPPC)	Annual fees savings account (% of GDPPC)	Number of documents to open checking account (out of 5)	Number of documents to open savings account (out of 5)
Peru	4	81.88	2.00	1.66	0.53	0.00	0.00	1.44	0.50	2.42	1.87
Philippines	4	41.84	2.00	14.54	11.88	14.54	11.88	0.00	0.00	3.17	2.20
Poland	2	28.65	2.53	0.00	0.00	0.00	—	0.24	0.00	1.00	2.00
Romania	4	35.01	2.30	0.03	0.71	0.02	0.18	0.40	0.23	1.28	1.00
Sierra Leone	4	100.00	1.42	51.63	44.89	8.81	43.56	26.63	0.00	4.02	3.88
Slovak Republic	3	58.12	2.08	0.12	0.79	0.10	0.79	0.18	0.01	1.47	1.51
Slovenia	5	67.48	1.50	0.01	0.03	0.01	0.02	0.17	0.00	1.88	1.88
South Africa	3	70.09	2.27	0.00	1.06	0.00	0.28	2.13	0.91	3.45	3.07
Spain	4	63.75	1.53	0.00	0.00	0.00	0.00	0.19	0.04	1.00	1.00
Sri Lanka	3	52.19	1.80	15.76	3.54	4.77	0.84	0.73	0.00	2.62	1.00
Sweden	2	39.47	1.66	0.00	0.01	0.00	0.00	0.00	0.00	1.00	1.00
Switzerland	2	79.57	2.00	0.00	0.00	0.00	0.00	0.08	0.00	1.14	1.14
Thailand	3	38.36	2.48	6.74	0.41	0.31	0.31	1.29	1.29	1.23	1.23
Trinidad and Tobago	3	40.15	2.00	1.37	0.42	1.28	0.49	0.35	0.00	4.29	3.07
Tunisia	2	29.65	2.49	7.96	0.23	0.00	0.23	0.59	0.12	2.02	1.51
Turkey	3	50.14	2.20	0.00	0.00	0.00	0.00	0.30	0.14	3.20	2.40
Uganda	3	59.27	2.00	51.12	48.62	1.73	29.52	24.88	3.37	4.00	3.00
United Kingdom	2	17.46	3.00	0.22	0.002	0.002	0.002	0.23	0.00	2.00	2.00
Uruguay	4	48.52	1.75	1.77	1.48	0.00	2.28	2.05	1.13	3.28	2.91
Venezuela, R. B. de	2	27.47	1.51	6.38	0.86	4.04	0.00	0.52	0.00	3.02	3.02
Zambia	3	46.28	1.80	0.00	7.87	0.00	7.87	9.07	7.79	4.28	4.00
Zimbabwe	4	28.24	2.00	3.64	2.06	0.00	0.69	10.70	6.55	4.13	4.72

(continued)

Table A.4 Barriers to deposit services *(continued)*

	Number of banks responding	Physical access		Affordability						Eligibility	
		Deposit market share (respondents share out of total system) 2004	Locations to open deposit account (out of 3)	Minimum amount to open checking account (% of GDPPC)	Minimum amount to open savings account (% of GDPPC)	Minimum amount to be maintained in checking account (% of GDPPC)	Minimum amount to be maintained in savings account (% of GDPPC)	Annual fees checking account (% of GDPPC)	Annual fees savings account (% of GDPPC)	Number of documents to open checking account (out of 5)	Number of documents to open savings account (out of 5)
Minimum	1	4.63	1.00	0.00	0.00	0.00	0.00	0.00	0.00	1.00	1.00
5th percentile	1	13.68	1.50	0.00	0.00	0.00	0.00	0.00	0.00	1.00	1.00
Median	3	44.56	2.00	0.62	0.88	0.00	0.45	0.30	0.00	2.53	2.00
Average	3	48.25	2.14	11.09	7.79	3.85	5.65	2.36	0.55	2.49	2.13
Maximum	6	100.00	3.00	141.84	70.92	123.77	73.83	26.63	7.79	4.57	4.72
95th percentile	5	89.08	3.00	57.17	45.26	14.23	31.36	11.69	3.38	4.15	3.92

Note: Indicators are obtained from a bank-level survey, as discussed in box 1.5 and Beck, Demirgüç-Kunt, and Martinez Peria (2007a), and are weighted country-level averages. The first column gives the number of banks that responded to the survey from each country. Deposit market share is the total deposits of all the banks in the sample divided by total deposits of the banking system of a country. The data on bank deposits is taken from Bankscope. Locations to open deposit account take the value 1 if an account can be opened at headquarters only; 2 if at headquarters or a branch; and 3 if at headquarters, branches, or a nonbranch outlet. Minimum amount to open (be maintained in) a checking (savings) account is the minimum balance required to open (maintain) a checking (savings) account. Annual fees checking (savings) account are the fees associated with maintaining a checking (savings) account. The affordability indicators are expressed as a share of GDP per capita (GDPPC). Documents needed to open a checking (savings) account consist of identification, payment slip, letter of reference, proof of domicile, and any "other" document a bank requires. This indicator varies from 1 to 5 depending on the number of documents required. Data for countries in which only one bank responded are not shown but are included in the descriptive statistics at the end of the table. Data are available at http://econ.worldbank.org/programs/finance.
— = data not available.

Table A.5 Barriers to loan services: consumer and mortgage loans

| | | Physical access | | Affordability | | | | Eligibility | |
	Number of banks responding	Loan market share (respondents share out of total system) 2004	Locations to submit loan applications (out of 5)	Minimum amount consumer loan (% of GDPPC)	Fees consumer loan (% of GDPPC)	Minimum amount mortgage loan (% of GDPPC)	Fees mortgage loan (% of GDPPC)	Days to process consumer loan applications	Days to process mortgage loan applications
Albania	5	64.24	2.03	214.29	7.17	535.19	7.36	9.64	11.69
Argentina	2	19.89	5.00	7.64	3.44	97.55	0.75	2.00	4.82
Armenia	4	47.28	2.00	14.74	1.98	234.16	9.19	4.83	10.95
Australia	2	33.59	5.00	7.31	0.52	41.12	0.80	1.00	2.59
Bangladesh	5	56.51	2.12	25.70	0.23	1412.52	0.18	9.44	33.48
Belarus	3	71.63	2.00	3.28	0.89	0.00	1.43	8.06	8.74
Belgium	3	68.57	2.45	5.34	0.00	86.18	0.95	2.70	5.24
Bolivia	4	58.87	2.74	109.00	3.45	1124.84	3.48	5.36	15.03
Bosnia and Herzegovina	4	58.96	2.73	18.54	1.47	484.92	1.49	5.36	16.65
Brazil	4	48.61	4.85	1.96	3.44	151.08	9.06	1.00	13.62
Bulgaria	3	31.65	3.42	14.24	1.45	213.32	1.49	4.88	6.84
Cameroon	5	81.36	2.14	78.53	6.21	1544.77	5.84	4.87	16.97
Chile	2	36.05	5.00	8.29	0.88	213.20	1.09	3.84	70.63
China	2	23.63	2.00	54.94	0.00	—	0.00	20.00	20.00
Colombia	5	45.65	3.47	16.40	0.97	150.48	1.39	2.51	5.14
Croatia	4	63.69	3.43	3.90	1.76	183.04	1.17	2.42	4.53
Czech Republic	2	43.00	3.13	10.22	0.70	84.65	0.60	1.00	6.66
Denmark	2	48.81	5.00	0.00	2.00	0.00	1.59	0.73	4.56
Dominican Republic	2	42.61	4.67	13.02	0.82	176.10	6.27	1.84	17.55
Egypt, Arab Rep. of	2	32.08	2.81	5.84	0.01	0.00	0.01	5.38	38.72
Ethiopia	4	85.37	2.00	178.16	0.00	712.65	0.68	5.41	15.00
France	2	30.08	4.00	3.22	1.00	6.36	1.00	4.87	24.67

(continued)

Table A.5 Barriers to loan services: consumer and mortgage loans *(continued)*

		Physical access			Affordability				Eligibility	
	Number of banks responding	Loan market share (respondents share out of total system) 2004	Locations to submit loan applications (out of 5)	Minimum amount consumer loan (% of GDPPC)	Fees consumer loan (% of GDPPC)	Minimum amount mortgage loan (% of GDPPC)	Fees mortgage loan (% of GDPPC)	Days to process consumer loan applications	Days to process mortgage loan applications
Gabon	3	—	4.76	0.00	109.24	0.00	109.24	7.00	15.00
Georgia	5	80.26	2.46	34.53	1.40	290.71	0.73	3.31	4.56
Germany	3	23.72	3.42	0.43	2.23	107.10	1.00	1.00	5.02
Ghana	4	68.72	2.63	111.94	2.04	1320.35	2.01	9.50	10.00
Greece	3	58.36	5.00	11.99	2.30	80.86	6.70	1.00	5.43
Hungary	3	42.43	3.29	4.77	3.71	29.00	1.59	5.66	19.94
India	4	37.75	2.44	28.79	1.19	145.17	0.74	4.17	9.45
Indonesia	4	40.38	3.10	31.68	1.67	225.90	1.46	4.94	6.07
Iran, Islamic Rep. of	2	28.51	2.67	11.24	15.00	11.24	16.00	4.33	15.62
Israel	2	34.75	4.58	0.03	—	16.65	0.40	1.00	12.08
Italy	4	19.04	2.69	8.47	0.38	33.89	1.03	2.01	22.44
Japan	4	24.52	3.42	3.81	0.00	11.65	0.56	1.95	1.95
Jordan	3	80.36	2.05	147.67	1.00	362.27	0.95	2.68	7.24
Kenya	3	47.61	3.27	186.42	1.84	4206.32	1.00	2.52	7.00
Korea	6	73.54	3.78	4.19	0.37	4.19	0.37	1.88	2.36
Lebanon	3	38.00	4.60	32.95	1.05	409.00	1.95	1.58	9.26
Lithuania	5	86.77	4.25	6.31	0.71	65.83	0.67	2.41	8.48
Madagascar	5	74.59	2.16	24.06	2.62	290.98	4.69	8.55	15.00
Malawi	3	59.73	2.12	222.36	1.00	1738.08	17.37	1.72	14.16
Malaysia	1	10.22	3.00	31.42	0.63	125.69	0.00	14.00	14.00
Malta	4	58.34	4.20	19.26	0.45	275.38	0.27	1.34	2.74
Mexico	3	45.74	4.20	7.54	1.81	298.56	1.40	5.01	28.25
Moldova	3	48.32	2.54	31.11	2.05	428.58	1.09	1.36	3.90
Mozambique	2	40.34	2.15	30.71	1.00	71.53	1.00	8.66	34.21
Nepal	5	42.40	2.00	1153.17	0.94	2147.93	1.00	3.71	9.5

Table A.5 Barriers to loan services: consumer and mortgage loans *(continued)*

		Physical access		Affordability (LOANS)				Eligibility	
	Number of banks responding	Loan market share (respondents share out of total system) 2004	Locations to submit loan applications (out of 5)	Minimum amount consumer loan (% of GDPPC)	Fees consumer loan (% of GDPPC)	Minimum amount mortgage loan (% of GDPPC)	Fees mortgage loan (% of GDPPC)	Days to process consumer loan applications	Days to process mortgage loan applications
Nigeria	3	29.31	2.78	81.79	3.83	408.96	3.67	3.59	14.75
Pakistan	3	44.02	3.09	146.71	0.14	954.59	0.08	20.71	28.44
Peru	4	76.40	3.21	21.08	1.83	410.39	6.50	1.94	3.81
Philippines	4	43.17	2.36	330.55	1.46	763.35	4.37	10.13	12.21
Poland	2	28.77	3.43	3.66	6.15	32.50	2.27	3.00	9.35
Romania	4	24.66	2.00	6.10	5.51	197.64	1.07	2.53	14.35
Sierra Leone	4	100.00	1.77	143.55	2.07	5157.40	1.00	1.73	4.66
Slovak Republic	3	51.93	3.64	10.26	0.60	71.15	0.85	1.75	4.67
Slovenia	5	70.68	2.13	1.13	1.22	94.90	1.30	1.13	7.60
South Africa	3	69.39	5.00	7.27	0.48	142.37	0.47	1.46	5.55
Spain	4	66.73	5.00	9.95	1.85	100.19	0.89	1.00	3.22
Sri Lanka	3	51.10	2.90	36.10	0.34	51.64	1.83	7.34	20.61
Sweden	2	22.43	4.28	1.14	0.21	11.49	0.11	1.72	1.72
Switzerland	2	59.19	3.12	0.11	0.00	22.57	0.00	1.44	1.56
Thailand	3	36.16	2.00	265.43	1.43	42.74	0.60	15.49	24.59
Trinidad and Tobago	3	50.27	4.62	7.71	1.33	93.03	1.02	1.33	7.50
Tunisia	2	29.08	2.00	18.41	0.80	18.41	1.40	9.00	45.00
Turkey	3	38.33	4.15	11.83	0.95	165.37	2.16	2.94	5.00
Uganda	3	46.87	2.00	205.75	2.68	—	—	1.38	—
United Kingdom	2	18.46	5.00	6.05	1.11	59.56	1.66	1.00	14.32
Uruguay	4	59.16	2.26	32.62	0.00	355.97	1.57	8.51	14.42
Venezuela, R. B. de	2	29.26	2.00	0.00	0.00	0.00	0.00	9.15	19.65
Zambia	3	34.41	2.00	—	2.41	—	—	—	—
Zimbabwe	4	43.45	2.85	24.08	3.05	—	—	1.46	—

(continued)

Table A.5 Barriers to loan services: consumer and mortgage loans *(continued)*

		LOANS							
		Physical access			Affordability			Eligibility	
	Number of banks responding	Loan market share (respondents share out of total system) 2004	Locations to submit loan applications (out of 5)	Minimum amount consumer loan (% of GDPPC)	Fees consumer loan (% of GDPPC)	Minimum amount mortgage loan (% of GDPPC)	Fees mortgage loan (% of GDPPC)	Days to process consumer loan applications	Days to process mortgage loan applications
Minimum	1	5.61	1.77	0.00	0.00	0.00	0.00	0.73	1.00
5th percentile	1	14.43	2.00	0.03	0.00	0.00	0.01	1.00	1.67
Median	3	43.17	3.05	13.63	1.08	143.77	1.09	2.94	9.45
Average	3	45.19	3.23	56.79	3.07	428.58	3.70	4.58	12.68
Maximum	6	100.00	5.00	1153.17	109.24	5157.40	109.24	20.71	70.63
95th percentile	5	80.46	5.00	215.50	6.16	1631.76	9.11	14.10	33.70

Note: Indicators are obtained from a bank-level survey as discussed in box 1.5 and Beck, Demirgüç-Kunt, and Martínez Pería (2007a), and are weighted country-level averages. The first column gives the number of banks that responded to the survey from each country. Loan market share is the total loans of all the banks in the sample divided by total loans of the banking system of a country. The data on bank loans is taken from Bankscope. Locations to submit loan applications take the value 1 if application can be submitted at headquarters only; 2 if at headquarters or a branch; 3 if at headquarters, branches, or a nonbranch outlet; 4 if at headquarters, branches, nonbranch outlets, or electronically; and 5 if at headquarters, branches, nonbranch outlets, electronically, or over the phone. Minimum amount consumer (mortgage) loan is the smallest amount of loan banks make, and fees consumer (mortgage) loan are the fees associated with consumer (mortgage) loans. Minimum loan amount and fees are expressed as a share of gross domestic product per capita (GDPPC). The last two columns show the number of days banks take to process a typical consumer (mortgage) loan application. Data for countries in which only one bank responded are not shown but are included in the descriptive statistics at the end of the table. Data are available at http://econ.worldbank.org/programs/finance. — = data are unavailable.

Table A.6 Barriers to loan services: business and SME loans

| | | | | LOANS | | | | | |
| | | Physical access | | Affordability | | | | Eligibility | |
	Number of banks responding	Loan market share (respondents share out of total system) 2004	Locations to submit loan applications (out of 5)	Minimum amount business loan (% of GDPPC)	Fees business loan (% of GDPPC)	Minimum amount SME loan (% of GDPPC)	Fees SME loan (% of GDPPC)	Days to process business loan applications	Days to process SME loan applications
Albania	5	64.24	2.03	2263.77	7.33	1358.23	7.33	16.05	14.50
Argentina	2	19.89	5.00	971.72	1.56	151.87	1.56	7.82	5.26
Armenia	4	47.28	2.00	1042.28	0.19	860.58	0.00	9.94	7.62
Australia	2	33.59	5.00	10.06	3.03	10.06	1.29	7.19	7.19
Bangladesh	5	56.51	2.12	55.28	6.46	174.4	2.62	34.55	43.26
Belarus	3	71.63	2.00	7.12	1.15	0.00	1.15	7.34	6.20
Belgium	3	68.57	2.45	28.29	2.30	28.29	2.30	3.60	3.60
Bolivia	4	58.87	2.74	759.35	3.48	795.48	3.61	23.26	9.70
Bosnia and Herzegovina	4	58.96	2.73	573.97	1.20	711.11	1.10	14.70	8.86
Brazil	4	48.61	4.85	19.19	2.10	8.08	2.10	10.32	3.63
Bulgaria	3	31.65	3.42	130.35	2.05	95.79	2.27	21.38	13.38
Cameroon	5	81.36	2.14	16393.68	81.39	947.92	81.39	12.91	9.31
Chile	2	36.05	5.00	178.74	3.57	121.70	1.09	10.00	13.87
China	2	23.63	2.00	—	0.00	—	0.00	50.00	40.00
Colombia	5	45.65	3.47	2131.83	0.23	242.96	0.09	11.00	8.22
Croatia	4	63.69	3.43	146.24	0.94	22.58	1.30	11.89	4.65
Czech Republic	2	43.00	3.13	4.96	0.70	4.96	0.70	8.05	10.84
Denmark	2	48.81	5.00	0.00	1.73	0.00	2.00	1.00	1.00
Dominican Republic	2	42.61	4.67	89.32	1.25	43.52	1.32	6.67	13.04
Egypt, Arab Rep. of	2	32.08	2.81	14.61	0.35	0.00	0.00	19.29	14.43
Ethiopia	4	85.37	2.00	981.67	0.64	878.77	0.64	14.55	14.55
France	2	30.08	4.00	6.36	1.00	6.36	1.00	18.22	10.00
Gabon	3	—	4.76	0.00	100.35	0.00	100.35	15.08	15.08

(continued)

Table A.6 Barriers to loan services: business and SME loans *(continued)*

		Physical access		Affordability				Eligibility	
								LOANS	
	Number of banks responding	Loan market share (respondents share out of total system) 2004	Locations to submit loan applications (out of 5)	Minimum amount business loan (% of GDPPC)	Fees business loan (% of GDPPC)	Minimum amount SME loan (% of GDPPC)	Fees SME loan (% of GDPPC)	Days to process business loan applications	Days to process SME loan applications
Georgia	5	80.26	2.46	2345.59	1.01	2480.08	1.10	5.03	5.62
Germany	3	23.72	3.42	0.00	0.62	0.00	0.62	3.87	4.25
Ghana	4	68.72	2.63	1044.39	1.31	1448.07	1.54	19.07	29.20
Greece	3	58.36	5.00	13.98	2.43	33.96	2.43	4.77	2.23
Hungary	3	42.43	3.29	58.00	3.31	58.00	1.51	10.04	7.66
India	4	37.75	2.44	57.77	0.93	145.17	0.84	19.98	10.75
Indonesia	4	40.38	3.10	0.00	0.90	1853.19	1.46	16.59	9.68
Iran, Islamic Rep. of	2	28.51	2.67	11.24	15.00	11.24	16.00	10.64	10.64
Israel	2	34.75	4.58	1.67	45.80	1.67	45.80	1.79	1.79
Italy	4	19.04	2.69	4.49	4.74	7.24	4.74	19.26	18.12
Japan	4	24.52	3.42	30.98	0.00	11.75	0.00	11.39	10.14
Jordan	3	80.36	2.05	354.70	1.03	445.26	1.03	8.16	7.91
Kenya	3	47.61	3.27	193.78	1.57	166.44	2.10	5.66	5.66
Korea, Rep. of	6	73.54	3.78	16.99	0.29	16.99	0.29	2.73	2.73
Lebanon	3	38.00	4.60	4470.83	5.40	1154.76	4.95	15.61	15.61
Lithuania	5	86.77	4.25	17.54	0.88	17.54	0.67	9.83	8.62
Madagascar	5	74.59	2.16	17.27	3.56	17.27	3.56	18.60	15.46
Malawi	3	59.73	2.12	306.05	1.32	1929.34	1.00	15.39	3.71
Malta	4	58.34	4.20	529.00	0.28	355.91	0.28	5.64	5.69
Mexico	3	45.74	4.20	101.93	1.27	87.80	1.61	15.70	9.86
Moldova	3	48.32	2.54	64216.77	1.34	71.78	1.43	7.31	4.31
Mozambique	2	40.34	2.15	28.61	0.75	28.61	1.00	25.84	25.84
Nepal	5	42.40	2.00	19407.57	18.57	2970.18	16.86	9.53	10.94

Table A.6 Barriers to loan services: business and SME loans *(continued)*

	Number of banks responding	Physical access		LOANS				Eligibility	
		Loan market share (respondents share out of total system) 2004	Locations to submit loan applications (out of 5)	Affordability					
				Minimum amount business loan (% of GDPPC)	Fees business loan (% of GDPPC)	Minimum amount SME loan (% of GDPPC)	Fees SME loan (% of GDPPC)	Days to process business loan applications	Days to process SME loan applications
Nigeria	3	29.31	2.78	0.00	1.35	81.79	4.14	8.24	11.49
Pakistan	3	44.02	3.09	1526.04	0.12	234.25	0.19	31.98	33.63
Peru	4	76.40	3.21	429.43	0.16	54.35	0.16	10.63	3.71
Philippines	4	43.17	2.36	920.23	1.41	916.66	1.41	44.13	33.29
Poland	2	28.77	3.43	0.00	2.35	0.54	2.31	12.00	12.43
Romania	4	24.66	2.00	124.83	1.03	124.83	1.06	12.45	12.45
Sierra Leone	4	100.00	1.77	218.23	1.76	243.89	2.07	11.53	9.52
Slovak Republic	3	51.93	3.64	50.91	1.13	57.89	1.13	3.06	3.54
Slovenia	5	70.68	2.13	5.21	0.38	5.21	0.95	4.19	3.89
South Africa	3	69.39	5.00	15.98	0.65	15.98	0.65	2.73	4.13
Spain	4	66.73	5.00	19.35	1.06	19.35	1.10	1.83	1.83
Sri Lanka	3	51.10	2.90	20.56	2.29	20.56	2.09	15.57	10.04
Sweden	2	22.43	4.28	0.00	0.21	0.00	0.22	2.28	2.28
Switzerland	2	59.19	3.12	11.28	0.00	11.28	0.00	3.24	3.24
Thailand	3	36.16	2.00	0.00	0.55	3.21	0.94	22.46	23.74
Trinidad and Tobago	3	50.27	4.62	8.30	1.24	8.30	1.14	10.41	7.32
Tunisia	2	29.08	2.00	92.07	1.50	92.07	1.50	20.60	22.60
Turkey	3	38.33	4.15	74.26	1.94	18.57	1.41	13.75	4.61
Uganda	3	46.87	2.00	7039.03	1.51	3141.17	2.25	5.15	4.47
United Kingdom	2	18.46	5.00	26.12	1.32	6.05	1.32	12.32	10.47
Uruguay	4	59.16	2.26	32.62	0.00	32.62	0.00	31.52	31.45
Venezuela, R. B. de	2	29.26	2.00	0.00	0.00	0.00	0.00	11.40	11.40
Zambia	3	34.41	2.00	—	2.23	—	2.43	10.67	8.33
Zimbabwe	4	43.45	2.85	263.49	2.54	240.12	2.54	7.91	3.91

(continued)

Table A.6 Barriers to loan services: business and SME loans *(continued)*

		Physical access		Affordability (LOANS)				Eligibility	
	Number of banks responding	Loan market share (respondents share out of total system) 2004	Locations to submit loan applications (out of 5)	Minimum amount business loan (% of GDPPC)	Fees business loan (% of GDPPC)	Minimum amount SME loan (% of GDPPC)	Fees SME loan (% of GDPPC)	Days to process business loan applications	Days to process SME loan applications
Minimum	1	5.61	1.77	0.00	0.00	0.00	0.00	1.00	1.00
5th percentile	1	14.43	2.00	0.00	0.00	0.00	0.00	1.99	1.99
Median	3	43.17	3.05	55.28	1.26	39.86	1.28	10.64	9.09
Average	3	45.19	3.23	2259.06	4.73	337.58	4.67	12.68	11.03
Maximum	6	100.00	5.00	64216.77	100.35	3141.17	100.35	50.00	43.26
95th percentile	5	80.46	5.00	9845.42	15.54	1876.04	16.13	31.54	31.54

Note: Indicators are obtained from a bank-level survey, as discussed in box 1.5 and Beck, Demirgüç-Kunt, and Martinez Peria (2007a), and are weighted country-level averages. The first column gives the number of banks that responded to the survey from each country. Loan market share is the total loans of all the banks in the sample divided by total loans of the banking system of a country. The data on bank loans is taken from Bankscope. Locations to submit loan applications take the value 1 if the application can be submitted at headquarters only; 2 if at headquarters or a branch; 3 if at headquarters, branches, or nonbranch outlets; 4 if at headquarters, branches, nonbranch outlets, or electronically; and 5 if at headquarters, branches, nonbranch outlets, electronically, or over the phone. Minimum amount business (SME) loan is the smallest amount of loan banks make to businesses (SMEs), and Fees business (SME) loan are the fees associated with business (SME) loans. Minimum loan amount and fees are expressed as a share of gross domestic product per capita (GDPPC). The last two columns show the number of days banks take to process a typical business loan and a typical SME loan application. Data for countries in which only one bank responded are not shown but are included in the descriptive statistics at the end of the table. Data are available at http://econ.worldbank.org/programs/finance. — = data are not available.

Table A.7 Barriers to payment services

Country	Number of banks that have responded	Deposit market share (respondents share out of total system) 2004	Cost to transfer funds internationally (% of $250)	Amount of fee for using ATM cards (% of $100)
Albania	5	91.42	7.70	0.0003
Algeria	1	91.00	—	0.21
Argentina	2	17.90	0.75	0.00
Armenia	4	59.63	6.14	0.07
Australia	2	32.59	8.05	0.00
Austria	1	11.46	3.45	0.00
Bangladesh	5	56.98	1.93	0.00
Belarus	3	74.58	1.27	0.00
Belgium	3	72.56	0.12	0.00
Bolivia	4	58.04	13.47	0.26
Bosnia and Herzegovina	4	64.04	3.79	0.01
Brazil	4	64.35	14.85	0.11
Bulgaria	3	34.87	5.24	0.13
Cameroon	5	83.83	9.15	0.00
Chile	2	35.50	20.00	0.00
China	2	23.33	2.67	0.12
Colombia	5	50.48	11.67	0.19
Croatia	4	63.42	3.57	0.00
Czech Republic	2	43.00	3.99	0.19
Denmark	2	72.71	4.09	0.00
Dominican Republic	2	39.27	20.00	5.70
Egypt, Arab Rep. of	2	32.05	0.76	0.00
El Salvador	1	24.74	1.23	0.06
Estonia	1	6.51	11.26	0.00
Ethiopia	4	93.73	1.87	0.00
France	2	26.23	5.12	0.00
Gabon	3	—	4.85	0.00
Georgia	5	85.71	7.03	0.13
Germany	3	31.91	1.12	0.00
Ghana	4	69.49	14.70	0.19
Greece	3	56.92	7.42	0.00
Hungary	3	53.09	3.60	—
India	4	36.87	6.49	0.00
Indonesia	4	44.73	2.83	0.00
Iran, Islamic Rep. of	2	29.86	—	0.00
Israel	2	36.17	8.15	0.23
Italy	4	22.79	7.39	0.00
Japan	4	29.63	13.24	0.00

(continued)

Table A.7   Barriers to payment services *(continued)*

Country	Number of banks that have responded	Deposit market share (respondents share out of total system) 2004	Cost to transfer funds internationally (% of $250)	Amount of fee for using ATM cards (% of $100)
Jordan	3	83.61	5.37	0.00
Kenya	3	43.82	8.43	0.15
Korea	6	68.95	7.05	0.22
Lebanon	3	38.00	9.76	0.00
Lithuania	5	88.87	8.72	0.00
Madagascar	5	72.44	4.30	0.00
Malawi	3	82.36	6.42	0.08
Malaysia	1	10.38	—	0.13
Malta	4	44.56	5.59	0.03
Mauritius	1	4.63	—	—
Mexico	3	48.95	8.66	0.40
Moldova	3	40.16	11.19	0.00
Mozambique	2	48.78	4.25	0.22
Nepal	5	37.86	7.10	0.00
New Zealand	1	16.75	6.63	0.33
Nigeria	3	32.22	6.17	0.50
Norway	1	19.30	3.56	0.00
Pakistan	3	47.50	2.10	0.60
Peru	4	81.88	6.68	0.24
Philippines	4	41.84	2.27	0.00
Poland	2	28.65	7.10	0.00
Portugal	1	13.93	—	0.00
Romania	4	35.01	17.43	0.00
Sierra Leone	4	100.00	6.86	0.00
Slovak Republic	3	58.12	4.38	0.19
Slovenia	5	67.48	2.88	0.00
South Africa	3	70.09	9.53	0.34
Spain	4	63.75	6.39	0.00
Sri Lanka	3	52.19	7.14	0.03
Swaziland	1	43.40	14.40	.
Sweden	2	39.47	8.16	0.00
Switzerland	2	79.57	3.17	0.00
Thailand	3	38.36	4.97	0.00
Trinidad and Tobago	3	40.15	3.74	0.05
Tunisia	2	29.65	5.19	0.00
Turkey	3	50.14	6.34	0.00
Uganda	3	59.27	0.55	0.19
United Kingdom	2	17.46	9.56	0.00

Table A.7 Barriers to payment services *(continued)*

Country	Number of banks that have responded	Deposit market share (respondents share out of total system) 2004	Cost to transfer funds internationally (% of $250)	Amount of fee for using ATM cards (% of $100)
Uruguay	4	48.52	7.18	0.14
Venezuela, R. B. de	2	27.47	12.00	0.10
Zambia	3	46.28	3.24	0.13
Zimbabwe	4	28.24	3.77	1.04
Minimum	1	4.63	0.12	0.00
5th percentile	1	13.68	1.01	0.00
Median	3	44.56	6.34	0.00
Average	3	48.25	6.63	0.17
Maximum	6	100.00	20.00	5.70
95th percentile	5	89.08	14.75	0.42

Note: Indicators are obtained from a bank-level survey, as discussed in box 1.5 and Beck, Demirgüç-Kunt, and Martinez Peria (2007a), and are weighted country-level averages. The first column gives the number of banks from each country that responded to the survey. Deposit market share is the total deposits of all the banks in the sample divided by total deposits of the banking system of a country. The data on bank deposits is taken from Bankscope. Cost to transfer funds internationally is the amount of fees banks charge to transfer funds internationally. The fee is expressed as percentage of $250. Amount of fee for using ATM cards is the fee banks charge consumers for using an ATM card. The fee is expressed as percentage of $100. Data are available at http://econ.worldbank .org/programs/finance. — = data are not available.

References

Abiad, Abdul, and Ashoka Mody. 2005. "Financial Reform: What Shakes It? What Shapes It?" *American Economic Review* 95 (11): 66–88.

Acemoglu, Daron, and Simon Johnson. 2005. "Unbundling Institutions." *Journal of Political Economy* 113 (5): 949–95.

Acemoglu, Daron, Simon Johnson, and James Robinson. 2001. "The Colonial Origins of Comparative Development: An Empirical Investigation." *American Economic Review* 91 (5): 1369–1401.

———. 2002. "Reversal of Fortunes: Geography and Institutions in the Making of the Modern World Income Distribution." *Quarterly Journal of Economics* 117 (4): 1231–94.

Adams, Dale, Douglas Graham, and J. D. von Pischke. 1984. *Undermining Rural Development with Cheap Credit.* Boulder, CO: Westview Press.

Adams, Dale, and J. D. von Pischke. 1992. "Microenterprise Credit Programs: Déja Vu." *World Development* 20 (10): 1463–70.

Adasme, Osvaldo, Giovanni Majnoni, and Myriam Uribe. 2006. "Access and Risk: Friends or Foes? Lessons from Chile." Policy Research Working Paper 4003, World Bank, Washington, DC.

Aggarwal, Reena, Aslı Demirgüç-Kunt, and Maria Soledad Martinez Peria. 2006. "Do Workers' Remittances Promote Financial Development?" Policy Research Working Paper 3957, World Bank, Washington, DC.

Aggarwal, Reena, Leora Klapper and Peter Wysocki. 2005. "Portfolio Preferences of Foreign Institutional Investors." *Journal of Banking and Finance* 29 (12): 2919–46.

Aghion, Philippe, and Patrick Bolton. 1997. "A Theory of Trickle-Down Growth and Development." *Review of Economic Studies* 64 (2): 151–72.

Aghion, Philippe, Eve Caroli, and Cecilia Garcia-Penalosa. 1999. "Inequality and Economic Growth: The Perspective of New Growth Theories." *Journal of Economic Literature* 37 (4): 1615–60.

Aghion, Philippe, Thibault Fally, and Stefano Scarpetta. 2006. "Credit Constraints as a Barrier to the Entry and Post-Entry Growth of Firms: Lessons from Firm-Level Cross

Country Panel Data." Working paper, Harvard University, Economics Department, Boston, MA.

Aghion, Philippe, Peter Howitt, and David Mayer-Foulkes. 2005. "The Effect of Financial Development on Convergence: Theory and Evidence." *Quarterly Journal of Economics* 120 (1): 173–222.

Ahlin, Christian, and Robert M. Townsend. 2007. "Using Repayment Data to Test across Models of Joint Liability Lending." *Economic Journal* 117 (517): F11-F51.

Alesina, Alberto, and Dani Rodrik. 1994. "Distributive Politics and Economic Growth." *Quarterly Journal of Economics* 109 (2): 465–90.

Allayannis, George, Greg Brown, and Leora Klapper. 2003. "Capital Structure, Foreign Debt and Financial Risk: Evidence from East Asia." *Journal of Finance* 58 (6): 2667–2710.

Allen, Franklin, Rajesh Chakrabarti, Sankar De, Jun Qian, and Meijun Qian. 2006. "Financing Firms in India." Policy Research Working Paper 3975, World Bank, Washington, DC. Wharton Financial Institutions Center Working Paper 06-08, University of Pennsylvania, Philadelphia.

Allen, Franklin, and Douglas Gale. 2000. *Comparing Financial Systems*. Cambridge, MA: MIT Press.

Allen, Franklin, Jun Qian, and Meijun Qian. 2005. "Law, Finance, and Economic Growth in China." *Journal of Financial Economics* 77 (1): 57–116.

———. 2008. "China's Financial System: Past, Present, and Future." In *China's Great Economic Transformation*, ed. Thomas Rawski and Loren Brandt, New York: Cambridge University Press, forthcoming.

Aportela, Francisco. 1999. "Effects of Financial Access on Savings by Low-Income People." Working paper, MIT, Cambridge, MA.

Armendáriz de Aghion, Beatriz, and Jonathan Morduch. 2005. *The Economics of Mirofinance.* Cambridge, MA: MIT Press.

Ashraf, Nava, Xavier Giné, and Dean Karlan. 2007. "Finding Missing Markets: An Evaluation of a Horticultural Export and Credit Program in Kenya." Working paper, World Bank, Washington, DC.

Ashraf, Nava, Dean Karlan, and Wesley Yin. 2003. "A Review of Commitment Savings Products in Developing Countries." Asian Development Bank, Manila, Philippines.

———. 2006a. "Deposit Collectors." *Advances in Economic Analysis and Policy* 6 (2): 1483–83.

———. 2006b. "Female Empowerment: Further Evidence from a Commitment Savings Product in the Philippines." Working paper, Yale University, Economics Department, New Haven, CT.

———. 2006c. "Tying Odysseus to the Mast: Evidence from a Savings Commitment Product in the Philippines." *Quarterly Journal of Economics* 121 (2): 635–72.

Ayyagari, Meghana, Aslı Demirgüç-Kunt, and Vojislav Maksimovic. 2006a. "How Important Are Financing Constraints? The Role of Finance in the Business Environment." Policy Research Working Paper 3820, World Bank, Washington, DC.

———. 2006b. "What Determines Protection of Property Rights: An Analysis of Direct and Indirect Effects." Policy Research Working Paper 3940, World Bank, Washington, DC.

———. 2007a. "Firm Innovation in Emerging Markets: Role of Governance and Finance." Policy Research Working Paper 4157, World Bank, Washington, DC.

———. 2007b. "Formal versus Informal Finance: Evidence from China." Working paper, Development Research Group, World Bank, Washington, DC.

———. 2007c. "How Well Do Institutional Theories Explain Firms' Perceptions of Property Rights?" *Review of Financial Studies,* forthcoming.

Banerjee, Abhijit V., and Esther Duflo. 2004. "Do Firms Want to Borrow More? Testing Credit Constraints Using a Directed Lending Program." CEPR Discussion Paper 4681. Centre for Economic Policy Research, London.

———. 2005. "Growth Theory through the Lens of Development Economics." In *Handbook of Economic Growth,* vol. 1, part A, ed. Philippe Aghion and Steven Durlauf, 473–552. Amsterdam: Elsevier.

Banerjee, Abhijit V., and Andrew F. Newman. 1993. "Occupational Choice and the Process of Development." *Journal of Political Economy* 101 (2, April): 274–98.

Barth, James R., Gerard Caprio, Jr., and Ross Levine. 2006. *Rethinking Bank Regulation: Till Angels Govern.* New York: Cambridge University Press.

Bebczuk, Ricardo. 2007. "Loan Size and Loss Predictability in Argentina." Working paper, Universidad Nacional de la Plata, La Plata, Argentina.

Beck, Thorsten. 2003. "Financial Dependence and International Trade." *Review of International Economics* 11 (2): 296–316.

Beck, Thorsten, and Augusto de la Torre. 2007. "The Basic Analytics of Access to Financial Services." *Financial Markets, Institutions, and Instruments* 16 (2): 79–117.

Beck, Thorsten, and Aslı Demirgüç-Kunt. 2006. "Small and Medium-Size Enterprises: Access to Finance as a Growth Constraint." *Journal of Banking and Finance* 30 (11): 2931–43.

Beck, Thorsten, Aslı Demirgüç-Kunt, Luc Laeven, and Ross Levine. 2005. "Finance, Firm Size and Growth." Policy Research Working Paper 3485, World Bank, Washington, DC.

Beck, Thorsten, Aslı Demirgüç-Kunt, Luc Laeven, and Vojislav Maksimovic. 2006. "The Determinants of Financing Obstacles." *Journal of International Money and Finance* 25 (6): 932–52.

Beck, Thorsten, Aslı Demirgüç-Kunt, and Ross Levine. 2000. "A New Database on the Structure and Development of the Financial Sector." *World Bank Economic Review* 14 (3): 597–605. Updated version available at econ. worldbank.org/programs/finance.

———. 2003. "Finance, Law and Endowments." *Journal of Financial Economics* 70 (2): 137–81.

———. 2005. "Law and Firms' Access to Finance." *American Law and Economics Review* 7 (1): 211–52.

———. 2006. "Bank Supervision and Corruption in Lending." *Journal of Monetary Economics* 53 (8): 2131–63.

———. 2007. "Finance, Inequality, and the Poor." *Journal of Economic Growth* 12 (1): 27–49.

Beck, Thorsten, Aslı Demirgüç-Kunt, and Vojislav Maksimovic. 2004. "Bank Competition and Access to Finance: International Evidence." *Journal of Money, Credit, and Banking* 36 (3, part 2): 627–48.

———. 2005. "Financial and Legal Constraints to Firm Growth: Does Firm Size Matter?" *Journal of Finance* 60 (1): 137–77.

———. 2006. "The Influence of Financial and Legal Institutions on Firm Size." *Journal of Banking and Finance* 30 (11): 2995–3015.

———. Forthcoming. "Financing Patterns Around the World: Are Small Firms Different?" *Journal of Financial Economics.*

Beck, Thorsten, Aslı Demirgüç-Kunt, and Maria Soledad Martinez Peria. 2007a. "Banking Services for Everyone? Barriers to Bank Access and Use around the World." Policy Research Working Paper 4079, World Bank, Washington, DC.

———. 2007b. "Reaching Out: Access to and Use of Banking Services across Countries." *Journal of Financial Economics* 85 (1): 234–66.

Beck, Thorsten, and Luc Laeven. 2006. "Institution Building and Growth in Transition Economies." *Journal of Economic Growth* 11 (2): 157–86.

Beck, Thorsten, and Ross Levine. 2002. "Industry Growth and Capital Allocation: Does Having a Market- or Bank-Based System Matter? *Journal of Financial Economics* 64 (2): 147–80.

———. 2005. "Legal Institutions and Financial Development." In *Handbook of New Institutional Economics*, ed. Claude Menard and Mary M. Shirley. Norwell MA: Kluwer Academic Publishers.

Beck, Thorsten, Ross Levine, and Alex Levkov. 2007. "Big Bad Banks? The Impact of U.S. Branch Deregulation in Income Distribution." Policy Research Working Paper 4330, World Bank, Washington, DC.

Beck, Thorsten, Ross Levine, and Norman Loayza. 2000. "Finance and the Sources of Growth." *Journal of Financial Economics* 58 (1): 261–300.

Becker, Bo, and David Greenberg. 2005. "Financial Development and International Trade." Working Paper, University of Illinois, Urbana-Champaign, College of Business.

Beegle, Kathleen, Rajeev Dehejia, and Roberta Gatti. 2007. "Child Labor and Agricultural Shocks." *Journal of Development Economics* 81 (1): 80–96.

Beinhocker, Eric D. 2006. *The Origin of Wealth: Evolution, Complexity, and the Radical Remaking of Economics*. Cambridge, MA: Harvard Business School Press.

Bekaert, Geert, Campbell R. Harvey, and Christian Lundblad. 2005. "Does Financial Liberalization Spur Growth?" *Journal of Financial Economics* 77 (1): 3–55.

Benavente, José Miguel, Alexander Galetovic, and Ricardo Sanhueza. 2006. "FOGAPE: An Economic Analysis." Working paper 222, University of Chile, Economics Department, Santiago.

Benavides, Guillermo, and Alberto Huidobro. 2005. "Are Loan Guarantees Effective? The Case of Mexican Government Banks." http://ssrn.com/abstract=637385.

Bennett, Fred, Alan Doran, and Harriett Billington. 2005. "Do Credit Guarantees Lead to Improved Access to Financial Services? Recent Evidence from Chile, Egypt, India, and Poland." Policy Division Working Paper, U.K. Department for International Development, Financial Sector Team, London.

Berger, Allen N., Aslı Demirgüç-Kunt, Ross Levine, and Joseph G. Haubrich. 2004. "Bank Concentration and Competition: An Evolution in the Making." *Journal of Money, Credit, and Banking* 36 (3): 433–654.

Berger, Allen N., W. Scott Frame, and Nathan H. Miller. 2005. "Credit Scoring and the Availability, Price, and Risk of Small Business Credit." *Journal of Money, Credit, and Banking* 37 (2): 191–222.

Berger, Allen N., Iftekhar Hasan, and Leora F. Klapper. 2004. "Further Evidence on the Link between Finance and Growth: An International Analysis of Community Banking and Economic Performance." *Journal of Financial Services Research* 25 (2/3): 169–202.

Berger, Allen N., and Gregory F. Udell. 1998. "The Economics of Small Business Finance: The Roles of Private Equity and Debt Markets in the Financial Growth Cycle." *Journal of Banking and Finance* 22 (6-8): 613–73.

———. 2006. "A More Complete Conceptual Framework for SME Financing." *Journal of Banking and Finance* 30 (11): 2945–66.

Bertrand, Marianne, Dean S. Karlan, Sendhil Mullainathan, Eldar Shafir, and Jonathan Zinman. 2005. "What's Psychology Worth? A Field Experiment in the Consumer Credit Market." Discussion Paper 918, Yale University Economic Growth Center, New Haven, CT.

Bertrand, Marianne, Antoinette Schoar, and David Thesmar. 2007. "Banking Deregulation and Industry Structure: Evidence from the French Banking Reforms of 1985." *Journal of Finance* 62 (2): 597–628.

Besley, Tim J. 1994. "How Do Market Failures Justify Interventions in Rural Credit Markets?" *World Bank Research Observer* 9 (1): 27–47.

Besley, Tim J., and S. Coate (1995). "Group Lending, Repayment Incentives, and Social Collateral." *Journal of Development Economics* 46 (1): 1–18.

Bester, Helmut. 1985. "Screening versus Rationing in Credit Markets with Imperfect Information." *American Economic Review* 75 (4): 850–55.

Biais, Bruno, and Enrico Perotti. 2002. "Machiavellian Privatization." *American Economic Review* 92 (1): 240–58.

Biggs, Tyler, and Manju Kedia Shah. 2006. "African SMEs, Networks, and Manufacturing Performance." *Journal of Banking and Finance* 30 (11): 3040–66.

Birdsall, Nancy. 2007. "Income Distribution: Effects on Growth and Development." In *International Handbook of Development Economics*, ed. Amitava K. Dutt and Jaime Ros. Aldershot: Edward Elgar, forthcoming.

Blundell, Richard, Stephen R. Bond, and Costas Meghir. 1996. "Econometric Models of Company Investment." In *The Econometrics of Panel Data: A Handbook of the Theory with Applications,* ed. László Matyas and Patrick Sevestre. Boston: Kluwer Academic Publishers.

Bonaccorsi di Patti, Emilia, and Giovanni Dell'Ariccia. 2004. "Bank Competition and Firm Creation." *Journal of Money, Banking, and Credit* 36 (2): 225–51.

Bond, Philip, and Ashok Rai. 2002. "Collateral Substitute in Microfinance." Working paper, Northwestern University, Institute for Advanced Study, Evanston, IL.

Bond, Stephen R., and John Van Reenen. 1999. "Microeconomic Models of Investment and Employment." In *Handbook of Econometrics*, vol. 5, ed. James J. Heckman and Edward E. Leamer. Amsterdam: Elsevier Science, North-Holland.

Bonin, John P., Iftekhar Hasan, and Paul Wachtel. 2005. "Bank Privatization and Performance: Evidence from Transition Countries." *Journal of Banking and Finance* 29 (1): 31–53.

Boot, Arnoud, and Anjolein Schmeits. 2005. "The Competitive Challenge in Banking." Working paper 2005-08, Amsterdam Center for Law and Economics, Amsterdam.

Bourguignon, François. 2001. "Pareto-Superiority of Unegalitarian Equilibria in Stiglitz's Model of Wealth Distribution with Convex Savings Function." *Econometrica* 49 (6): 1469–75.

———. 2003. "The Growth Elasticity of Poverty Reduction: Explaining Heterogeneity across Countries and Time Periods." In *Inequality and Growth: Theory and Policy Implications,* ed. Theo Eicher and Stephen Turnovsky. Cambridge, MA: MIT Press.

———. 2004. "The Poverty-Growth-Inequality Triangle." Working paper, World Bank, Washington, DC.

Boyd, John, Ross Levine, and Bruce Smith. 2001. "The Impact of Inflation on Financial Sector Performance." *Journal of Monetary Economics* 47 (2): 221–48.

Boyreau-Debray, Genevieve. 2003. "Financial Intermediation and Growth—Chinese Style." Policy Research Working Paper 3027, World Bank, Washington, DC.

Boyreau-Debray, Genevieve, and Shang-Jin Wei. 2005. "Pitfalls of a State-Dominated Financial System: The Case of China." NBER Working Paper 11214, National Bureau of Economic Research, Cambridge, MA.

Braun, Matias, and Claudio Raddatz. 2007. "The Politics of Financial Development: Evidence from Trade Liberalization." *Journal of Financial Economics,* forthcoming.

Brown, Michael, Tulio Jappelli, and Marco Pagano. 2006. "Information Sharing and Credit: Firm-Level Evidence from Transition Countries." Swiss National Bank, Zurich.

Burgess, Robin, and Rohinde Pande. 2005. "Can Rural Banks Reduce Poverty? Evidence from the Indian Social Banking Experiment." *American Economic Review* 95 (3): 780–95.

Burkart, Mike, Tore Ellingsen, and Mariassunta Giannetti. 2004. "What You Sell Is What You Lend? Explaining Trade Credit Contracts." Stockholm School of Economics, Stockholm.

Burkart, Mike, Fausto Panunzi, and Andrei Shleifer. 2003. "Family Firms." *Journal of Finance* 58 (5): 2167–202.

Calvo, Guillermo. 1998. "Capital Flows and Capital-Market Crises: The Simple Economics of Sudden Stops." *Journal of Applied Economics* 1 (November): 35–54.

Caprio, Gerard, and Aslı Demirgüç-Kunt. 1997. "The Role of Long-Term Finance: Theory and Evidence." *World Bank Economic Review* 10 (2): 291–321.

Caprio, Gerard, Jonathan Fiechter, Robert Litan, and Michael Pomerleano, eds. 2004. *The Future of State-Owned Financial Institutions.* Washington, DC: Brookings Institute.

Caprio, Gerard, and Patrick Honohan. 2004. "Can the Unsophisticated Market Provide Discipline." In *Market Discipline across Countries and Industries,* ed. William C. Hunter, George G. Kaufman, Claudio Borio, and Kostas Tsatsaronis, 349–62. Cambridge, MA: MIT Press.

Caskey, John, Clemente Ruiz Duran, and Tova Maria Solo. 2006. "The Urban Unbanked in Mexico and the United States." Policy Research Working Paper 3835, World Bank, Washington, DC.

Cetorelli, Nicola, and Philip E. Strahan. 2004. "Finance as a Barrier to Entry: Bank Competition and Industry Structure in Local U.S. Markets." Working paper 2004-04 (January), Federal Reserve Bank of Chicago, Chicago, IL.

Chari, Anusha, Paige Ouimet, and Linda Tesar. 2005. "The Stock Market Valuation of Corporate Control: Evidence from Cross-Border Mergers and Acquisitions in Emerging Markets." University of Michigan, Department of Economics, Ann Arbor, MI.

Chen, Shaohua, Ren Mu, and Martin Ravallion. 2006. "Are There Lasting Impacts of a Poor-Area Development Program?" Policy Research Working Paper 4084, World Bank, Washington, DC.

Chen, Shaohua, and Martin Ravallion. 2004. "How Have the World's Poorest Fared since the Early 1980s?" *World Bank Research Observer* 19 (2): 141–69.

Chiquier, Loic, Olivier Hassler, and Michael Lea. 2004. "Mortgage Securities in Emerging Markets." Policy Research Working Paper 3370, World Bank, Washington, DC.

Christen, Robert Peck, Veena Jayadeva, and Richard Rosenberg. 2004. "Financial Institutions with a Double Bottom Line: Implications for the Future of Microfinance." CGAP Occasional Paper 8, Consultative Group to Assist the Poorest, Washington DC.

Claessens, Stijn. 2006. "Access to Financial Services: A Review of the Issues and Public Policy Objectives." *World Bank Research Observer* 21 (2): 207–40.

Claessens, Stijn, Aslı Demirgüç-Kunt, and Harry Huizinga. 2001. "How Does Foreign Entry

Affect the Domestic Banking Market?" *Journal of Banking and Finance* 25 (5): 891–911.

Claessens, Stijn, Gergely Dobos, Daniela Klingebiel, and Luc Laeven. 2003. "The Growing Importance of Networks in Finance and its Effects on Competition." In *Innovations in Financial and Economic Networks,* ed. A. Nagurney, 110–35. Northampton, MA: Edward Elgar Publishers.

Claessens, Stijn, and Eric Feijen. 2006. "Financial Sector Development and the Millennium Development Goals." World Bank Working Paper 89, Washington, DC.

———. 2007. "Finance and Hunger: Empirical Evidence of the Agricultural Productivity Channel." Policy Research Working Paper 4080, World Bank, Washington, DC.

Claessens, Stijn, Erik Feijen, and Luc Laeven. 2007. "Political Connections and Preferential Access to Finance: The Role of Campaign Contributions." *Journal of Financial Economics,* forthcoming.

Claessens, Stijn, and Luc Laeven. 2003. "Financial Development, Property Rights, and Growth." *Journal of Finance* 58 (6): 2401–36.

———. 2004. "What Drives Bank Competition? Some International Evidence." *Journal of Money, Credit, and Banking* 36 (3): 563–83.

Claessens, Stijn, and Neeltje van Horen. 2007. "Location Decision of Foreign Banks and Competitive Advantage." Policy Research Working Paper 4113, World Bank, Washington, DC.

Clarke, George R. G., Robert Cull, and Maria Soledad Martinez Peria. 2006. "Foreign Bank Participation and Access to Credit across Firms in Developing Countries." *Journal of Comparative Economics* 34 (4): 774–95.

Clarke, George R. G., Robert Cull, Maria Soledad Martinez Peria, and Susana M. Sanchez. 2005. "Bank Lending to Small Businesses in Latin America: Does Bank Origin Matter?" *Journal of Money, Credit, and Banking* 37 (1): 83–118.

Clarke, George, L. Colin Xu, and Heng-fu Zou. 2006. "Finance and Income Inequality: What Do the Data Tell Us?" *Southern Economic Journal* 72 (3): 578–96.

Coffee, John C. 2002. "Racing towards the Top? The Impact of Cross-Listings and Stock Market Competition on International Corporate Governance." Columbia Law and Economics Working Paper 205, Columbia University, New York (May 30).

Cole, Shawn. 2004. "Fixing Market Failures or Fixing Elections? Agricultural Credit in India." Harvard Business School, Cambridge, MA.

Coleman, B. 1999. "The Impact of Group Lending in Northeast Thailand." *Journal of Development Economics* 60 (1): 105-42.

Collard, Sharon, and Elaine Kempson. 2005. *Affordable Credit: The Way Forward.* Bristol, U.K.: Policy Press and Joseph Rowntree Foundation.

Costa, Ana Carla, and Joao de Mello. 2006. "Judicial Risk and Credit Market Performance: Micro Evidence from Brazilian Payroll Loans." NBER Working Paper 12252, National Bureau of Economic Research, Cambridge, MA.

Cotler, Pablo, and Chris Woodruff. 2007. "The Impact of Short-Term Credit on Microenterprises:

Evidence from the Bimbo Program in Mexico." Working Paper, University of California at San Diego, School of International Relations and Pacific Studies.

Cull, Robert, Aslı Demirgüç-Kunt, and Jonathan Morduch. 2007. "Financial Performance and Outreach: A Global Analysis of Leading Microbanks." *Economic Journal* 117 (517): F107–F133.

Cull, Robert, and L. Colin Xu. 2000. "Bureaucrats, State Banks, and the Efficiency of Credit Allocation: The Experience of Chinese State-Owned Enterprises." *Journal of Comparative Economics* 28 (1): 1–31.

———. 2003. "Who Gets Credit? The Behavior of Bureaucrats and State Banks in Allocating Credit to Chinese SOEs." *Journal of Development Economics* 71 (2): 533–59.

———. 2005. "Institutions, Ownership, and Finance: The Determinants of Profit Reinvestment among Chinese Firms." *Journal of Financial Economics* 77 (1): 117–46.

Cumming, Douglas, Daniel Schmidt, and Uwe Walz. 2006. "Legality and Venture Governance around the World," Working paper, University of Frankfurt, Department of Economics.

Dahl, Drew, Douglas Evanoff, and Michael F. Spivey. 2000. "Does the Community Reinvestment Act Influence Lending? An Analysis of Changes in Bank Low-Income Mortgage Activity." Working Paper 2000–06, Federal Reserve Board of Chicago.

Daley-Harris, Sam. 2006. "State of the Microcredit Summit Campaign Report 2006." http://www.microcreditsummit.org/pubs/reports/socr/2006.htm.

Da Rin, Marco, Giovanna Nicodano, and Alessandro Sembenelli. 2004. "Public Policy and the Creation of Active Venture Capital Markets." Innocenzo Gasparini Institute for Economic Research Working Paper 270, Milan, Italy.

Deaton, Angus. 2005. "Measuring Poverty in a Growing World (or Measuring Growth in a Poor World)." *Review of Economics and Statistics* 87 (1): 1–19.

Degryse, Hans, and Steven Ongena. 2005. "Distance, Lending Relationships, and Competition." *Journal of Finance* 60 (1): 231–66.

De Haas, Ralph, and Ilko Naaborg. 2005. "Does Foreign Bank Entry Reduce Small Firms' Access to Credit? Evidence from European Transition Economies." Working Paper 50, De Nederlandsche Bank, Amsterdam.

Dehejia, Rajeev, Heather Montgomery, and Jonathan Morduch. 2005. "Do Interest Rates Matter? Credit Demand in the Dhaka Slums." Working paper, New York University, Department of Economics, New York.

De Janvry, Alain, Craig McIntosh, and Elisabeth Sadoulet. 2006. "The Supply and Demand Side Impacts of Credit Market Information." Working paper, University of California, Berkeley, Agricultural and Resource Economics, Berkeley, CA.

De la Torre, Augusto, Juan Carlos Gozzi, and Sergio Schmukler. 2007. "Innovative Experiences in Access to Finance: Market Friendly Roles for the Visible Hand?" Policy Research Working Paper 4326, World Bank, Washington, DC.

De la Torre, Augusto, Maria Soledad Martinez Peria, and Sergio Schmukler. 2007. "Bank Financing to Small and Medium Enterprises: Survey

Results from Argentina and Chile." Working paper, World Bank, Development Research Group, Washington, DC.

De la Torre, Augusto, and Sergio Schmukler. 2004. "Coping with Risks through Mismatches: Domestic and International Financial Contracts for Emerging Economies." *International Finance* 7 (3): 349–90.

De Luna Martinez, Jose. 2005. "Workers' Remittances to Developing Countries: A Survey with Central Banks on Selected Public Policy Issues." Policy Research Working Paper 3638, World Bank, Washington, DC.

De Mel, Suresh, David McKenzie, and Christopher Woodruff. 2007. "Returns to Capital in Microenterprises: Evidence from a Field Experiment." Policy Research Working Paper 4230, World Bank, Washington, DC.

De Meza, David, and David C. Webb. 1987. "Too Much Investment: A Problem of Asymmetric Information." *Quarterly Journal of Economics* 102 (2): 281–92.

Demirgüç-Kunt, Aslı, and Edward Kane. 2002. "Deposit Insurance around the Globe? Where Does It Work?" *Journal of Economic Perspectives* 16 (2): 175–95.

Demirgüç-Kunt, Aslı, Leora Klapper, and Giorgios Panos. 2007. "The Origins of Self-Employment." Working paper, World Bank, Development Research Group, Washington, DC.

Demirgüç-Kunt, Aslı, and Ross Levine. 2001. *Financial Structure and Economic Growth: A Cross-Country Comparison of Banks, Markets and Development.* Cambridge, MA: MIT Press.

———. 2007. "Finance and Economic Opportunity." Working paper, World Bank, Development Research Group, Washington, DC.

Demirgüç-Kunt, Aslı, Luc Laeven, and Ross Levine. 2004. "Regulations, Market Structure, Institutions, and the Cost of Financial Intermediation." *Journal of Money, Credit, and Banking* 36 (3): 593–622.

Demirgüç-Kunt, Aslı, Ernesto Lopez-Cordova, Maria Soledad Martinez Peria, and Christopher Woodruff. 2007. "Remittances and Banking Services. Evidence from Mexico." Working paper World Bank, Development Research Group, Washington, DC.

Demirgüç-Kunt, Aslı, Inessa Love, and Vojislav Maksimovic. 2006. "Business Environment and the Incorporation Decision." *Journal of Banking and Finance* 30 (11): 2967–93.

Demirgüç-Kunt, Aslı, and Vojislav Maksimovic. 1998. "Law, Finance, and Firm Growth." *Journal of Finance* 53 (6): 2107–37.

———. 1999. "Institutions, Financial Markets, and Firm Debt Maturity." *Journal of Financial Economics* 54 (3): 295–336.

———. 2002. "Funding Growth in Bank-Based and Market-Based Financial Systems: Evidence from Firm-Level Data." *Journal of Financial Economics* 65 (3): 337–63.

Demirgüç-Kunt, Aslı, and Maria Soledad Martinez Peria. 2007. "Remittances and the Use of Banking Services. Evidence from El Salvador." Working paper, World Bank, Development Research Group, Washington, DC.

De Nicolo, Gianni, Patrick Honohan, and Alain Ize. 2005. "Dollarization of the Banking System:

Good or Bad?" *Journal of Banking and Finance* 1647–1727.

Desai, Mihir, and Alberto Moel. 2007. "Czech Mate: Expropriation and Investor Protection in a Converging World." *Review of Finance*, forthcoming.

Detragiache, Enrica, Poonam Gupta, and Thierry Tressel. 2006. "Foreign Banks in Poor Countries: Theory and Evidence." Working Paper 06/18, International Monetary Fund, Washington, DC.

Diamond, Douglas. W. 1984. "Financial Intermediation and Delegated Monitoring." *Review of Economic Studies* 51 (3): 393–414.

Dinç, Serdar. 2005. "Politicians and Banks: Political Influences on Government-Owned Banks in Emerging Countries." *Journal of Financial Economics* 77 (2): 453–79.

Djankov, Simeon, Rafael La Porta, Florencio Lopez-de-Silanes, and Andrei Shleifer. 2005. "The Law and Economics of Self-Dealing." NBER Working Paper 11883. National Bureau of Economic Research, Cambridge, MA.

Djankov, Simeon, Caralee McLiesh, Tatiana Nenova, and Andrei Shleifer. 2003. "Who Owns the Media?" *Journal of Law and Economics* 46 (October): 341–82.

Djankov, Simeon, Caralee McLiesh, and Andrei Shleifer. 2007. "Private Credit in 129 Countries." *Journal of Financial Economics* 84 (2): 299–329.

Djankov, Simeon, Edward Miguel, Yingyi Qian, Gerard Roland, and Ekaterina Zhuravskaya. 2005. "Who Are Russia's Entrepreneurs?"

Journal of the European Economic Association 3 (2–3): 587–97.

Dollar, David, and Aart Kraay. 2002. "Growth is Good for the Poor." *Journal of Economic Growth* 7 (3): 195–225.

Doran, Alan, and Jacob Levitsky. 1997. "Credit Guarantee Schemes for Small Business Lending: A Global Perspective." Graham Bannock and Partners Ltd., London.

Dorn, Helmut. 2005. "Practices and Policies in Credit Guarantee Programs in the EU." Powerpoint presentation at the EU Workshop on SME Credit Guarantee Systems, October 26–28, 2005, Shanghai, China. http://info .worldbank.org/etools/docs/library/202079/ Helmut%5FDorn%5FPractices%5Fand% 5FPolicies%5Fin%5FCredit%5FGuarantee% 5FPrograms%5Fin%5Fthe%5FEU.pdf.

Duflo, Esther, and Michael Kremer. 2005. "Use of Randomization in the Evaluation of Development Effectiveness." In *Evaluating Development Effectiveness*, ed. O. Feinstein, G. K. Ingram, and G. K. Pitman, vol. 7, 205–32. London, U.K.: Transaction Publishers.

Ellison, Anna, Sharon Collard, and Rob Forster. 2006. "Illegal Lending in the U.K." Research Report URN 06/1883, U.K. Department of Trade and Industry, London.

Emran, M. Shahe, AKM Mahbub Morshed, and Joseph Stiglitz. 2006. "Microfinance and Missing Markets." Working paper, Columbia University, Department of Economics, New York.

European Commission (2005). "Public Opinion in Europe on Financial Services." *Special*

Eurobarometer 230. http://europa.eu.int/ comm/consumers/cons_int/fina_serv/cons_ experiences/background_en.htm.

Evans, David S., and Richard Schmalensee. 2005. *Paying with Plastic,* 2d ed. Cambridge, MA: MIT Press.

Fafchamps, Marcel. 2004. *Market Institutions in Sub-Saharan Africa: Theory and Evidence.* Cambridge, MA: MIT Press.

Feijen, Eric, and Enrico C. Perotti. 2005. "The Political Economy of Financial Fragility." CEPR Discussion Paper 5317, Centre for Economic Policy Research, London.

Ferri, Giovanni, Li-Gang Liu, and Giovanni Majnoni. 2001. "The Role of Rating Agencies Assessments in Less Developed Countries: Impact of the Proposed Basel Guidelines." *Journal of Banking and Finance* 25 (1): 115–48.

Field, Erica, and Maximo Torero. 2006. "Do Property Titles Increase Access to Credit among the Urban Poor? Evidence from a Nationwide Titling Program." Working paper, Harvard University, Department of Economics, Cambridge, MA.

Firpo, Janine. 2005. "Banking the Unbanked: Technology's Role in Delivering Accessible Financial Services to the Poor." In *Electronic Banking with the Poor,* ed. Stuart Mathison. Foundation for Development Cooperation. https://securesites.golden-orb.com/websites .golden-orb.com/fdc/100462.php.

Fisman, Raymond J. 2003. "Ethnic Ties and the Provision of Credit: Relationship-Level Evidence from African Firms." *Advances in Economic Analysis and Policy* 3 (1).

Fisman, Raymond J., and Inessa Love. 2003. "Trade Credit, Financial Intermediary Development, and Industry Growth." *Journal of Finance* 58 (1): 353–74.

Flug, Karnit, Antonio Spilimbergo, and Erik Wachtenheim. 1998. "Investment in Education: Do Economic Volatility and Credit Constraints Matter?" *Journal of Development Economics* 55 (2): 465–81.

Forbes, Kristin. 2000. "A Reassessment of the Relationship between Inequality and Growth." *American Economic Review* 90 (4): 869–87.

Freund, Caroline, and Nikola Spatafora. 2005. "Remittances: Transaction Costs, Determinants, and Informal Flows." Policy Research Working Paper 3704, World Bank, Washington, DC.

Galiani, Sebastian, and Ernesto Schargrodsky. 2005. "Property Rights for the Poor: Effects of Land Titling." Working paper, Centro de Investigacion en Finanzas, Buenos Aires.

Galor, Oded, and Joseph Zeira. 1993. "Income Distribution and Macroeconomics." *Review of Economic Studies* 60 (1): 35–52.

Genesis. 2005a. "An Inter-Country Survey of the Relative Costs of Bank Accounts." Johannesburg.

———. 2005b. "Measuring Access to Transaction Banking Services in the Southern Customs Union: An Index Approach." Johannesburg.

Gertler, Paul, David Levine, and Enrico Moretti. 2003. "Do Microfinance Programs Help Families Insure Consumption against Illness?" Center for International and Development Economics Research Working Paper, University of California, Berkeley.

Ghatak, Maithreesh, and Timothy Guinnane. 1999. "The Economics of Lending with Joint Liability: Theory and Practice." *Journal of Development Economics* 60 (1): 195–228.

Giannetti, Mariassunta, and Steven Ongena. 2005. "Financial Integration and Entrepreneurial Activity: Evidence from Foreign Bank Entry in Emerging Markets." Working Paper 498, European Central Bank, Frankfurt, Germany.

Gibson, John, Geua Boe-Gibson, Halahingano Rohorua, and David McKenzie. 2006. "Efficient Financial Services for Development in the Pacific." Working paper, World Bank, Development Research Group, Washington, DC.

Gibson, John, David McKenzie, and Halahingano Rohorua. 2006." How Cost-Elastic Are Remittances? Estimates from Tongan Migrants in New Zealand?" Working paper, World Bank, Development Research Group, Washington, DC.

Giné, Xavier. 2005. "Access to Capital in Rural Thailand: An Estimated Model of Formal vs. Informal Credit." Policy Research Working Paper 3502, World Bank, Washington, DC.

Giné, Xavier, Pamela Jakiela, Dean Karlan, and Jonathan Morduch. 2006. "Microfinance Games." Policy Research Working Paper 3959, World Bank, Washington, DC.

Giné, Xavier, and Dean Karlan. 2006. "Group vs. Individual Liability: A Field Experiment in the Philippines." Policy Research Working Paper 4008, World Bank, Washington, DC.

Giné, Xavier, and Inessa Love. 2006. "Do Reorganization Costs Matter for Efficiency? Evidence from a Bankruptcy Reform in Colombia." Policy Research Working Paper 3970, World Bank, Washington, DC.

Giné, Xavier, and Robert Townsend. 2004. "Evaluation of Financial Liberalization: A General Equilibrium Model with Constrained Occupation Choice." *Journal of Development Economics* 74 (2): 269–307.

Giné, Xavier, Robert Townsend, and James Vickery. 2007. "Patterns of Rainfall Insurance Participation in Rural India." Working Paper, World Bank, Development Research Group, Washington, DC.

Giné, Xavier, and Dean Yang. 2007. "Insurance, Credit and Technology Adoption: A Field Experimental Approach." Working Paper, World Bank, Development Research Group, Washington, DC.

Goldberg, Nathanael, and Dean Karlan. 2005. "The Impact of Microfinance: A Review of Methodological Issues." Yale University, Department of Economics, New Haven, CT.

Goldstein, Morris, and Philip Turner. 2004. *Controlling Currency Mismatches in Emerging Markets.* Washington, DC: Institute for International Economics.

Gonzalez-Vega, Claudio. 2003. "Deepening Rural Financial Markets: Macroeconomic, Policy and Political Dimensions." Presented to the USAID-WOCCU Conference: *Paving the Way Forward for Rural Finance: An*

International Conference on Best Practices. Washington DC, March 2003. http://www.basis.wisc.edu/rfc/.

Goodwin-Groen, Ruth. 2007. *The National Credit Act and Its Regulations in the Context of Access to Finance in South Africa.* Johannesburg: Finmark Trust.

Gormley, Todd A. 2004. "Banking Competition in Developing Countries: Does Foreign Bank Entry Improve Credit Access?" Working paper, Washington University, John M. Olin School of Business, St. Louis.

Gormley, Todd A., Simon H. Johnson, and Changyong Rhee. 2006. "Corporate Bonds: A Spare Tire in Emerging Markets?" Working paper, Washington University, John M. Olin School of Business, St. Louis.

Gozzi, Juan Carlos, Ross E. Levine, and Sergio L. Schmukler. 2007. "Internationalization and the Evolution of Corporate Valuation." *Journal of Financial Economics*, forthcoming.

Gracey, A. D. 2001. *Guarantee Mechanisms for Financing Innovative Technology: Survey and Analysis.* Luxembourg: European Commission.

Graham, Teresa. 2004. *Review of the UK Small Firms Loan Guarantee Scheme.* London: Her Majesty's Stationery Office. http://www.hm-treasury.gov.uk/independent_reviews/graham.

Green, Anke. 2003. "Credit Guarantee Schemes for Small Enterprises: An Effective Instrument to Promote Private Sector-Led Growth?" SME Technical Working Paper 10. Vienna: United Nations Industrial Development Organization.

Green, Richard K., and Susan M. Wachter. 2005. "The American Mortgage in Historical and International Context." *Journal of Economic Perspectives* 19 (4): 93–114.

Greenwood, Jeremy, and Boyan Jovanovic. 1990. "Financial Development, Growth, and the Distribution of Income." *Journal of Political Economy* 98 (5): 1076-1107.

Greif, Avner. 1993. "Contract Enforceability and Economic Institutions in Early Trade: The Maghribi Traders' Coalition." *American Economic Review* 83 (3): 525–48.

Grose, Claire, and Felice B. Friedman. 2006. "Promoting Access to Primary Equity Markets: A Legal and Regulatory Approach." Policy Research Working Paper 3892, World Bank, Washington, DC.

Guadamillas, Mario. 2007. "Balancing Competition and Cooperation in Retail Payment Systems." Powerpoint presentation. http://info.worldbank.org/etools/library/latestversion.asp?240389.

Guarcello, Lorenzo, Fabrizia Mealli, and Furio Rosati. 2003. "Household Vulnerability and Child Labour: The Effects of Shocks, Credit Rationing, and Insurance." Working paper, Understanding Children's Work Research Project, Washington DC. http://www.ucw-project.org/pdf/publications/standard_CL_and_Vulnerability.pdf.

Gupta, Nandini, and Kathy Yuan. 2003. "Financial Dependence, Stock Market Liberalizations, and Growth." William Davidson Institute Working Paper 562, University of Michigan, Ann Arbor.

Haber, Stephen. 2005. "Political Institutions and Financial Development: Evidence from the Economic Histories of Mexico and the United States." Stanford Center for International Development Working Paper 268, Stanford University, Palo Alto, CA.

Haber, Stephen, and Aldo Musacchio. 2005. "Contract Rights and Risk Aversion: Foreign Banks and the Mexican Economy, 1997–2000." Stanford University, Department of Economics, Palo Alto, CA

Halac, Marina, and Sergio Schmukler. 2004. "Distributional Effects of Crises: The Financial Channel." *Economia* 5 (1): 1–67.

Hanson, James A. 2004. "The Transformation of State-Owned Banks." In *The Future of State-Owned Financial Institutions,* ed. Gerard Caprio, Jonathan Fiechter, Robert Litan, and Michael Pomerleano. Washington DC: Brookings Institution Press.

Harrison, Ann, Inessa Love, and Margaret McMillan. 2004. "Global Capital Flows and Financing Constraints." *Journal of Development Economics* 75 (1): 269–301.

Harrison, Ann, and Margaret McMillan. 2003. "Does Direct Foreign Investment Affect Domestic Firm Credit Constraints?" *Journal of International Economics* 61 (1): 73–100.

Haselmann, Rainer F. H., Katharina Pistor, and Vikrant Vig. 2006. "How Law Affects Lending." Columbia Law and Economics Working Paper 285. Columbia University, New York.

Haselmann, R., and P. Wachtel. 2006. "Institutions and Bank Behavior." Stern Economics Working Paper 06-16, New York University, New York.

Helms, Brigit, and Xavier Reille. 2004. "Interest Rate Ceilings and Microfinance: The Story So Far." CGAP Occasional Paper 9, Consultative Group to Assist the Poorest, Washington, DC.

Hernández-Coss, Raúl. 2005. "The U.S.-Mexico Remittance Corridor: Lessons on Shifting from Informal to Formal Remittance Systems." World Bank, Financial Sector, Washington, DC.

Hernández-Coss, Raúl, Chinyere Egwuagu, Jennifer Isern, and David Porteous. 2005. "AML/CFT Regulation: Implications for Financial Service Providers that Help Low-Income People." CGAP Focus Note 29, Consultative Group to Assist the Poorest, Washington, DC.

Himmelberg, Charles P., R. Glenn Hubbard, and Inessa Love. 2002. "Investor Protection, Ownership, and the Cost of Capital." Policy Research Working Paper 2834, World Bank, Washington, DC.

Honohan, Patrick. 2001. "Perverse Effects of an External Ratings-Related Capital Adequacy System." *Economic Notes* 30 (3): 359–72.

———, ed. 2003. *Taxation of Financial Intermediation: Theory and Practice for Developing Countries.* New York: Oxford University Press.

———. 2004. "Financial Sector Policy and the Poor." Working Paper 43, World Bank, Washington, DC.

———. 2005a. "Banking Sector Crises and Inequality." Policy Research Working Paper 3659, World Bank, Washington, DC.

———. 2005b. "Measuring Microfinance Access: Building on Existing Cross-Country Data."

Policy Research Working Paper 3606, World Bank, Washington, DC.

———. 2006. "Household Financial Assets in the Process of Development." Policy Research Working Paper 3965, World Bank, Washington DC.

Honohan, Patrick, and Thorsten Beck. 2007. *Making Finance Work for Africa*. Washington, DC: World Bank.

Hubbard, Glenn. 1998. "Capital Market Imperfections and Investment." *Journal of Economics Literature* 36 (1): 193–225.

Huybens, Elisabeth, and Bruce Smith. 1998. "Financial Market Frictions, Monetary Policy, and Capital Accumulation in a Small Open Economy." *Journal of Economic Theory* 81: 353–400.

———. 1999. "Inflation, Financial Markets, and Long-Run Real Activity." *Journal of Monetary Economics* 43 (2): 283–315.

Jacoby, Hanan G. 1994. "Borrowing Constraints and Progress through School: Evidence from Peru." *Review of Economic Studies* 76 (1): 151–60.

Jacoby, Hanan G., and Emmanuel Skoufias. 1997. "Risk, Financial Markets, and Human Capital in a Developing Country." *Review of Economic Studies* 64 (3): 311–35.

Jain, Sanjay, and Ghazala Mansuri. 2003. "A Little at a Time: The Use of Regularly Scheduled Repayments in Microfinance Programs." *Journal of Development Economics* 72 (1): 253–79.

Jaumdally, Adnan Ally Mamode. 1999. "Discussion: Speculation and Gambling." *International Journal of Islamic Financial Services* 1 (2).

http://islamic-finance.net/journals/journal2/art5.pdf.

Jayaratne, Jith, and Phil Strahan. 1996. "The Finance-Growth Nexus: Evidence from Bank Branch Deregulation." *Quarterly Journal of Economics* 111 (3): 639–70.

Jensen, Michael. 1988. "Agency Costs of Free Cash Flow, Corporate Finance, and the Market for Takeovers." *American Economic Review* 76 (2): 323–29.

Jeong, Hyeok, and Robert Townsend. 2003. "Growth and Inequality: Model Evaluation Based on Estimation-Calibration Strategy." Institute of Economic Policy Research Paper 05.10, University of Southern California, Los Angeles.

Jin, Li, and Stewart C. Myers. 2006. "R^2 around the World: New Theory and New Tests." *Journal of Financial Economics* 79 (2): 257–92.

Johnson, Susan. 2007. "Gender and Microfinance: Guidelines for Good Practice." http://www.gdrc.org/icm/wind/gendersjonson.html.

Johnston, Don, and Jonathan Morduch. 2007. "Microcredit vs. Microsaving: Evidence from Indonesia." http://siteresources.worldbank.org/INTFR/Resources/Microcredit_versus_Microsaving_Evidence_from_Indonesia.pdf.

Karlan, Dean. 2005. "Using Experimental Economics to Measure Social Capital and Predict Financial Decisions." *American Economic Review* 95 (5): 1688–99.

———. 2007. "Social Connections and Group Banking." *Economic Journal* 117 (517): F52–F84.

Karlan, Dean, and Martin Valdivia. 2006. "Teaching Entrepreneurship: Impact of Business Training on Microfinance Clients and Institutions." Yale University, Department of Economics, New Haven, CT.

Karlan, Dean, and Jonathan Zinman. 2006a. "Expanding Credit Access: Using Randomized Supply Decisions to Estimate the Impacts." Yale University, Department of Economics, New Haven, CT.

———. 2006b. "Observing Unobservables: Identifying Information Asymmetries with a Consumer Credit Field Experiment." Yale University, Department of Economics, New Haven, CT.

———. Forthcoming. "Credit Elasticities in Less Developed Countries: Implications for Microfinance." *American Economic Review.*

Keeton, W. 1979. *Equilibrium Credit Rationing.* New York: Garland Press.

Kempson, Elaine, Claire Whyley, John Caskey, and Sharon Collard. 2000. "In or Out? Financial Exclusion: A Literature and Research Review." Financial Services Authority, London.

Khandker, Shahidur R. 2003. "Microfinance and Poverty: Evidence Using Panel Data from Bangladesh." Policy Research Working Paper 2945, World Bank, Washington, DC.

Khwaja, Asim Ijaz, and Atif Mian. 2005. "Do Lenders Favor Politically Connected Firms? Rent Provision in an Emerging Financial Market." *Quarterly Journal of Economics* 120 (4): 1371–411.

Klapper, Leora. 2006. "The Role of Reverse Factoring in Supplier Financing of Small and Medium Sized Enterprises." *Journal of Banking and Finance* 30 (11): 3111–30.

Klapper, Leora, Luc Laeven, and Raghuram Rajan. 2006. "Entry Regulation as a Barrier to Entrepreneurship." *Journal of Financial Economics* 82 (3): 591–629.

KPMG Management Consulting. 1999. *An Evaluation of the Small Firms Loan Guarantee Scheme.* London: U.K. Department of Trade and Industry.

Kroszner, Randall S., and Philip E. Strahan. 1999. "What Drives Deregulation? Economics and Politics of the Relaxation of Bank Branching Restrictions." *Quarterly Journal of Economics* 114 (4): 1437–67.

Kuijs, Louis. 2005. "Investment and Saving in China." Policy Research Working Paper 3633, Washington, DC, World Bank.

Kumar, Anjali. 2005. *Access to Financial Services in Brazil.* World Bank, Washington, DC.

Kuznets, Simon. 1955. "Economic Growth and Income Inequality." *American Economic Review* 45 (1): 1–28.

———. 1963. "Quantitative Aspects of the Economic Growth of Nations." *Economic Development and Cultural Change* 11 (2): 1–80.

Laeven, Luc. 2003. "Does Financial Liberalization Reduce Financing Constraints?" *Financial Management* 2003 (Spring): 5–34.

Laeven, Luc, and Christopher Woodruff. 2007. "The Quality of the Legal System, Firm Ownership, and Firm Size." *Review of Economics and Statistics,* forthcoming.

La Porta, Rafael, Florencio Lopez-de-Silanes, and Andrei Shleifer. 1999. "Corporate Ownership around the World." *Journal of Finance* 54 (2): 471-517.

———. 2006. "What Works in Securities Laws?' *Journal of Finance* 61 (1): 1–32.

La Porta, Rafael, Florencio Lopez-de-Silanes, Andrei Shleifer, and Robert W. Vishny. 1997. "Legal Determinants of External Finance." *Journal of Finance* 52 (3): 1131–50.

———. 1998. "Law and Finance." *Journal of Political Economy* 106 (6): 1113–55.

La Porta, Rafael, Florencio Lopez-de-Silanes, and Guillermo Zamarripa. 2003. "Related Lending." *Quarterly Journal of Economics* 118 (1): 231–68.

Larraín, C., and J. Quiroz. 2006. "Estudio para el fondo de garantía de pequeños empresarios." Santiago: Banco Estado.

Leeds, Roger, and Julie Sunderland. 2003. "Private Equity Investing In Emerging Markets." *Journal of Applied Corporate Finance* 15 (4): 8–16.

Levine, Ross E. 2002. "Bank-Based or Market-Based Financial Systems: Which Is Better?" *Journal of Financial Intermediation* 11 (1): 1–30.

———. 2005. "Finance and Growth: Theory and Evidence." In *Handbook of Economic Growth*, ed. Philippe Aghion and Steven Durlauf. Amsterdam: North-Holland Elsevier Publishers.

Levine, Ross E., and Sergio L. Schmukler. 2007a. "Internationalization and Stock Market Liquidity." *Review of Finance* 10 (1): 153–87.

———. 2007b. "Migration, Spillovers, and Trade Diversion: The Impact of Internationalization on Domestic Market Liquidity." *Journal of Banking and Finance* 31 (6): 1595–1612.

Levitsky, Jacob. 1997. "SME Guarantee Schemes: A Summary." *The Financier* 4 (1 and 2): 5–11. http://www.the-financier.com.

Levy-Yeyati, Eduardo, and Alejandro Micco. 2007. "Concentration and Foreign Penetration in Latin American Banking Sectors: Impact on Competition and Risk." *Journal of Banking and Finance* 31 (6): 1633–47.

Levy-Yeyati, Eduardo, Alejandro Micco, and Ugo G. Panizza. 2006. "State-Owned Banks: Do They Promote or Depress Financial Development and Economic Growth?" http://ssrn.com/abstract=629384.

Li, Hongyi, Lyn Squire, and Heng-fu Zou. 1998. "Explaining International and Intertemporal Variations in Income Inequality." *Economic Journal* 108 (446): 26–43.

Li, Hongyi, Lixin Colin Xu, and Heng-fu Zou. 2000. "Corruption, Income Distribution, and Growth." *Economics and Politics* 12 (2): 155–82.

Littlefield, Elizabeth, Jonathan Morduch, and Syed Hashemi. 2003. "Is Microfinance an Effective Strategy to Reach the Millennium Development Goals." CGAP Focus Note 24. Consultative Group to Assist the Poorest, Washington, DC.

Love, Inessa, 2003. "Financial Development and Financing Constraints: International Evidence from the Structural Investment Model." *Review of Financial Studies* 16 (3): 765–91.

Love, Inessa, and Natalia Mylenko. 2003. "Credit Reporting and Financing Constraints." Policy Research Working Paper 3142, World Bank, Washington, DC.

Love, Inessa, Lorenzo A. Preve, and Virginia Sarria-Allende. 2007. "Trade Credit and Bank Credit: Evidence from Recent Financial Crises." *Journal of Financial Economics* 83 (2): 453–69.

Luoto, Jill, Craig McIntosh, and Bruce Wydick. 2007. "Credit Information Systems in Less-Developed Countries: A Test with Microfinance in Guatemala." *Economic Development and Cultural Change* 55 (2): 313–34.

Malesky, Edmund, and Markus Taussig. 2005. "Where Is Credit Due? Companies, Banks, and Locally Differentiated Investment Growth in Vietnam." http://homepage.mac.com/markustaussig/. Public/MaleskyTaussig.pdf.

Mankin, N. Gregory, David Romer, and David N. Weil. 1992. "A Contribution to the Empirics of Economic Growth." *Quarterly Journal of Economics* 107 (2): 407–37.

Martinez Peria, Maria Soledad, and Ashoka Mody. 2004. "How Foreign Participation and Market Concentration Impact Bank Spreads: Evidence from Latin America." *Journal of Money, Credit, and Banking* 36 (3): 510–37.

Maurer, Noel, and Stephen Haber. 2004. "Related Lending and Economic Performance: Evidence from Mexico." Working paper, Stanford University, Department of Economics, Palo Alto, CA.

McKenzie, David J., and Christopher Woodruff. 2007. "Experimental Evidence on Returns to Capital and Access to Finance in Mexico." Working paper, World Bank, Development Research Group, Washington, DC.

Mian, Atif. 2006. "Distance Constraints: The Limits of Foreign Lending in Poor Economies." *Journal of Finance* 61 (3): 1465–1505.

Micco, Alejandro, Ugo Panizza, and Monica Yañez. 2007. "Bank Ownership and Performance: Does Politics Matter?" *Journal of Banking and Finance* 31 (1): 219–41.

Miller, Margaret, ed. 2003. *Credit Reporting Systems and the International Economy*. Cambridge, MA: MIT Press.

Mitton, Todd. 2006. "Why Have Debt Ratios Increased for Firms in Emerging Markets?" Working paper, Brigham Young University, School of Management, Provo, Utah.

Moran, Theodore H. 2005. "How Does FDI Affect Host Country Development." In *Does Foreign Direct Investment Promote Development?*, ed. Theodore H. Moran, Edward M. Graham, and Magnus Blomström, 281–313. Washington DC: International Institute of Economics.

Morck, Randall K., and Lloyd Steier. 2005. "The Global History of Corporate Governance: An Introduction." NBER Working Paper 11062, National Bureau of Economic Research, Cambridge, MA.

Morck, Randall, and Bernard Yeung. 2003. "Family Control and the Rent-Seeking Society." William Davidson Institute Working Paper 585, University of Michigan, Ann Arbor, MI.

Morck, Randall K., Bernard Yeung, and W. Yu. 2000. "The Information Content of Stock Markets: Why Do Emerging Markets Have

Synchronous Stock Movements?" *Journal of Financial Economics* 58 (1-2): 215–60.

Morduch, Jonathan. 1998. "Does Microfinance Really Help the Poor? New Evidence from Flagship Programs in Bangladesh." Princeton University, Department of Economics, Princeton, NJ.

———. 1999. "The Microfinance Promise." *Journal of Economic Literature* 37 (4): 1569–1614.

———. 2006 "Microinsurance: The Next Revolution?" In *Understanding Poverty*, ed. Abhijit V. Banerjee, Roland Benabou, and Dilip Mookherjee. New York: Oxford University Press.

Nenova, Tatiana. 2003. "The Value of Corporate Voting Rights and Control: A Cross-Country Analysis." *Journal of Financial Economics* 68 (3): 325–51.

North, Douglass C., John Joseph Wallis, and Barry R. Weingast. 2006. "A Conceptual Framework for Interpreting Recorded Human History." NBER Working Paper 12795, National Bureau of Economic Research, Cambridge, MA.

Obaidullah, Mohammed. 2005. *Islamic Financial Services*. Jeddah: King Abdulazziz University.

Omiccioli, Massimo. 2005. "Trade Credit as Collateral." Temi di discussione (Economic Working Papers) 553, Bank of Italy, Economic Research Department, Rome.

Ortiz-Molina, Hernan, and Maria Fabiana Penas. 2006. "Lending to Small Businesses: The Role of Loan Maturity in Addressing Information Problems." Working paper, University of British Columbia, Sauder School of Business Working Paper, Vancouver.

Pande, Rohini, and Christopher Udry. 2006. "Institutions and Development: A View from Below." Working paper, Yale University, Department of Economics, New Haven, CT.

Paulson, Anna, Robert M. Townsend, and Alexander Karaivanov. 2006. "Distinguishing Limited Liability from Moral Hazard in a Model of Entrepreneurship." *Journal of Political Economy* 114 (1): 100–144.

Peachey, Stephen, and Alan Roe. 2006. "Access to Finance: Measuring the Contribution of Savings Banks." World Savings Banks Institute, Brussels, Belgium.

Perotti, Enrico C., and Paolo F. Volpin. 2004. "Lobbying on Entry." CEPR Working Paper 4519, Centre for Economic Policy Research, London.

Perotti, Roberto. 1992. "Fiscal Policy, Income Distribution, and Growth. "Working Paper 636, Columbia University, Department of Economics, New York.

———. 1993. "Political Equilibrium, Income Distribution, and Growth." *Review of Economic Studies* 60 (4): 755–76.

———. 1996. "Income Distribution and Growth." *Journal of Economic Growth* 1 (2): 149–87.

Persson, Torsten, and Guido Tabellini. 1994. "Is Inequality Harmful for Growth?" *American Economic Review* 84 (3): 600–21.

Pitt, M. M., and S. R. Khandker. 1998. "The Impact of Group-Based Credit Programs on Poor Households in Bangladesh: Does the Gender of Participants Matter?" *Journal of Political Economy* 106 (5): 958–96.

Policis. 2004. "The Effect of Interest Rate Controls in Other Countries." U.K. Department of Trade and Industry, London.

———. "Economic and Social Risks of Consumer Credit Market Regulation: A Comparative Analysis of the Regulatory and Consumer Protection Frameworks for Consumer Credit in France, Germany and the U.K." London, U.K. http://www.policis.com/Economic%20and%20Social%20Risks%20of%20Consumer%20Credit%20Market%20Regulation.pdf.

Porteous, David. 2005. "The Access Frontier as an Approach and Tool in Making Markets Work for the Poor." Finmark Trust, South Africa.

———. 2006. "The Enabling Environment for Mobile Banking in Africa." Bankable Frontier Associates. http://www.bankablefrontier.com/assets/ee.mobil.banking.report.v3.1.pdf.

Powell, Andrew P., Nataliya Mylenko, Margaret Miller, and Giovanni Majnoni. 2004. "Improving Credit Information, Bank Regulation, and Supervision: On the Role and Design of Public Credit Registries." Policy Research Working Paper 3443, World Bank, Washington, DC.

Prahalad, C. K. 2004. *The Fortune at the Bottom of the Pyramid: Eradicating Poverty through Profits.* Philadelphia: Wharton School Publishing.

Qian, Jun, and Philip E. Strahan. 2007. "How Law and Institutions Shape Financial Contracts: The Case of Bank Loans." *Journal of Finance*, forthcoming.

Quintyn, Marc, Silvia Ramirez, and Michael Taylor. 2007. "The Fear of Freedom: Politicians and the Independence and Accountability of Financial Sector Supervisors." IMF Working Paper 07/25, Inernational Monetary Fund, Washington, DC.

Rajan, Raghuram. 2006a. "The Persistence of Underdevelopment: Constituencies and Competitive Rent Preservation." Working Paper, University of Chicago, Graduate School of Business, Chicago.

———. 2006b. "Separate and Unequal." *Finance and Development* 43 (1): 56–57.

Rajan, Raghuram, and Luigi Zingales. 1998. "Financial Dependence and Growth." *American Economic Review* 88 (3): 559–87.

———. 2003. *Saving Capitalism from the Capitalists.* New York: Crown Business.

Ravallion, Martin. 2001. "Growth, Inequality, and Poverty: Looking beyond Averages." *World Development* 29 (11): 23–49.

———. 2004. "Pro-Poor Growth: A Primer." World Bank, Development Research Group, Washington, DC.

Rioja, Felix, and Neven Valev. 2004a. "Does One Size Fit All? A Reexamination of the Finance and Growth Relationship." *Journal of Development Economics* 74 (2): 429–47.

———. 2004b. "Finance and the Sources of Growth at Various Stages of Economic Development." *Economic Inquiry* 42 (1): 127–40.

Robinson, Marguerite. 2001. *The Microfinance Revolution: Sustainable Banking for the Poor.* Washington, DC: World Bank.

Rocha, Roberto, and Gregorio Impavido. 2006. "Competition and Performance in the Hungarian Second Pillar." Policy Research Working Paper 3876, World Bank, Washington, DC.

Rocha, Roberto, and Craig Thorburn. 2007. *Developing Annuity Markets: The Experience of Chile*. Washington DC: World Bank.

Roth, Jim, Michael McCord, and Dominic Liber. 2007. "The Landscape of Microinsurance in the World's 100 Poorest Countries." Microinsurance Centre, Appleton, WI.

Rousseau, Peter, and Paul Wachtel. 2005. "Economic Growth and Financial Depth: Is the Relationship Extinct Already?" Stern School of Business Working Paper 05-15, New York University, New York.

Rubenstein, David M. 2006. "Have Emerging Markets Finally Left Behind their Second Class Citizenship for Private Equity Investors?" Presentation to EMPEA Conference, May. The Carlyle Group, Washington, DC

Rutherford, Stuart. 1998. "The Savings of the Poor: Improving Financial Services in Bangladesh." *Journal of International Development* 10 (1): 1–15.

Sapienza, Paula. 2004. "The Effects of Government Ownership on Bank Lending." *Journal of Financial Economics* 72 (2): 357–84.

Schiantarelli, Fabio. 1995. "Financial Constraints and Investment: A Critical Review of Methodological Issues and International Evidence. In *Is Bank Lending Important for the Transmission of Monetary Policy?*, ed. Joe Peek and Eric Rosengren. Federal Reserve Bank of Boston, Boston, MA.

Schulz, Heiner. 2006. "Foreign Banks in Mexico: New Conquistadors or Agents of Change?" Wharton Financial Institutions Center Working Paper 06-11, Philadelphia.

Semenova, Maria. 2006. "Information Sharing in Credit Markets: Incentives for Incorrect Information Reporting." Working paper, Higher School of Economics, Moscow, Russia.

Shim, Ilhyock. 2006. "Corporate Credit Guarantees in Asia." *BIS Quarterly Review* (December): 85–98.

Sorge, Marco, and Chendi Zhang. 2006. "Credit Information Quality and Corporate Debt Maturity: Theory and Evidence." Policy Research Working Paper 4239, World Bank, Washington, DC.

Stiglitz, Joseph, and Andrew Weiss. 1981. "Credit Rationing in Markets with Imperfect Information." *American Economic Review* 71 (3): 393–410.

Stulz, Rene. 1990. "Managerial Discretion and Optimal Financing Policies." *Journal of Financial Economics* 26 (1): 3–27.

Tirole, Jean. 2006. *The Theory of Corporate Finance*. Princeton, NJ: Princeton University Press.

Townsend, Robert, and Kenichi Ueda. 2006. "Financial Deepening, Inequality and Growth: A Model-Based Quantitative Evaluation." *Review of Economic Studies* 73 (1): 251–93.

U.K. Department of Trade and Industry. 2003. "Fair, Clear and Competitive: The Consumer Credit Market in the 21st Century." White Paper CM 6040, Her Majesty's Stationery Office, London.

U.K. Competition Commission. 2006. *Home Credit Market Investigation*. London.

U.S. General Accounting Office. 1996. "A Comparison of SBA's 7(a) Loans and Borrowers with Other

Loans and Borrowers." Report to the U. S. Senate Committee on Small Business, GAO/RCED-96-222, Government Printing Office, Washington, DC. (NB: Since 2004, this agency has been known as the Government Accountability Office.)

———. 2001. "Small Business Administration Section 7(a) General Business Loans Credit Subsidy Estimates." Briefing before the Staffs of the Senate and House Committees on Small Business, July 31, 2001. GPO, Washington, DC. www.gao.gov/cgi-bin/getrpt?GAO-01-1095R.

———. 2003. "Small Business Administration: Progress Made but Improvements Needed in Lender Oversight." Testimony before the Committee on Small Business and Entrepreneurship, U.S. Senate, April 20, 2003. GAO-03-720T. GPO, Washington DC.

Visaria, Sujata. 2006. "Legal Reform and Loan Repayment: Microeconomic Impact of Debt Recovery Tribunals in India." Institute for Economic Development Working Papers DP157, Boston University, Boston, MA.

Weiss, Andrew, and Georgiy Nikitin. 2004. "Foreign Portfolio Investment Improves Performance: Evidence from the Czech Republic." *Topics in Economic Analysis & Policy* 4 (1): Art. 15.

Williamson, Steven D. 1987. "Costly Monitoring, Loan Contracts and Equilibrium Credit Rationing." *Quarterly Journal of Economics* 102 (1): 135–46.

World Bank. 2001. *Finance for Growth. Policy Choices in a Volatile World*. Washington, DC.

———. 2004. *India: Scaling Up Access to Finance for India's Rural Poor*. Washington, DC.

———. 2006a. *Equity and Development: World Development Report 2006*. Washington, DC.

———. 2006b. *The Role of Postal Networks in Expanding Access to Financial Services*. Washington, DC.

———. Various years. *World Development Indicators*. Washington, DC.

Wurgler, Jeffrey. 2000. "Financial Markets and the Allocation of Capital." *Journal of Financial Economics* 58 (1–2):187–214.

Wydick, Bruce. 1999. "Credit Access, Human Capital, and Class Structure Dynamics." *Journal of Development Studies* 35 (6): 131–52.

Yang, Dean. 2007. "International Migration, Remittances, and Household Investment: Evidence from Philippine Migrants' Exchange Rate Shocks." *Economic Journal*, forthcoming.

Yoo, JaeHoon. 2007. *Developing SME Exchanges*. Washington, DC: World Bank.

Zarutskie, Rebecca. 2005. "Evidence on the Effects of Bank Competition on Firm Borrowing and Investment." Working paper, Duke University, Fuqua School of Business, Durham, NC.

Zecchini, Salvatore, and Marco Ventura. 2006. "Public Credit Guarantees and SME Finance." ISAE Working Paper 73, Instituto di Studi e Analisi Economica, Rome.

Zia, Bilal. 2007. "Export Incentives, Financial Constraints, and the (Mis)Allocation of Credit: Micro-Level Evidence from Subsidized Export Loans." *Journal of Financial Economics*, forthcoming.

Index